The First Information War

The First Information War

Col. S.C. Narang (Retd.)

PRASHANT PUBLISHING HOUSE
DELHI-110094

Published by :
Prashant Publishing House
C-34, 28 Foota Road, Gali-3,
West Karwal Nagar, Delhi-110094
Phone : 011-22963970, Mob. : 9810396373
e-mail.: prashantpublishinghouse@gmail.com

The First Information War

First Published 2015

ISBN 978-93-80565-58-3

PRINTED IN INDIA
Published by Mr. R.K. Jha M/s Prashant Publishing House and Published at H.S. Offset House Press, Delhi.

Contents

Preface

The history of warfare is described in three waves. During the agrarian revolution, warfare was fought by a warrior class based on information. With the industrial revolution, the war changed to mass destruction. Nation states used mass armies to protect and expand their societies through wars with high casualties. In the information age, warfare changes to Information War.

The Art of War is one of the oldest books on military strategy in the world. Like a work of mathematics or science, much of the work is dedicated to defining its concepts in what has been described as a series of formulas. It is the first and one of the most successful works on strategy and has had a huge influence on Eastern and Western military thinking, business tactics, and beyond. Sun Tzu was the first to recognize the importance of positioning in strategy and that position is affected both by objective conditions in the physical environment and the subjective opinions of competitive actors in that environment.

Information warfare is often thought of as being defined by a particular target setudecision makers, information, information processes, and information systems. The "battlespace" associated with IW has been a constantly expanding one, moving far beyond traditional military situations. In some quarters, IW has even been associated with the leveraging of information technologies to achieve greater effectiveness and efficiency.

This has stretched the meaning of IW to the breaking point and has sowed more confusion than enlightenment. For this reason, this treatment of the subject uses the term "information strategies" to refer to the recognition and utilization of information and information technologies as an instrument of national power that can be independent of, or complementary to, military presence and operations.

The scope, or battlespace, of information warfare and strategy (IWS) can be defined by the players and three dimensionsùthe nature of their interactions, the level of their interactions, and the arena of their interactions. Nation states or combinations of nation states are not the only players. Non-state actors (including political, ethnic, and religious groups; organized crime; international and transnational organizations; and even individuals empowered by information technology) are able to engage in information attacks and to develop information strategies to achieve their desired ends.

Even though information warfare has been used for centuries, current doctrine, policies, and guidance provide little help for the warrior to understand first, what information warfare is, and secondly, how to do it.

—*Editor*

1

The Art of War

The Art of War is one of the oldest books on military strategy in the world. Like a work of mathematics or science, much of the work is dedicated to defining its concepts in what has been described as a series of formulas. It is the first and one of the most successful works on strategy and has had a huge influence on Eastern and Western military thinking, business tactics, and beyond. Sun Tzu was the first to recognize the importance of positioning in strategy and that position is affected both by objective conditions in the physical environment and the subjective opinions of competitive actors in that environment. He taught that strategy was not planning in the sense of working through a todo list, instead it requires quickly responding appropriately to changing conditions. Planning works in a controlled environment, but in a competitive environment, competing plans collide creating situations that no one plans. The book was first translated into a European language in 1782 by French Jesuit Jean Joseph Marie Amiot, and had possibly influenced Napoleon, and even the planning of Operation Desert Storm. Leaders as diverse as Mao Zedong, General Pervez Musharraf, Vo Nguyen Giap, and General Douglas MacArthur have claimed to have drawn inspiration from the work. The Art of War has also been applied, with much success, to business and managerial strategies.

ANNOTATIONS

Before the bamboo scroll version was discovered by archaeologists in April 1972, the most cited version of The Art of

War was the Annotation of Sun Tzu's Strategies by Cao Cao, the founder of the Kingdom of Wei. In the preface, he wrote that previous annotations were not focused on the essential ideas. Other annotations cited in official history books include Shen You (1762-04)'s Sun Tzu's Military Strategy, Jia Xu's Copy of Sun Tzu's Military Strategy, Cao Cao and Wang Ling's Sun Tzu's Military Strategy. The Book of Sui documented seven books named after Sun Tzu. An annotation by Du Mu also includes Cao Cao's annotation. Li Jing's The Art of War is said to be a revision of Sun Tzu's strategies. Annotations by Cao Cao, Du Mu and Li Quan were translated into Tangut language before 1040 AD.

After the movable type printer was invented, The Art of War (with Cao Cao's annotations) was published as a military text book, known as Seven Military Classics with six other strategy books. A book named Ten Schools of The Art of War Annotations was published before 1161 AD. As a required reading military textbook since the Song Dynasty, Seven Military Classics has many annotations. More than 30 differently annotated versions of this book exist today. Vernacular Chinese became increasingly popular in the late 1920s. Annotations in Vernacular Chinese began to appear after this time. Some of these works were translated from other languages, such as Japanese.

The two most common traditional Chinese versions of the Art of War, (the Complete Specialist Focus and Military Bible versions) were the sources for early translation into English and other languages. It was not until the 1970s that these works were compiled with more recent archeological discoveries into a single more complete version in Taipei. The resulting work is known as the Complete Version of Sun Tzu's Art of War for the National Defence Research Investigation Office has been the source for more recent and complete translations.

Quotations

So it is said that if you know your enemies and know yourself, you will fight without danger in battles. If you only know yourself, but not your opponent, you may win or may lose. If you know neither yourself nor your enemy, you will always endanger yourself.

This has been more tersely interpreted and condensed into the modern proverb: If you know both yourself and your enemy, you can come out of hundreds of battles without danger.

Many people interpret this sentence as 'If you know both sides, you will win a hundred times in one hundred battles. This translation is incorrect. The word '?' in Chinese means 'danger'. '?' in this sentence is better interpreted as 'numerous' rather than 'hundred'.

Furthermore, knowing both sides doesn't guarantee winning. Since in the beginning paragraph of chapter four, Sun Tsu wrote 'Hence, we can well predict who would win but there is no strategy guaranteeing winning'. The reason of the uncertainty is quite simple. How about dealing with the opponent who knows both sides better than you do? Similar verses have also been borrowedin a manner construing skilfulness as victory "without fighting" for example: Therefore one hundred victories in one hundred battles is not the most skilful. Seizing the enemy without fighting is the most skilful. And, the most famous quotation: All warfare is based on deception.

Military Applications

In many East Asian countries, The Art of War was part of the syllabus for potential candidates of military service examinations. Various translations are available. During the Sengoku era in Japan, a daimyo named Takeda Shingen (1521-1573) is said to have become almost invincible in all battles without relying on guns, because he studied The Art of War. The book even gave him the inspiration for his famous battle standard "Furinkazan" (Wind, Forest, Fire and Mountain), meaning fast as the wind, silent as a forest, ferocious as fire and immovable as a mountain.

The translator Samuel B. Griffith offers a chapter on "Sun Tzu and Mao TseTung" where The Art of War is cited as influencing Mao's On Guerilla Warfare, On the Protracted War, and Strategic Problems of China's Revolutionary War and includes Mao's quote: "We must not belittle the saying in the book of Sun Wu Tzu, the great military expert of ancient China, 'Know your enemy and know yourself and you can fight a thousand battles without disaster.'" During the Vietnam War, some Vietcong officers studied The Art of War, and reportedly could recite entire passages from memory. The Department of the Army in the United States, through its Command and General Staff College, has directed all units to maintain libraries within their respective headquarters for the continuing education of personnel in the art of war. The Art of War is specifically mentioned by name as an example of works to be maintained at each individual unit, and staff duty officers are obliged to prepare short papers for presentation to other officers on their readings.

Applicability Outside the Military

Since at least the 1980s, The Art of War has been applied to fields well outside the military. Much of the text is about how to fight wars without actually having to do battle: it gives tips on how to outsmart one's opponent so that physical battle is not necessary. As such, it has found application as a training guide for many competitive endeavours that do not involve actual combat. The book has gained popularity in corporate culture; there have been a variety of business books written applying its lessons to "office politics" and corporate strategy. Many Japanese companies make the book required reading for their key executives. The book is also popular among Western business management, who have turned to it for inspiration and advice on how to succeed in competitive business situations.

The Art of War has also been the subject of various law books and legal articles on the trial process, including negotiation tactics and trial strategy. It has also crept its way into sport: Australian cricket coach John Buchanan handed out excerpts from the book to his players before a match against England in 2001, and the book is allegedly a favourite of University of South Carolina football head coach Steve Spurrier.

Former Brazilian football coach, and current coach of the Portuguese national football team Luiz Felipe Scolari uses the book to plot his football strategy. In the 2002 FIFA World Cup he gave each of his players copies. In the recent 2006 FIFA World Cup in Germany he used the book to plan his team's win against

England. On the popular reality television show Survivor: China, participants were given copies as a source of strategy and advice. It has found use in political campaigning as well; Republican election strategist Lee Atwater claimed he travelled everywhere with it.

Some have also interpreted The Art of War as providing methods for developing social strategies, such as social relationships, maintaining romantic relationships, and seduction. The book stresses subtlety and always making it appear like one is trying to achieve something other than one's actual intention. The use of individual quotations from the book as a source of fortune cookielike proverbs and not seeing the general coherence of the text has been criticized by many scholars of Chinese history. The book has also gained influence among players of strategy games, including TCGs, collectible miniatures games, and realtime strategy games.

PRINCIPLES OF WAR: A HISTORICAL PERSPECTIVE

The principles of war: Objective, Offensive, Mass, Economy of Force, Maneuver, Unity of Command, Security, Surprise, Simplicity. Military officers first learn of these principles as lieutenants and seek to refine their understanding throughout their careers. They hold a place of importance in our doctrine-based force and serve as a "guiding light" to those who would seek success on the battlefield. To facilitate an understanding of these principles, I will briefly address three basic questions. 1) What constitutes a "principle?" 2) Where did they come from? 3) And, what is their significance to the warfighter today? The principles of war are not expressed in neat algebraic formulas nor do they possess the same characteristics as the laws of nature and science.

We teach that these principles should not be adhered to blindly and that each principle may apply directly to one situation and not at all to another. Many even argue that since war is an art and not a science, in the truest sense of the word, principles do not apply to war. But war is both art and science. "Science consists of knowing; art of doing." Regardless, "no art exists without certain fundamental truths, which can be derived from analysis, from logic, and from the successes and failures of those who have plied the art." The bottom line is this: a "principle" of war is, in practice, a guide to action concerning the application of combat power, rather than an unquestioned truth with universal application to every single military operation."

Antonine-Henri Jomini was probably the first individual whose writings led to the concept that a small set of principles could serve as a guide for the commander to succeed on the battlefield. Jomini wrote, "The fundamental principles upon which rest all good combinations of war have always existed, and to them all others should be referred for the purpose of arriving at their respective merits. These principles are unchangeable; they are independent of the arms employed, of times, and of places." Following WWI, the British adopted the first official list of principles of war, due greatly to the influence of J.F.C. Fuller, which included eight items: Maintenance of the Objective, Offensive Action, Surprise, Concentration, Economy of Force, Security, Mobility, and Co-Operation. In 1921, when the U.S. War Department listed principles of war in Training Regulation 10-5, eight of the nine principles listed were identical to those of British origin. However, between the years of 1928 and 1949, not a single definitive list of the principles of war appeared in any official U. S. Army doctrine manual. The list of nine principles that we currently use today did not appear in the U.S. Army Field Service Regulations until 1949.

It is also interesting to note that the principles of war are not the same throughout the major militaries of the world. The U.S. military currently holds that there are nine principles, the French only three, and the British and Russian military, ten. These principles, even though there is a great degree of similarity in name, are different in definition and application across the board.

This historical perspective highlights several issues. First, the very concept that a certain limited number of "principles", by which warfare should be conducted in all situations and for all times, even exists and can be codified into nine, ten, or eleven principles has always been and still is under debate. Even if a set of "principles of war" do exist, their exact number, content, and definition is a second area of disagreement. Finally, history reveals that even in our own experience as a military, there has not been homogeneous thought about the concept or the content of the principles of war. Russell Glenn provides an excellent summary in his article, "No More Principles of War?" He states, "History reveals that the principles of war have frequently been the subject of long and often inspired debate; their character, number, and definition have changed repeatedly. They took their present form in U.S. Army doctrine only 49 years ago. On the one hand, this span is but a fraction of the years spent in their study. On the other, much has transpired since 1949. One may legitimately ask whether the principles as they stand could meet the needs of U.S. armed forces half a century from now." We, too, should consider the same question, but more specifically, will they meet the needs of the information-based warrior?

Revolution in Military Affairs

Exactly what is a Revolution in Military Affairs? In his article "Calvary to Computer, The Pattern of Military Revolutions", Andrew Krepinevich describes an RMA as "what occurs when the application of new technologies into a significant number of military systems combines with innovative operational concepts and organizational adaptation in a way that fundamentally alters the characteristics and conduct of conflict. It does so by producing a dramatic increase—often an order of magnitude or greater—in the combat potential and military effectiveness of armed forces." The key proponents of the current information-based RMA state that a combination of high-tech sensors, robust information systems, focused intelligence, stealth technologies, advanced C4, and precision weapons will enable the commander to "see and understand everything on a battlefield, and if you see the battlefield, you will win the war." Admiral William A. Owens, former Vice Chairman of the JCS, was one of the early advocates of the information-based RMA. He believed that if the U.S. armed forces could integrate its currently procured subsystems into a higher "systems-of-systems," it would be able to achieve and sustain "information dominance." By communicating this information rapidly throughout the forces they would be able to react with speed, precision, and accuracy that would produce a devastating effect upon the enemy and "propel the U.S. military to a qualitatively new order of military power." In relation to the principles of war, it is critically important to note that it is often the operational innovation, or doctrinal changes, that prove to be more important to the full development of the RMA than is the element of technology itself.

The Principles of War: A New Paradigm

Guiding principles are important to any organization for they form a paradigm that serves as the basis for the way in which its members think and act. In our doctrine-based military, the principles of war serve to form our paradigm concerning the art of war. We must choose our words and definitions carefully, for they convey to our soldiers what we hold to be true about our profession. If the information-based RMA has the potential to deliver on its promises, then we must begin to embrace it by reexamining the underlying elements of our doctrine, the principles of war. The following paragraphs will examine six of the principles which may be most effected by the emergence of information-based warfare.

MASS

The purpose of mass is to concentrate the effects of combat power at the place and time to achieve decisive results. The advent of the information-based RMA may cause us to think of the principle of mass in a significantly different manner. Most will agree that the tactics used by the 8th Air Force in WWII, in which hundreds of B-17 bombers delivered thousands of tons of bombs on the factories and towns of Germany in the attempt to destroy one single target, is a thing of the past. Today, with the advent of high-tech weapons systems, soldiers no longer talk of massing forces, but of massing effects. It is no longer required to bring forces into the same geographical area to bring their effects to bear on the same target and, in fact, on the modern battlefield it may be dangerous as well. Consider Colonel Phillip Meilinger's statement that "the result of the trend towards 'airshaft accuracy' in air war is a denigration in the importance of mass." He goes on to say that, in reality, what we have been seeking all along is not mass (any large amount or number) but density (mass per unit volume).

It is a waste of resources to "over-destroy" the target, but neither do we want to have to come back again to finish the job another day. What we ultimately desire to achieve is the right effect on the right target at the right time. Mass has nothing to do with one F-117 Stealth Fighter delivering a precision-guided weapon down the airshaft of a telecommunications building with the resulting effect of destroying the main critical node contained in that building. That particular attack involved one airplane delivering one weapon, but had the same effect as hundreds of B-17s.

We should reconsider the concept of mass as used by Napoleon and WW II air campaign planners and refine our understanding of this principle for three reasons. First, precision guided weapons are expensive, and in the climate of reduced budgets we must be somewhat judicious in the employment of these weapons. In an attempt to destroy a peer competitor's information infrastructure, we may soon realize that the number of targets required to be hit could place a strain on the number of available weapons. That is not to mention the possibility of fighting a second major regional conflict within a short period of time, as our current military strategy requires. Second, if we are required to resort to physical destruction of information-based targets, they are likely to be located (or co-located) in urban areas that have a highly concentrated civilian population. In this instance we will probably not be able to employ a large amount of non-precision firepower (traditional mass) because the American people will require that we avoid civilian casualties. Third, a significant factor of the information-based RMA will be speed with which wars are won or lost. If our objective is to bring strategic paralysis to our enemy before he has the chance to do the same to us, we must deliver the right weapon to the right target the first time. Logistical constraints will demand that we not bring more than we need, which may leave some targets uncovered, and we may not be given a second chance if peer competitor is equally successful at attacking us. We should begin to think in terms of "density," rather than "mass," as this word more fully exemplifies the concept of rapid precision strike that the US military will need to embrace as this information-based RMA unfolds.

Objective

The purpose of the objective is to direct every military operation toward a clearly defined, decisive, and attainable objective. Field Manual 100-5, Operations, published by the U.S. Army, states as its first sentence in the explanation of the principle of objective, "The ultimate military purpose of war is the destruction of the enemy's armed forces and will to fight." However, the information-based RMA, with its promise of the capability to render the enemy "strategically paralyzed" in a relatively short period of time focuses less on the enemy's armed forces and more on his leadership, C2, and infrastructure. In addition, the continuing improvements in sensors, the "sensor-to-shooter" information systems, and the accuracy of precision weapons means that in the future more of the enemy's forces will be seen and more of what is seen can be destroyed. John Orme states, "Once the (information-based) RMA power has demonstrated the ability to kill nearly all of what it sees, simply communicating to the enemy that 'we know where you are' may be enough to persuade them to surrender or withdraw." So, even though the principle of the objective will retain its importance, the information-based RMA may serve to refocus it away from the long standing concept of the destruction of the enemy's armed forces.

Another aspect to consider is time, that is, when in the course of a conflict should one consider the principle applicable? Traditionally, commanders have thought of the objective in predominantly physical terms, such as a ridgeline, an enemy force, or as a condition to be achieved, such as air superiority. This paradigm tells us the "objective" is achieved primarily by "force-on-force" and does not apply until hostilities are eminent. However, with the advent of the information-based RMA, the early struggle for information dominance may begin by simply inserting a computer virus into the enemy's C4I networks. This could occur days, weeks, or even months before the onset of forces being employed. Thus, commanders may now wish to consider their "objectives" much sooner than in the past, as well as thinking of this principle as much in "intangible", as well as tangible, ways.

Offensive

The purpose of an offensive action is to seize, retain, and exploit the initiative. Throughout the history of warfare theorists have sought to determine the stronger position in war, the offensive or the defensive. Traditionally, most have agreed with Clausewitz, "we must say that the defensive form of warfare is intrinsically stronger than the offensive." However, the information-based RMA will reinforce the principle of the offensive and possibly reverse this long-held axiom. It has always been clear to military commanders that you do not achieve victory in most conflicts without some offensive action. The offensive also allows the commander to maintain the initiative, forcing the enemy to react rather than act as he wishes, and denying him the opportunity to pursue his own objectives.

Maintaining and exploiting the initiative is all about attaining information dominance. The "fog of war," which serves to paralyze the commander and leads to inaction, is due primarily to a lack of information concerning his opponent. He is reluctant to act for fear of failure, but knows that he must do something or forfeit the initiative. The information-based RMA, by establishing information dominance, will serve to lift the "fog" for the commander relative to his opponent and make him more eager to act. Major Aresenio T. Gumahad states, "These future warriors will quickly outflank and outmaneuver an enemy with knowledge of its position and combat situation. With information age weapons at their disposal they will engage an enemy precisely and decisively." This confidence in the individual commander's ability to seize and maintain the initiative will provide a synergistic effect on the battlefield and serve to propel the "order of magnitude" effects this RMA will produce.

Also, the age old requirement for the offense to concentrate forces in order to break through the defence is greatly reduced under the information-based RMA. John Orme predicts, "With continued improvements in the range and accuracy of weaponry and the effectiveness of command and coordination, it will become increasingly possible for the offense to concentrate fire but not forces before the enemy, which may shift the eternal contest between offense and defence decisively in favour of the attacker." Another aspect which will favour the offensive is the speed in which an information-based RMA force will be able to act. Wars may no longer last months or even years. The requirement to establish information dominance early in a conflict may require a massive preemptive attack on the enemy's information infrastructure as well as his capability to retaliate in kind. One who waits too long may find himself unable to launch credible resistance very soon after hostilities breakout. These issues considered, the information-based RMA should cause us to examine the traditional balance between the offensive and the defensive roles of warfare.

Economy of Force

The purpose of the economy of force is to allocate minimum essential combat power to secondary objectives. At the heart of the current concept of economy of force is the need to preserve combat power for sustained and follow-on operations. This principle focuses one to think of a campaign primarily in a sequential nature in which several enabling objectives are achieved prior to ultimately arriving at the final goal. Lt Col Frederick Strain, USAF, in his article "The New Joint Warfare" describes it this way, "Each phase establishes the requisite environment or conditions for the next operation. Developing campaign plans designed to "peel the onion" layer by layer to get to the centre of gravity is old thinking." The Gulf War demonstrated the capability to attack the enemy at all levels-strategic, operational, and tactical-simultaneously, in a brief period of time, and effectively "locked out" many of Saddam's options very early in the conflict. As the information-based RMA unfolds, warfare will become less sequential and more simultaneous, promoting the concept of parallel attack in future campaign operations.

The information-based RMA may require us to think differently about the concept of reserve forces also. The following comments by General Dennis Reimer, Chief of Staff of the US Army help to illustrate this point, "We talk now about situational awareness...if we can do that (achieve it) we can change the way we operate. If you go to Ft. Leavenworth they teach in terms of operations when there is uncertainty and risk you keep a large reserve. Generally, most of the Army students will tell you it's two (units) up and one (unit) back. That's the way it has been for a long time. But if you can take that risk out of there, you can get more of your combat systems in the fight." The primary reason to keep forces in reserve is to preserve combat power to be able to counter the unpredictable nature of the enemy. If information dominance renders the enemy significantly more predictable, the logic for a reserve force becomes less valid. The result is that the information-based RMA will allow JFCs to employ forces in a more simultaneous than sequential manner, as well as employing more of the force from the onset of hostilities.

Unity of Command

The purpose of unity of command is to ensure unity of effort under one responsible commander for every objective. Military units have traditionally been hierarchical organizations with the commander at the top and many successive layers to the bottom. In a hierarchy there are strictly defined lines of communication, known as "the chain of command," in which data and information go up and commands come back down. New data is routed to commanders, who assess its impact and then direct an organizational response. However, members of a hierarchy routinely act on incomplete information because they receive only the command and not the information underlying it. Therefore, subsequent decisions on the lower levels are likely to be made on incomplete or late data resulting in uninformed action.

Another characteristic of a hierarchy is that each successive level upward in the chain of command is likely to have a "bigger picture" of the battlefield than the last, thus rendering the commander the most capable individual in the unit to make decisions. However, consider the effect the information-based RMA will have on this hierarchical structure. What if the individual at the lower level was able to acquire the same "big picture" as the individual at the top? Before, the individual acted without question because all he received was a command without the underlying information, now this may no longer be true. Imagine, as well, the situation described by Major James K. Morningstar, "It is easy to envision brigade commanders having to fight the urge to bypass less experienced battalion and company commanders to guide platoon leaders at objectives via direct digital links." The information-based RMA will force our "chain of command" to function more like a network (in a pure network, all individuals are equal and autonomous, all possible lines of communication can be used, there is no leader, any individual can interact directly with any other individual, and all decisions are reached by consensus) resulting in a more flattened and responsive command structure. In this sense, the information-based RMA may challenge our current "hierarchical" concept of unity of command.

Surprise

The purpose of surprise is to strike the enemy at a time or place or in a manner for which it is unprepared. The principle of surprise will be defined in two entirely different ways depending on whether or not we are fighting a peer-competitor. If we are engaging an adversary who has not mastered the information-based RMA, the principle of surprise could be an important aspect of the way we will employ force. Throughout the history of warfare the element of surprise has been the exception rather than the rule. Forces were seldom surprised because of their ability to understand the enemy and to plan for his most likely courses of action. However, by achieving information dominance early on in the conflict, we will be able to "see" and "engage" the enemy's forces, while denying him that same capability. This ability to "surprise at will" may cause the enemy to withdraw or surrender simply by communicating to him that "we know where you are." In this instance surprise may become the norm, rather than the exception, for an information-based RMA power.

Conversely, with the capability of a peer-competitor to employ surveillance technologies and rapidly communicate information to his forces, the ability to "surprise at will" will probably not be a realistic option. In this type of conflict the principle of surprise will be defined by two key elements: stealth and speed. "Stealth strengthens the attacker by restoring the prospects for surprise, perhaps close to the levels prevailing before the invention of radar, while accuracy radically diminishes the number of aircraft and tonnage of bombs needed to destroy a given set of targets." For example, in Operation DESERT STORM F-117 Stealth Fighters flew more than 1,250 sorties, attacking valuable strategic targets in downtown Baghdad, without losing a single aircraft. Additionally, the speed at which information-based RMA forces will be able to act will allow them to continually operate inside the enemy's decision cycle always leaving our opponent a step behind.

DEVELOPMENT OF MILITARY STRATEGY

Early Military Strategy

The principles of military strategy can be found as far back as 500 BC in the works of Sun Tzu and Chanakya. The campaigns of Alexander the Great, Chandragupta Maurya, Hannibal, Qin Shi Huang, Julius Cæsar, Zhuge Liang, and Khalid ibn alWalid demonstrate strategic planning and movement. Mahan describes in the preface to The Influence of Sea Power upon History how the Romans used their sea power to effectively block the sea lines of communication of Hannibal with Carthage; and so via a maritime strategy achieved Hannibal's removal from Italy, despite never beating him there with their legions.

In 1520 Niccolò Machiavelli's Dell'arte della guerra (Art of War) dealt with the relationship between civil and military matters and the formation of the grand strategy. In the Thirty Years' War, Gustavus Adolphus of Sweden demonstrated advanced operational strategy that led to victories in Holy Roman Empire area. It was not until the 18th century that military strategy was subjected to serious study. In the Seven Years' War (1756-1763), Frederick the Great improvised a "strategy of exhaustion" to hold off his opponents and conserve his Prussian forces. Assailed from all sides by France, Austria, Russia and Sweden, Frederick exploited his central position which enabled him to move his army along interior lines and concentrate against one opponent at a time.

Unable to achieve victory, he was able to stave off defeat until a diplomatic solution was reached. Frederick's "victory" led to great significance being placed on "geometric strategy" which emphasized lines of manoeuvre, awareness of terrain and possession of critical strongpoints.

Genghis Khan and the Mongols

As a counterpoint to European developments in the strategic art, the Mongol Emperor Genghis Khan provides a useful example. Genghis' successes, and those of his successors, were based upon manoeuvre and terror. The point of Genghis' strategic assault was nothing less than the psychology of the opposing population. By a steady and meticulous implementation of this strategy, Genghis and his descendants were able to conquer most of Eurasia. The building blocks of Genghis' army and his strategy were his tribal levies of mounted archers and (just as important) the vast horseherds of Mongolia. Each archer had at least one extra horse; (it was an average five horses per man) thus the entire army could move with incredible rapidity. Moreover since horse milk and horse blood were the staples of the Mongolian diet, Genghis' horseherds functioned not just as his means of movement but also as his logistical tail. All other necessities could be foraged and plundered. It was not until well into the 20th century that any army was able to match the rapidity of deployment of Genghis' armies. Compared to the armies of Genghis, all other armies were heavy and comparatively immobile. Through manoeuver and continuous assault, Chinese, Persian, Arab and Eastern European armies could be stressed until they broke, and then annihilated in pursuit.

When confronted with a fortified city, the Mongol imperatives of manoeuver and speed required that it be quickly subdued. Here the fear engendered by the awful reputation of the Mongolians helped. So too did primitive biological warfare. A trebuchet or other type of ballista weapon would be used to launch dead animals and corpses into a barricaded city, spreading disease and death among the inhabitants. If a particular town or city displeased the Mongolian Khan, everyone in the city would be killed to set an example for all other cities. This could be called a form of psychological warfare. Note that of the above list of strategic terms, even this elementary summary indicates that the Mongols strategy was directed towards an objective (that schwerpunkt (main focus) being nothing less than the psychology of the opposing population) achieved through the offensive; the offensive was characterized by concentration of forces, manoeuvre, surprise and simplicity.

Napoleonic Strategy

The French Revolution and the Napoleonic Wars that followed revolutionized military strategy. The impact of this period was still to be felt in the American Civil War and the early phases of World War I. With the advent of cheap small arms and the rise of the drafted citizen soldier, armies grew rapidly in size to become massed formations. This necessitated dividing the army first into divisions and later into corps. Along with divisions came divisional artillery; lightweight, mobile and with great range and firepower. The rigid formations of pikemen and musketeers firing massed volleys gave way to light infantry fighting in skirmish lines. Napoleon I of France took advantage of these developments to pursue a brutally effective "strategy of annihilation" that cared little for the mathematical perfection of the geometric strategy. Napoleon invariably sought to achieve decision in battle, with the sole aim of utterly destroying his opponent, usually achieving success through superior manouevre. As ruler and general he dealt with the grand strategy as well as the operational strategy, making use of political and economic measures.

While not the originator of the methods he used, Napoleon very effectively combined the maneuver and battle stages into one event. Before this, General Officer had considered the approach to battle a separate event. However, Napoleon used the maneuver to battle to dictate how and where the battle would progress. The Battle of Austerlitz was a perfect example of this maneuver. Napoleon withdrew from a strong position to draw his opponent forward and tempt him into a flank attack, weakening his centre. This allowed the French army to split the allied army and gain victory. Napoleon used two primary strategies for the approach to battle. His "Maneuver De Derrière" was intended to place the

French Army across the enemy's lines of communications. This forced the opponent to either march to battle with Napoleon or attempt to find an escape route around the army. By placing his army into the rear, his opponents supplies and communications would be cut. This had a negative effect on enemy morale. Once joined, the battle would be one in which his opponent could not afford defeat. This also allowed Napoleon to select multiple march routes into a battle site. Initially, the lack of force concentration helped with foraging for food and sought to confuse the enemy as to his real location and intentions. This strategy, along with the use of forced marches created a morale bonus that played heavily in his favour.

The "indirect" approach into battle also allowed Napoleon to disrupt the linear formations used by the allied armies. As the battle progressed enemy committed their reserves to stabilize the situation, Napoleon would suddenly release the flanking formation to attack the enemy. His opponents, being suddenly confronted with a new threat and with little reserves, had no choice but to weaken the area closest to the flanking formation and draw up a battle line at a right angle in an attempt to stop this new threat. Once this had occurred, Napoleon would mass his reserves at the hinge of that right angle and launch a heavy attack to break the lines. The rupture in the enemy lines allowed Napoleon's cavalry to flank both lines and roll them up leaving his opponent no choice but to surrender or flee.

The second strategy used by Napoleon I of France when confronted with two or more enemy armies was the use of the central position. This allowed Napoleon to drive a wedge to separate the enemy armies. He would then use part of his force to mask one army while the larger portion overwhelmed and defeated the second army quickly. He would then march on the second army leaving a portion to pursue the first army and repeat the operations. This was designed to achieve the highest concentration of men into the primary battle while limiting the enemy's ability to reinforce the critical battle. The central position had a weakness in that the full power of the pursuit of the enemy could not be achieved because the second army needed attention.

So overall the preferred method of attack was the flank march to cross the enemies logistics. Napoleon used the central position strategy during the Battle of Waterloo Hundred Days. Napoleon masked Arthur Wellesley, 1st Duke of Wellington and massed against the Prussian army, and then after the Ligny battle was won, Napoleon attempted to do the same to the Allied/English army located just to the south of Waterloo. His subordinate was unable to mask the defeated Prussian army, who reinforced the Waterloo battle in time to defeat Napoleon and end his domination of Europe. It can be said that the Prussian Army under Gebhard Leberecht von Blücher used the "maneuver de derrière" against Napoleon who was suddenly placed in a position of reacting to a new enemy threat.

Napoleon's practical strategic triumphs, repeatedly leading smaller forces to defeat larger ones, inspired a whole new field of study into military strategy. In particular, his opponents were keen to develop a body of knowledge in this area to allow them to counteract a masterful individual with a highly competent group of officers, a General Staff. The two most significant students of his work were Carl von Clausewitz, a Prussian with a background in philosophy, and AntoineHenri Jomini, who had been one of Napoleon's staff officers. Clausewitz's On War has become the bible of strategy, dealing with political, as well as military, leadership. His most famous assertion being:

"War is not merely a political act, but also a real political instrument, a continuation of policy carried out by other means."

Clausewitz dismissed "geometry" as an insignificant factor in strategy, believing instead in the Napoleonic concept of victory through battle and destruction of the opposing force, at any cost. However, he also recognized that limited warfare could influence policy by wearing down the opposition through a "strategy of attrition". In contrast to Clausewitz, AntoineHenri Jomini dealt mainly with operational strategy, planning & intelligence, the conduct of the campaign, and "generalship" rather than "statesmanship". He proposed that victory could be achieved by occupying the enemy's territory rather than destroying his army. As such, geometric considerations were prominent in his theory of strategy. Jomini's two basic principles of strategy were to concentrate against fractions of the enemy force at a time and to strike at the most decisive objective.

One notable exception to Napoleon's strategy of annihilation and a precursor to trench warfare were the Lines of Torres Vedras during the Peninsular campaign. French Armies lived off the land and when they were confronted by a line of fortifications which they could not out flank, they were unable to continue the advance and were forced to retreat once they had consumed all the provisions of the region in front of the lines.

The Peninsular campaign was notable for the development of another method of warfare which went largely unnoticed at the time, but would become far more common in the 20th century. That was the aid and encouragement the British gave to the Spanish to harass the French behind their lines which led them to squander most of the assets of their Iberian army in protecting the army's line of communications. This was a very cost effective move for the British, because it cost far less to aid Spanish insurgents than it did to equip and pay regular British army units to engage the same number of French troops. As the British army could be correspondingly smaller it was able to supply its troops by sea and land without having to live off the land as was the norm at the time. Further, because they did not have to forage they did not antagonise the locals and so did not have to garrison their lines of communications to the same extent as the French did. So the strategy of aiding their Spanish civilian allies in their guerrilla or 'small war' benefited the British in many ways, not all of which were immediately obvious.

PRINCIPLES OF WAR IN A CHANGING WORLD

The 20th century has seen veritable successive 'revolutions' in warfare, starting with the advent of air power in World War I, and cemented by aircraft carriers further extending this reach across the oceans by World War II. This was followed by the introduction of nuclear weapons, development of nuclear warfighting doctrines, growth of missile and electronic warfare, and a move towards increasing coordination and jointness between the single Services.

In the last two decades, technological advances have provided near real-time situational awareness and minimal sensor-shooter cycle, even as the reach, accuracy and lethality of modern weapons have attained unprecedented levels. Over this period, the 'ways and means' of war have undergone constant transformation. The ends for which war was waged have also expanded, from territorial ambitions to increasing geostrategic spheres of influence, to pursuit of religious-ideological conflicts, and again a reversion towards safeguarding of territorial and socioeconomic interests. The nature of war, as seen through its ways, means and ends, has probably traversed its largest arc of change in the last 100 years. The evolutionary trends of war led to several assessments, even before 9/11, of the emerging nature of 21st century warfare. This was appreciated as being more diverse and divisive, with the ways, means and ends of war continuing to change, along with traditional rationale and actors, and expectations of a transmutation of conflict, from total to limited war, from inter-state to intra-state war, and from regular, structured warfare to irregular warfare.

Wars of choice were assessed to more likely dominate the 21st century, with significant effort required to keep them limited amidst a danger of cascading effect upon wider areas in the world. The tragic events of 9/11 and the ensuing wars against (and by) terrorism have exemplified these earlier estimates and the wider spectrum of modern war. In the constant evolution of the nature of war, it is reasonable to expect that changes would be reflected in revision of not only the doctrines of warfighting, but also the underlying Principles of War (PoW). However, whilst warfighting doctrines have undergone significant changes in the last two decades, there has been little debate on the corresponding evolution of the PoW, which provide the (conceptual) foundation for building these warfighting doctrines. Areview of the prevailing PoW, in the light of the current nature and spectrum of war, would reveal significant deficiencies and point out the revisions necessary for the principles to have continued relevance in the 21st century. The PoW have been codified from the time of Sun Tzu, and evolved/ refined by Napoleon, Clausewitz, J.F.C. Fuller, and thence given institutionalised definition and interpretation by various nations and militaries. The fact that there is still no consensus on a single list of PoW underscores the complexities in addressing war across time and space.

A glance at the table shows there is a fair degree of commonality in the list and understanding of the PoW amongst the various nations, though some emphases and nuances would naturally vary. In the modern spectrum of war, however, some of these principles appear excessively focused on conventional, unlimited, war, and do not adequately cover the imperatives of other forms of significant changes in the last two decades, there has been little debate on the corresponding war, such as limited conventional war and sub-conventional war, which are both more widespread and more likely in the post-Cold War geostrategic environment.

Conventional limited wars are restricted in aim, scope and methods, and may require a broader canvas and interpretation of the PoW to meet their specific requirements. Sub-conventional war, where at least one actor is a nonstate and the war is characterised by an irregular and covert fabric such as for terrorism, militancy, insurgency, proxy war and civil war, may also need a more flexible interpretation of the PoW, especially since such warfare may take place in own territory and impose limitations on the applicability of the PoW.

However, even this would be more relevant for fighting against sub-conventional forces, rather than in the waging of such form of warfare, since the latter is the domain of mostly non-state actors who do not follow established norms and laws of war.

Hence, full application of the PoW to them would remain tenuous. Some of the existing PoW, with slight amendments, would retain their validity in this context, even whilst others may be seen to suffer from limitations in addressing the wider spectrum of modern war.

The principle of Selection and Maintenance of Aim is the primary PoW, which entails that the desired 'end-state' must be clearly defined and selection of the attainable aim done after careful cost-benefit analysis, keeping in mind the resources available. More often than not, this principle has been interpreted in purely military terms (since it is, after all, a principle of 'war').

But, accepting the Clausewitzian precept that war is an extension of politics by other means, the issue of politics can never be separated from the military objective.

Military aims would have to be situated in the political purpose for the use of force. In the era of 'total wars,' the selection and maintenance of aim/objective was relatively simpler, with full national resources being devoted to the war and all costs deemed acceptable, since the purpose was survival on one side and 'unconditional surrender' or annihilation on the other. But the nature of war itself has been changing, with total, unlimited war becoming a considerably lesser viable option. In an increasingly globalised and interdependent world, political restraints (including those of domestic pressures) would have a an increasingly globalised and interdependent world, political restraints (including those of domestic pressures) would have a major influence in the way war can be waged, and what sort of end-state can be achieved.

This is even more critical for countries that possess nuclear weapons. It can be argued that 'asymmetric warfare' has emerged primarily because of the politico-military restraints in an information age. The problem is that the 'endstate' is becoming less easy to define.

For example, the war against global terrorism might seek to rid the world of the scourge of terrorism. But it obviously remains unachievable without a major political-ideological campaign of ideas. Nuclear weapon states, in particular, have to seriously rethink the issue of military objectives and aims. Warfighting with nuclear weapons would defeat the very logic of war as a rational instrument of policy since it would destroy the very object it seeks to gain. Similarly, even a conventional war between nuclear weapon states would require redefinition of the traditional concepts of victory and defeat. Risk of escalation to nuclear weapons use can nullify what might have been seen as a 'decisive' military victory in a non-nuclear weapon environment. This has wide-ranging implications for the way wars can be fought. But, from the point of view of this examination, the critical point is that the very concept of 'victory' would need to be redefined in a war using conventional weapons and forces under a nuclear overhang. Countries placed in such situations would either have to avoid a direct war (as indeed the two superpowers did during the Cold War), or plan and fight a limited war (e.g. Sino-Russian border war 1969, and Indo-Pak Kargil War 1999). The former, avoidance of direct war, had led to the use of proxy wars; while the latter permits only a war with limited objectives. It is not surprising, therefore, that China has adopted a military doctrine of "local, border war under high-tech conditions." This, in turn, would require far greater synergy between political aims and military goals.

The military aim of modern war may accordingly require refinement, with consequent shift in focus onto attaining key objective areas that signify political victory or provide the post-war political leverage for conflict resolution, rather than seeking 'decisive' military victory as defined in the past. In the case of fighting insurgency/militancy/terrorism, the military objective may need to be similarly attuned to the political purpose, and limited to providing the modicum of security necessary for generating movement towards a politico-economic solution. An excessively ambitious aim, such as "stamping out all violent opposition" or "overthrow of the state" through the use of military force is more likely to fuel that very violence, and also provide non-state actors with an image of victory even if they merely survive or avoid total military defeat. This has been evinced in the ongoing Iraq War, where the desire to crush militant opposition has been faulted as an inappropriate and inapplicable politico-military aim and military strategy, and has probably instead contributed to deterioration of the security environment, rather than provide stability for attaining the political objectives.

The nature of modern warfare emphasises the need to synergise military objectives with political goals, with an inherent recognition of the fact that the latter could change frequently and demand similar readjustment of military objectives and strategy. Such continued synergy was demonstrated in the Indo-Pak Kargil War 1999, where Indian political desire to limit the war to the Indian side of the Line of Control (LoC) was supported by a military strategy to "contain-evict-deny," and included political clearance for use of air power in India's own territory. Inversely, political goals may also be affected by the military situation, and require reorientation according to the military gains or losses in order to derive the best 'end-state' possible, as seen in the India–Pakistan War 1971, where the capture of Dhaka was reportedly not part of the original aim. Hence, while "Selection and Maintenance of Aim" as a PoW remains at the core of modern warfare, its application has undergone significant change with the need for maintaining greater and constant synergy with the political purpose of the war, particularly in the case of limited and sub-conventional wars. Accordingly, the "aim" in the earlier Principle of War needs a more comprehensive and representative interpretation to encompass both political and military aims and, most importantly, the maintenance of synergy between them. The revisions in interpretation warrant a more appropriate term, such as Maintenance of Synergy in Politico-Military Aims.

The principle of Offensive Action, which is often held as the chief means of achieving victory, entails control over the purpose, scope, intensity and pace of operations, and retention of initiative at all times. This places a premium on early action, even preemption. But the nature of sub-conventional warfare, especially terrorism, inherently provides early initiative to the non-state actor. Preemptive action here is difficult, and may well prove counter-productive, such as in the case of faulty intelligence, or due to collateral damage in the apparent absence of adequate justification. This would push the civil populace to favour the non-state actors, as partly experienced in the current Iraq War, and provide strategic-level backlash for tactical actions. In such cases, a higher level of own security and rapid response capability would serve the war aims better than focus on offensive action per se. In the case of conventional limited war, with an inherently higher premium on preemption, there may be less scope for regaining the offensive or dictating fresh parameters against preemptive strike, within the limitations of time, area, scale and methods available.

This was seen in the Indo-Pak War in Kargil, 1999, wherein any Indian attempt to develop military offensive action beyond the tactical level purely on military logic could have escalated the war to the detriment of the war's politico-strategic objective. Hence, the view that offensive action per se is the means to attaining the initiative and freedom of action, and positive results thereby, needs adjustment. In the available technological environment, and ongoing techno-doctrinal focus on rapid response capability, the requirement is not so much on maintaining offensive action, but rather on the maintenance and exploitation of Freedom of Action (FoA) by a variety of measures, since the latter would provide broader options and initiative for decisive, including offensive, action. Freedom of Action has, accordingly, become a core principle across the spectrum of modern warfare, with the requirements extending from its attainment and maintenance for own forces, across all levels and dimensions of war, to the disruption and denial of similar freedom to the opponent. Freedom of Action would need to cover the various dimensions of war, viz. land, sea, air and information.

This would also entail the exploitation of own Freedom of Action by the employment of offensive doctrines, such as attainment and utilisation of favourable situation or air superiority, sea control, command of the air/sea, information superiority, escalation control/dominance, etc. The development and exploitation of Freedom of Action in all dimensions and theatres/ battlefields would require the support of robust physical and information security, sound logistics and administration, exercise of mobility, maintenance of initiative, suitable deployment of offensive forces, etc. Each of these aspects would need to be addressed in the military doctrines flowing from the overarching PoW, of maintenance and exploitation of Freedom of Action. It stands to reason that the side losing freedom of action would thereby lose its ability to influence the conduct of the war, and be forced to constantly react to the exercise of corresponding freedom by the opponent.

The principle of Mass/Concentration of Force is viewed as the concentration of combat power at the decisive time and place, to achieve decisive results. This principle has been highly valued, from Sun-Tzu through Napoleon to World War II, wherein it denoted the destructive power of a force. The principle of mass providing a distinct advantage is perhaps embedded in Napoleon's supposed remarks that even God is on the side of the bigger battalions! Mass, no doubt, denoted the killing power of a force, seen essentially in terms of quantity. This was the logic that gave the Roman Phalanx its distinct advantage in battle, and why modern militaries still look at a 3:1 favourable ratio of forces as a doctrinal parameter for successful offensive action. But, if viewed more closely, what we can observe is that killing power as a function of mass was true when the quantum of killing power in a unit element of force was limited. Hence, to maximise the overall impact of killing power, mass and concentration of force became a necessary principle.

In substance, since the accuracy, rate of fire, and range of the manmachine combination that produced the weapon system was limited, this was sought to be compensated by concentrating combat power, so that the friendly force could kill the maximum number of enemy forces/weapon systems. In battlefields that were concentrated in space, mass also provided enhanced moral power because of the emotional-psychological support derived from a greater number of friendly forces. Generation of mass, whether by massing more soldiers or by dispensing more projectiles onto the target, remained intrinsically important because of the limitations of range, target location and acquisition, accuracy and lethality of weapons, and the friction in war (that Clausewitz talked of). This also placed limits on the quantum of combat power that could be concentrated in time and space. In reality, however, the foundations of this principle started getting eroded with the advancement of technology. For example, the carnage at Verdun in World War I demonstrated how even a single machine gun could concentrate more firepower in the hands of a single soldier than what was possible earlier. Advances in military technology have been rapidly altering the traditional aggregative relation between quantum of forces and their combat power. Nowhere has this been more obvious than in the advent of air power, which provided the means to outflank the enemy from the third dimension. This changed the battlefield completely, and rendered the surface forces vulnerable except through acquiring a counter-outflanking capability with their own air power.

Even here, technological changes have determined a continuous expansion of the 'engagement zone', which itself challenges the traditional concept of concentration of force, as brought about by advances in air power. One element of this was air-to-air warfare becoming all-weather with beyond-visual-range (BVR) capability soon after the end of World War II. However, employment of air power against surface targets remained limited to what was essentially 'line-of-sight' targeting till recently, when improvements in targeting technology have enabled the application of combat power by diverse and geographically separated force elements. Space capabilities are expected to further expand this envelope, and in fact have already done so in the form of surveillance and information warfare, e.g. target spotting by an unmanned aerial vehicle (UAV), its classification and targeting by a centre possibly in another continent, and prosecution by a cruise missile launched from a submarine in another theatre, more than 1,000 km away. Expansion of the battlefield along with compression of time has provided a totally different dimension to concentration of combat power in time and space compared to what the principle of mass/concentration of force conveys. In determining the nature of change in this principle, we need to revisit the purpose of concentration of force and augmentation of combat power. Simply, this was to attain a certain destructive effect, wherein the massing of force appeared to provide the best means for attaining this end.

Consequently, this assumed the status of a PoW. The impact of advanced weapon technologies in terms of range, accuracy and lethality, synergised with parallel advancements in sensor and command and control (C2) technologies, has led to a situation wherein firepower-effect, as a derivative of cosmbat power, is no longer a summation of the mass of forces. All other things being equal, and leaving the intangibles like morale, etc. out of consideration for the time being, effective combat power could be denoted normatively by the equation:

Combat Power CP = Q x D x M

where Q is Quantity,

D is Destructive Power (a combination of range, accuracy and lethality) per unit weapon, and M is Mobility (or manoeuvre to enable concentration in time and space) It is obvious that if D, the destructive power of the force (weapon/soldier) is low, then Q, the quantity of force needed, would have to be high. In other words, a greater mass would be necessary to maintain the requisite combat power as constant. But, where D is higher, and M is developed, the Q quotient could be much lower, i.e. concentration of force would not be required, as the requisite combat power was being applied by the other components. The applicability of the above can be seen even in World War II, wherein the combination of German Panzer Divisions and aerial dive bombers in the Blitzkrieg in France, and Allied "thousand bomber raids" over Germany, were examples of augmenting combat power through enhancing Mobility, Destructive Power and Quantity, respectively.

The recent wars in Iraq and Afghanistan have further demonstrated the applicability of the above, wherein requisite combat power was attained with a lesser concentration of forces than would have been the case earlier, by a corresponding increase in precision strike, destructive power and mobility of the forces used. This fact has also been evident throughout military history, where lesser numbers of higher range and accuracy weapons, with higher rates of fire and speed of delivery, have habitually prevailed against larger concentration of opposing forces, due to their relatively higher concentration of firepower. But, since the weapons and systems in most wars, including the Napoleonic and two World Wars, tended to be comparable for the opposing sides, concentration of forces was perceived as providing the decisive edge, whereas it was actually the concentration of firepower enabled by the massing of forces that was responsible for this effect. In other words, it was the Q+Q, that is (Quality +Quantity) paradigm (both of firepower and manpower) that held the key.

The distinction is important today, when advanced military technologies have led to provision of unprecedented levels of discriminate destructive power in small larger concentration of lances, bows and arrows, and similarly for the British-Indian Army Lee Enfields against Indian-rebel forces with lances, muskets and swords in the War of Independence, 1857, and again in the machine-gun based carnage at Verdun in World War I. Throughout military history, lesser numbers of higher range and accuracy weapons, with higher rates of fire and speed of delivery, have habitually prevailed against larger concentration of opposing forces, due to their relatively higher concentration of firepower.

The source of that firepower could be naval, air or land power, which is also the central logic for joint operations. The most recent and dramatic example in support of the need to replace the existing principle of mass/concentration of force to one of concentration of firepower is to be found in the Iraq War where the United States reversed the traditionally accepted force ratios necessary for offensive action completely on their head. Similarly, the United States employed forces widely dispersed across the globe, ranging from home bases to warships and aircraft carriers, and special forces operating with missiles, UAVs, space assets, etc. in the 2001-02 War in Afghanistan, so as to bring firepower concentrated on specific tactical targets—even employing B-52 strategic bombers for close air support missions with the barest minimum military force deployed on land. This did not mean that the principle of concentration of force per se was ignored, but that its effect was attained through concentration of effective firepower, independent of the position and number of weapon firing platforms rather than from the aggregation of combat power platforms in time and space.

Today, two B-2s can provide the same effect, through accurate delivery of firepower, which required 50 B-52s a decade ago, and 1,000 bombers in World War II. Modern battlefields are expanding in space, even as they are contracting in time, due to the speed and reach of modern firepower. Hence, there will continue to be greater dispersion of forces, especially amongst naval and air platforms. This would seem to violate the principle of concentration of force, as understood hitherto. However, there is no contradiction if the principle is viewed instead as Concentration of Firepower, with its components being the emulative effect of the Quantity, Destructive Power and Mobility paradigm.

Economy of Effort is the principle requiring forces to be judiciously employed so as to maximise the effect of available resources, including through apportionment of resources between the main and secondary efforts. This has been seen as an adjunct to the principle of Concentration of Force (or firepower, as suggested above), and the focus is on the availability of forces. The core, however, relies on attaining the maximum effect for available resources, which also provides the conceptual foundation for the modern doctrine of "Effects-Based Operations." Hence, it may be more appropriate to view this principle instead as the Attainment of Effect, i.e. expand the current understanding from merely fullest use of available forces, to production of the desired effect through best employment of these resources, including by development of different strategies/tactics. For example, guerrilla warfare was developed in response to the adversary's superior force and firepower, wherein it neutralised own inferiority by exploiting potential strengths in relation to the prevailing environment (jungles, mountains, and now also urban areas). This, and also terrorist methods of waging war, such as 9/11 or the Madrid bombings, are not adequately covered under the principle of Economy of Force/Effort, but would be well supported by a shift in focus on production of effect using available resources. The relation between "Effect" and 'Force" may be considered as an equation:

$$E = F \times S$$

Where E is Effect, F is Force/Firepower, and S is Strategy

Thus, while the old principle of Economy of Effort sought to maximise the effect for a given force, it inherently accepted that this maximum effect need not correspond to what was required. This was in consonance with wars being 'total' or unlimited, where the emphasis was on maximum effective utilisation, rather than on utilisation for maximum (desired) effect. However, by shifting focus on attaining the desired effect, rather than on economising the effort, we emphasise the goal more than the means. Thus, the earlier 'economy' of effort would correspond to the component of strategy in the above equation, as a means to attaining the goal. However, strategy would also have other components, and not just judicious employment of forces. Effect could also be achieved by enhancing the firepower and other strategy quotients. Hence, attainment of effect would provide a more useful principle. The principle of Flexibility has been replaced by Manoeuvre, Initiative and/or Mobility by some countries. The principle is looked at in both active and reactive manner, leading to different interpretations and terms used by various nations. For example the US definition of manoeuvre is more active, in that it entails placing the enemy at disadvantage through the flexible application of own combat power at the strategic, operational and tactical levels of war. The Indian Army Doctrine is, however, somewhat reactive, in that it deems flexibility as the capability to react appropriately to changing situations. The Indian Maritime Doctrine is a mix of both, and views flexibility as the capacity to cope with a rapidly changing situation and seize fleeting opportunities, wherein it entails both physical mobility and reaction capability, with the latter accruing from planning, staff-work and the commander's mental outlook. In the various definitions/interpretations, we can see two themes: first, the ability to respond to change and, second, the ability to impose change. In essence, the principle of Flexibility/Manoeuvre/Initiative/Mobility all look at the Management of Change, both in imposition upon the enemy, by the use of manoeuvre and 'flexible' application of combat power, and in reacting to change that is imposed by the enemy or that occurs otherwise. The purpose, in both cases, is to derive advantage from a change in situation that could occur or be created by either side. The change may occur in the various dimensions of war, i.e. through forces arrayed on land, sea or air, and also at the various levels of warfare, viz. tactical, operational or strategic.

Thus, change may be introduced by the application or redeployment of physical forces in the three dimensions, by the timing of executing change, and also by the very rate of change. In fact, the rate of change or pace/tempo of battle is increasingly being recognised as a key factor in introducing and exploiting vulnerabilities in the enemy's Information-Decision-Action (IDA) Cycle, also leading to suggestions of time becoming an independent dimension of war. The 'manoeuvrist' concept of warfare, espoused in the UK Joint Warfare Doctrine, also envisages application of multiple lines of operation, in physical dimensions, at a higher speed and tempo, so as to overwhelm the enemy's mental and moral capability to cope/respond. It may be seen, therefore, that the current principle of flexibility, whilst constituting a valid concept, is inadequate as it does not address the advantages provided in imposing change on the enemy, which are inherent in the corresponding principles of initiative, manoeuvre, and mobility.

However, these latter principles on their part do not address the value of flexibility in enabling rapid and appropriate response to changes in situations that occur or are imposed by the enemy, or the developments in using time/tempo in unsettling the enemy's management of change. Hence, this principle needs to be expanded in scope, and the concepts of Flexibility, Initiative, Manoeuvre, and Mobility all subsumed into a more inclusive term, such as the Management of Change.

Cooperation/Unity of Command has been viewed as the coordination of efforts to attain a common goal. In India and UK, this is seen as emanating from 'jointness', wherein cooperation is the vehicle by which the necessary coordination is sought to be delivered. In the US interpretation of this PoW, coordination is sought to be attained by vesting a single commander with the requisite authority, viz. unity of command, which would allow him to direct all forces in coordinated action. The moot and common point here is in the need for coordination of effort and actions by multiple forces, of the same and also allied nations, so as to avoid mutual interference and synergise their effect upon the opponent. This clearly brings out that the principle is simply Coordination, as already adapted by Russia and China. The concepts of unity of command or cooperation are, thus, not principles in themselves, but merely the tools used to comply with the core, common principle and organisational method of attaining coordination. In an era of growing joint and combined complex and specialised operations, there is increasing focus on effective coordination, through a variety of means. This becomes even more valid in the case of limited conventional wars, where limitations in time, space or methods employable necessitate synchronisation of efforts, as also in subconventional wars, where there is likely to be a larger number of actors and resources involved, including non-military resources. In these cases, unity of command per se may not be feasible and is less likely to provide the result by itself.

Additional tools to strengthen coordination, through joint planning training, perspective and organisations, and experience of combined, multinational operations have accordingly become increasingly important. The principle of Security refers to protection of own forces from enemy action. In essence this points to the factor of vulnerability, in turn, therefore, this is aimed at enhancing own freedom of action. The utility of this concept is certainly evident, but not as an independent principle in the light of the arguments made earlier for replacing the principle of offensive action by Freedom of Action (FoA). It follows that this latter new principle of FoA would subsume the principle of security as well, wherein the concept of maintaining security is inherent in the maintenance of own FoA. The converse of the principle of security is also covered in FoA, viz. attacking the enemy's security through denying him FoA through manoeuvre and offensive counter-FoA operations. The principle of security is, thus, deemed limited in scope, and not worthy of categorisation as an independent principle. Its replacement and absorption by FoA would provide a more robust and inclusive principle.

The principle of Surprise has long been seen as a necessary force multiplier, to provide the decisive edge at strategic, operational and tactical levels of warfare. It entails catching the enemy off-balance and thereby forcing him to give battle in circumstances unfavourable to him. There is a growing realisation, however, that surprise is increasingly difficult to attain at the strategic and operational levels, as a result of the increasing transparency of the battlespace and effect of the Information Age. The reduced attainability of this condition in modern warfare would lead to its reduced applicability as a principle, which gravitates against its viability and status as an independent Principle of War. It is important to examine the purpose and limitations of surprise, in relation to modern warfare, to identify and rectify the flaw.

The purpose of surprise is, very evidently, to provide an advantage, by pushing the enemy 'off-balance'. The purpose itself indicates that surprise is only 'a', and not necessarily 'the', means to an end, let alone being considered as an end/goal in itself, even though it has been hitherto a primary means in attaining the above purpose. But, in the modern techno-tactical environment, the attainability and sustainability of surprise is coming increasingly under question, whereby combat power would still need to be applied in significant measure to achieve dominance and victory. A great deal would also depend upon a common but frequently ignored aspect of warfare, i.e. the enemy and his ability to cope with surprise. After all, once the initial surprise and possible dislocation due to it is over, the enemy could well convert the disadvantage of being tactically surprised into an advantage of his own, through a technological surprise or a counter-tactical surprise move. Hence, surprise also has to be converted into continuing operational/tactical advantage, rather than be limited to an initial action or early advantage, which has sometimes been deemed adequate. The foregoing does not lend support to the qualification of surprise per se as an independent principle. On the other hand, credible nuclear deterrence relies on reducing surprise and ensuring transparency to allow for successful deterrence.

The excessive focus on surprise as a PoW, and its centrality in avoiding casualties or attrition warfare, appears to have masked the fact that it is merely a tool and not the main principle, as borne out by its stated purpose of "catching the enemy off-balance." The principle, in fact, lies in pushing and then keeping the enemy 'off-balance', rather than in attaining surprise per se. This would require the generation of an asymmetry, which would allow application of combat power in own favour, and then sustaining the same so as to develop a favourable momentum (in other words, a continuing competitive advantage) in the war/battle and thereby attain the overall aims. Hence, it could also be expressed in terms of a 'competitive advantage' in strategic, operational, tactical and also technological terms. Technological asymmetry and surprise is perhaps even more important, but would provide its best value where the doctrine has been developed to support and exploit its potential, so that it can be used in ways superior to that of the enemy, even where the technological level of the opposing forces may be similar. Hence, the key point is the need for a more comprehensive concept, such as Generation and Sustenance of

Favourable Asymmetry, to provide the guidelines in waging of warfare in modern conditions. Surprise, as such, would be one facet of establishing continuing favourable asymmetry in the application of combat power, even while generation and sustenance of favourable asymmetry as a principle would employ a broader range of technical and tactical tools.

The attainment of favourable asymmetry has been the basic theme in warfare through history. The methods used have included use of surprise in terms of time and space, advantages of new technology, exploitation of operational art and environment, use of stratagem, information superiority, etc. Technological tools have arguably been as, if not more, effective than surprise in time and space, for generating favourable asymmetry. The Israeli actions at Beka'a Valley in June 1982 relied on integration of technology with doctrine, leading to spectacular results, and became the forerunner of modern joint operations and the "Revolution in Military Affairs." In World War II, Rommel preparation of the battlefield by RC-135 electronic surveillance aircraft, E-2C Hawkeye AWACS and UAVs, wherein the movement of Syrian forces were constantly tracked. This led to the destruction of 86 Syrian aircraft, 400 tanks and 24 SAM sites, against the loss of only one Israeli aircraft, in 96 hours. The attainment of favourable asymmetry has been the basic theme in warfare through history. The methods used have included use of surprise in terms of time and space, advantages of new technology, exploitation of operational art and environment, use of stratagem, information superiority, etc. marshalled his forces and used them in superior tactical manner to generate local favourable asymmetry against superior forces, mostly by sheer speed of advance.

However, he did not possess the means to sustain that advantage due to poor logistics back-up and inferior air power. The Allied forces, on the other hand, were able to generate sustained favourable asymmetry with air-land cohesion and better logistics, and were thereby able to push Rommel back. This revised approach to the PoW would also recognise logistics as an important ingredient in generating and sustaining favourable asymmetry. The use of pace and tempo of operations, discussed above in the context of flexibility/manoeuvre and the manoeuvrist approach to warfare, also provides another tool for generation of asymmetry, even in the absence of strategic or operational surprise. For example Op Cactus Lily, the Indian military strike through East Pakistan in 1971 in 12 days, led to the collapse of Pakistani defences and capture of 90,000 Pakistani military prisoners of war. It follows, therefore, that the attainment of favourable asymmetry sets the conditions for military victory and is its prerequisite at some stage of the operation. Further, its maintenance enables the avoidance of defeat by denying the enemy the conditions for victory. Asymmetry is not generated automatically through its potential or possession, but by the specific interaction in time and space against the opponent, employing various tools, such as the above. Hence, generation and sustenance of favourable asymmetry deserves to be viewed as an independent PoW, with surprise as its sub-set.

The principle of Administration primarily covers logistics, and also welfare and discipline. The use and value of Logistics in winning wars has been amply demonstrated throughout history, such as its effect on Rommel's operations in North Africa despite tactical superiority, and bears no further reiteration. Based on its time-tested central role in the history of warfare, and its continued relevance today, such as in expanding the reach and reducing the time for response of a force, logistics merits recognition as an independent principle of war. Its inclusion within the principle of administration, as presently done, tends to dilute the value of this concept and limit the scope as long as it is yoked to administration. The aspects of welfare and discipline, which have been dovetailed with logistics in the principle of administration, are certainly important, but need mix up with logistics, which stands on its own merit. In fact, welfare and discipline are more relevant to, and better covered under, the existing, separate principle of Maintenance of Morale, as they are contributory factors to the same. In the practice of maintenance of morale, another aspect that bears recognition is the new challenges thrown against it by the modern techno-tactical environment, where morale has to be maintained for forces spread across different dimensions and separated theatres, amidst higher intensity and increasing opaqueness of operations, and an increasingly deleterious and visible effect of war and its human cost. This is more so in the case of prolonged counter-insurgency and anti-terrorist warfare, in own and foreign lands.

There are a couple of principles that have been enunciated by some countries, but which do not have a parallel amongst other nations. These include "simplicity" in the USA, and "political mobilisation" in China. A closer look at these 'principles' reveals that they do not really merit independent status. Simplicity simply entails avoiding 'complexity' in military operations. In essence, it addresses the need to maintain clarity and cohesion at all levels, and avoidance of unnecessary complications. However, this principle is inherent in the application of the first PoW of aim/objective, and flows from the same, whilst also forming part of the execution of some others, such as "coordination" and "logistics." Hence, its value as an independent PoW is questionable, and it belongs more at the doctrinal level than amongst the higher PoW. Similarly, "political mobilisation" is inherent in the "maintenance of synergy" in politico-military aims.

THE AUSTRO-PRUSSIAN WAR-THE FIRST MODERN WAR

The Civil War featured a number of new innovations-ironclads, land mines, and so forth. It is often represented that the new rifle musket was one of these great innovations-that it made the old tactics obsolete, that thousands of lives were wasted by using 50 year old tactics. Although the tactics used weren't exactly Napoleonic in a Napoleon I sense, they were NOT modern either-an evolution not a revolution.

Major tactical change in the mid 19th century was pioneered by the Prussian army. Only they dared to make radical change. Developed in 1848, the Prussian Dreyse needle gun was a quick firing, bolt-action, breech-loading rifle that infantrymen could load and fire in a prone position. In 1863, the Prussians estimated that three hundred of their men armed with the needle gun were superior to 900 of the enemy armed with muzzle loaders. In a small engagement at Lundby in the 1864 Denmark War, 124 Prussians repulsed 180 attacking Danes, inflicted 88 casualties on them as they advanced from 250 meters to 150 meters. In 1866, Prussian troops armed with needle guns easily defeated an Austrian army equipped with muzzle-loading Lorenz rifles, weapons also used in the Civil War. Instead of using a long thin line of men to blast away at an opposing long thin line of men at close range, the Prussians used small company columns that sent men forward into skirmish lines to gain fire superiority.

The skirmish line would take advantage of the terrain, and the men, who had had extensive target practice, would take careful note of the range to the enemy and adjust their sights accordingly. The skirmish line was now the main effort, and the column existed primarily to lend support and to send troops forward to the skirmish line. These methods easily defeated the Austrians, who used columns of infantry for shock attacks.

At Podol, 400 Prussians defeated 2,000 Austrians, losing only 100 men compared to over 1,000 killed, wounded, and captured Austrians. (Austro p134) At Trautenau, an Austrian "victory", 5,000 Austrians were lost compared to 1,300 Prussians. (Austro p150) Austrian artillery was effective out to 5,000 meters, but the gunners were vulnerable to fire from the needle gun. One Austrian battery at Koniggratz lost 54 men and 68 horses to rifle fire in the course of several minutes, (Austro p 252) something the likes of which had not seen in the American Civil War. Although only one Prussian bullet out of 250 fired actually hit anyone-little different from the past-the Austrians lost 5 men to every one the Prussians lost-plus the rapid fire had an immense psychological impact on the enemy. (The Franco-Prussian War, Geoffrey Wawro p51) Prussian cavalry, despite facing rifled muskets, were effectively used against fleeing infantry and even successfully captured an enemy artillery battery. (Austro p262) Had Civil War armies faced the Prussians, they too would have been slaughtered.

Prussian Needle Gun

In response to these developments, the French army fielded the breech-loading Chassepot rifle which could fire 8 to 15 rounds per minute compared to the 4 to 5 rounds of the Prussian needle gun. (Franco p52) The Chassepot had a longer range as well. In the early skirmishes of the war, it was clear that the Chassepot was superior. In one instance, a French platoon held off a company, and in another, three Frenchmen stopped a column of Prussians. (Franco 87, 93) In addition to quick firing, breech loading rifles, the Franco-Prussian War in 1870 also featured breech-loading artillery, effective out to 3,800 meters, and the mitrailleuse, a crude machine gun mounted on an artillery carriage. The mitrailleuse mowed men down at a range of 1,200 yards firing 100 to 200 rounds per minute. (Franco 53) All of these weapons lead to a genuine tactical revolution. Prussian weapons and tactics were matched against even superior French small arms, and Prussian frontal attacks consistently failed. Newer, more lethal weapons had forced new tactics, and combat was less decisive. By the Franco-Prussian War, artillery and infantry could still co-operate in battle, but cavalry co-operating with infantry in the attack was no longer practical. Its use was now limited to screening the army. (Franco 61) Infantry fighting exclusively as skirmishers had made infantry fire even more deadly and the men more steady than if they were in closed order. Jean Colin in his classic "Transformations of Warfare" explains:

"Comparative isolation is good for the morale of a man from the time he finds himself in the zone of fire. If men are close to each other emotions are transmitted and hyper-excitement is reciprocally induced-this is very bad for the steadiness of the combatant.... If the intervals are large, the man who falls has plenty of room, is seen by a less number of people, and drags no one down in his fall; the moral(e) impression made on his comrades is slighter, their courage is less shaken."

French Chassepot

So all factors conspired to make combat less decisive. Much more so than during the American Civil War, the defence was now supreme, and an army with an average of one man per yard of front could be expected to hold its position. Shallow flanking moves became the key to success on the battlefield. In comparison, even behind entrenchments, Lee's army at Spotsylvania averaged

5 men per yard, and Civil War armies on occasion averaged 8 men per yard of front.

As weapons technology continued to advance, the indecisive trench warfare of the First World War was the next logical step. In 1914 the battle line stretched so far that there was no flank remaining to attack. Infantry units were still armed exclusively with rifles.

To break this deadlock, rifle units were replaced with units armed with a mix of weapons down to the squad level-grenades, flame throwers, mortars, and squad automatics, all used together for the purpose of fire suppression- keeping the enemy's head down. This allowed the infantry to move forward for the kill. This was the beginning of modern tactics like those still used today. The family tree of these modern tactics goes back to mid 19th century Europe-not to the American Civil War, which had no children.

Casualty Figures

Further proof that Civil War weapons were not as deadly as they are often portrayed can be found in casualty figures. Historians charting the lethality of weapons discovered a counter-intuitive trend. As the lethality of weapons increased, the percentage casualties for a constant unit of time has decreased. So while battles in the linear era produced casualties in the range of 10 to 40% per day, by World War II, casualties on the order of 1% per day were considered heavy. Let's take a look at some battles over a range of time periods to compare the losses-killed and wounded only-not captured or missing. (generally, figures are from David Chandler's Guide to the Battlefields of Europe)

A Rifled Musket Revolution?

But why compare Civil War tactics to those of the eighteenth century and Napoleon's time? After all, the rifled musket had changed everything. Right? That's what almost everyone says, and the majority is never wrong, now is it? John Hennessey, in his excellent book "Return to Bull", gives the conventional version of the effect of the rifled musket. He writes:

"Civil War tactics were largely the product of Napoleon Bonaparte. That meant, most particularly, that their theory was predicated in large part on the use of the bayonet. But in 1862, after First Manassas, Shiloh and Gaines Mill, the rifle musket, now in vogue on both sides, had rendered the bayonet charge impractical. While Napoleon's charging lines at Waterloo or Austerlitz had been exposed to musket fire for a hundred yards, the rifle muskets could ravage a charging line with accuracy from 350 yards in, and do damage at more than 500 yards. By 1862, most battle lines never made it close enough to engage in a classic hand-to-hand fight. Most soldiers found their bayonets more useful as candle holders or pot hooks than as weapons of death."

Not to pick on Mr. Hennessey, but he misunderstands Napoleonic tactics and the use of bayonet. In Napoleon's time, as well as in the Civil War, the bayonet was a psychological weapon-and a powerful one. With few exceptions, the bayonet charge was conducted only after achieving fire superiority-which created morale superiority. When the enemy line looked shaky was the time for a bayonet attack. An advance with cold steel would convince him that he had a pressing engagement further to the rear. The fact that bayonet wounds have always been rare does not prove that the bayonet was an ineffective weapon. It proves the exact opposite.

As we will see, Civil War rifle-muskets aren't all that they're cracked up to be. A major advance in small arms during the half century before was actually the percussion cap, which, unlike flints, were consistently reliable. A much higher percentage of shots after the first volley were fired successfully, and the infantryman could pay more attention to his aim without gunpowder burning near his eyes.

Rifled bullets also flew a straighter, more predictable course. But in one important respect the rifled musket was actually inferior to its predecessor. A bullet traveling down a smoothbore barrel would bounce around, with its final trajectory determined by its final bounce. But at fairly short range, 100 yards or less, the smoothbore was quite good, though, with between 40-75% of shots hitting a simulated line of cavalry in various peacetime experiments. At 200 yards, 18-30% of shots hit the target. The rifling in the new rifled muskets gave the bullet a much truer course, but they also created much more friction than in smoothbores, which lowered the muzzle velocity significantly. This meant that the bullet traveled a more parabolic course. So even though the bullet flew a *truer* course, its relatively slow speed meant that at long range the shooter had to estimate the range accurately to within a few yards in order to hit his target.

Jack Coggins writes, "A bullet fired by a kneeling man at the belt buckle of a man running toward him at an estimated range of 300 yards would pass over the head of a man 250 yards away. Thus, if the shooter had overestimated the range by as little as 50 yards he would have missed." In addition, the bullet would fall at the feet of a man 350 yards away. The further the range, the more vital the estimate of range was, and the more difficult the task became. Twentieth century studies show that people are quite bad at estimating ranges, with errors usually around 30%. (Ohio Dept of Natural Resources, Division of Wildlife website) Modern rifles are much better longer range weapons. While the rifled musket bullet would rise 43 inches over the line of sight, a World War II era M-1 rifle bullet would rise just 7.2 inches above the line of sight, making accurate range estimation much less important. (Coggins 38-9) Despite the flatter trajectory of modern bullets, even today, firefights rarely occur at ranges over 400 yards. The human eye is the reason for this. In fact, at 500 yards, a human face can only be made out as a light spot. (Hughes 26) Take a look across a football field. Do you think you could hit anything at 100 yards? What if someone was shooting at YOU? Brent Nosworthy's "Bloody Crucible of Courage" says that the Union army quit making adjustable sights for their rifle muskets because the men were too frightened in battle to remember to adjust them. Perhaps it wouldn't have mattered even if men could keep their wits in battle.

Many men were too frightened to even tell whether their weapon had fired. Not even noting the absence of a kick to their shoulder, a strong enough force to leave a bruise, men simply loaded one round on top of the other. SLA Marshall, in a flawed but important study of Korean War combat, found that a substantial portion of infantrymen in battle never fired their weapons; the fear of death simply overcame them. It is expecting a great deal for an infantryman to accomplish the simple task of loading and aiming a musket in battle. People are not designed to face that sort of danger. They are designed to run for their lives.

When you also figure that after some artillery fire and a volley or two of musketry there may have be so much smoke that men couldn't even see the enemy, how can you expect them to hit anything? It should be no surprise that Paddy Griffith in "Battle Tactics of the Civil War" calculated an average first volley of around 140 yards, little different from previous wars, and with little difference in lethality. When you consider that each man was eager to open fire, to do something seemingly constructive against the threat facing him, 140 yards was too far away for an effective volley.

So although rifle-muskets were an improvement over smoothbores, the advantage appears slight. Grady McWhiney's thesis that there was a rifle revolution and that the Confederates wasted their manpower in futile frontal assaults is dead wrong. The technology of rifled muskets didn't make combat indecisive. Other factors may have, however.

Napoleonic Tactics and Civil War Tactics

If you understand how Napoleon fought, you will see that Civil War tactics were different in a number of important ways. These differences perhaps explain the indecisive nature of Civil War combat.

In the gunpowder age, battle was rarely decisive; Napoleonic combat, the ultimate development of linear tactics, is the exception. To understand Napoleonic tactics, you first have to understand how and why they developed. To do that, you have to go back one hundred years before even Napoleon's time to the invention of the socket bayonet. Before then, an infantry battalion was an unwieldy and vulnerable combination of musketeers and pikemen, with the pikemen protecting the musketeers from enemy pikemen and cavalry. When the socket bayonet replaced the plug bayonet, musketeers shed themselves of pikemen because they could now protect themselves and still fire their muskets. Musketeers stretched themselves thinner, first into six ranks, then four, then three, and finally just two. It was still an awkward system in some ways, with difficulty deploying an army from the march into line of battle. In Marlborough's day, in the early 1700s, it took most of the day to prepare for battle, and it was impossible to surprise an enemy on the march. When battle began, the whole of the infantry would typically attack together simultaneously in two lines. The logical place for cavalry was still on the flanks. In battle, the cavalry would defeat the opposing enemy horsemen then attack the rear of the enemy infantry just like in the 1600s-but also much like during the Civil War, at least in theory. By Napoleon's time, however, this would change-thanks to advances in infantry tactics.

With the use of thinner battle lines-two or three ranks-a quicker system was developed to deploy from marching column into line of battle. Battle was becoming more practical, no longer a rare and consensual event. Frederick the Great perfected this system, marching and deploying on the enemy's flank for a devastating attack. If you have read about Frederick at Leuthen, you will see the similarities with Jackson's attack on the XI Corps at Chancellorsville, Early's attack at Cedar Creek, and Warren's attack at Five Forks. And if you have heard of Rossbach, then you might be skeptical of Longstreet's hoped-for turning movement at Gettysburg. Indeed, in many ways the Civil War looks more like the Seven Years War than it does the Napoleonic Wars. Let's take a look at change in the 18th century and the development of Napoleonic tactics, one feature at a time.

Artillery

There was plenty of room to improve upon mid-18th century tactics, and the defeated and humiliated French army lead the way with reform. The Austrians had already made great strides in reducing the weight of their guns, with their new pieces weighing only half as much as their predecessors.

The French adopted these concepts with the Gribeauval system. Frederick had already complaining in the Seven Years' War that the new Austrian artillery was killing off his highly trained infantry, who were re-known for their discipline and quick rate of fire. The new lighter field artillery had the potential to revolutionize warfare. There was no choice for a monarch but to enter into an artillery arms race-or else have his army slaughtered. Masses of the new mobile guns could be brought to bear against the enemy, blowing holes in his line and demoralizing his men.

Skirmishers

Frederick was also whining that Austrian light infantrymen sent ahead of their main line were picking off officers and men while taking cover behind trees and terrain features. With an army made in many cases of forcibly recruited Euro-trash held in bondage only by the threat of severe punishment, Frederick couldn't trust his men to go forward and skirmish. With the prospect of freedom, they might run away and never be seen again.

Frederick resisted this change, at least for a while. Other armies developed highly trained and motivated special units of light infantry too. Although skirmishers of the French Revolutionary Wars and Napoleonic times are often stereotyped as ill-trained levies good for nothing more than swarming in dense masses in front of the enemy line, modern historians dispute this. Whenever possible, skirmishers of the era were highly motivated, well trained, and good shots. Their calm, slow, well-aimed fire, combined with artillery, gradually wore down the enemy and un-nerved the survivors before the main attack.

Columns

A misunderstanding of early English-speaking historians has distorted our understanding of a major aspect of Napoleonic warfare-the use of columns. Focusing on the Peninsula War and relying almost exclusively on British sources, some historians came to the misguided conclusion that the French primarily used battalions of infantry for shock action in columns of attack. As early as the mid 1700s the French were keeping their second line in column formation to allow for a flexible response to problems or opportunities on the first line. During the 1777 Battle of Brandywine, the British army, generally thought of as conservative, advanced on the rebels in maneuver columns then deployed into line. By Napoleonic times French infantry, preceded by skirmishers, advanced toward the enemy in battalion-sized columns for more flexibility and maneuverability on the battlefield, allowing them to adjust to enemy deployments, better seize opportunities, or to attempt to flank the enemy line. Before contact with the enemy, however, the columns would *deploy* into line for the firefight. A bayonet charge in column formation was only done after gaining firepower superiority when the enemy troops looked shaky and on the verge of breaking. Against most armies, this method worked very well. The infantry's increased flexibility helped in other ways. The infantry columns also allowed much closer cooperation with the artillery, which was better able to mass against a portion of the enemy line or even move forward with the infantry. More importantly, closer co-operation with the cavalry was also possible. Unlike in the 18th century, cavalry could advance right along with the infantry.

Cavalry

While 18th century cavalry was placed exclusively on the flanks, the new infantry columns allowed the mounted arm to advance in columns directly in support of the infantry, and even change places with them to lead the attack. To protect themselves. enemy infantry would form squares, but in so doing they deprived themselves of much of their firepower and their ability to maneuver. If artillery could be brought forward, the enemy squares would be blasted out of existence. Either way, a massive hole was formed in the enemy line, and decisive victory was assured.

In terms of grand tactics, Napoleon would typically threaten the enemy's flank, forcing him to commit his reserve. He always kept a large reserve available, a vitally important part of his system, to either exploit success of stave off defeat. Most often, with the enemy reserve committed, Napoleon would send his own reserve into the weak point in the enemy line and secure a decisive victory. Co-operation among all three combat arms was key to Napoleon's system, and the reserve decided the battle. Does this sound like Civil War tactics to you? No! Civil War armies kept few reserves, and Civil War combat featured little in the way of combined arms cooperation. Civil War tactics were NOT Napoleonic. The new French tactics in Spain and Portugal didn't work out so well, and their old school British opponents may have never understood their intent.

Rough terrain complicated the system considerably. It was difficult to mass artillery batteries, and it was difficult for cavalry to support the infantry. Wellington sometimes sent as much as one third of his men forward as skirmishers, and the French could never gain superiority over them. Since Wellington kept his infantry hidden behind the reverse slope, the French maneuver columns blundered upon the British line and were surprised. Struggling to deploy into line and disorganized and shocked by the surprise encounter, the French received one or two close range volleys from their British opponents who then let out a cheer and charged. The British system worked consistently, except at Albeura-and at Waterloo, where the open terrain suited Napoleon's methods. Terrain explains much of the British success against the French. In part, terrain also explains why combined arms tactics were so rare during the Civil War, but we'll discuss that later. Perhaps because of the British success, and because of the bloody nature of Napoleon's later battles, post-Napoleonic military theorists became somewhat reactionary and supported tactics which looked backward to the 18th century.

2

World War I

WORLD WAR I: CAUSES

The reasons of World War I, which began in central Europe in late July 1914, incorporated intertwined factors, such as the conflicts and hostility of the four decades leading up to the war. Militarism, alliances, imperialism, and nationalism played biggest roles in the clash as well. The immediate origins of the war, though, place in the decisions taken through statesmen and generals throughout the Crisis of 1914, casus belli for which was the assassination of Archduke Franz Ferdinand of Austria and his wife through Gavrilo Princip, an irredentist Serb.

The crisis came after an extensive and hard series of diplomatic clashes flanked by the Great Powers (Italy, France, Germany, the British Empire, the Austria-Hungarian Empire, and Russia) in excess of European and colonial issues in the decade before 1914 that had left tensions high. In turn these diplomatic clashes can be traced to changes in the balance of power in Europe since, 1867. The more immediate reason for the war was tensions in excess of territory in the Balkans. Austria-Hungary competed with Serbia and Russia for territory and power in the area and they pulled the rest of the Great Powers into the clash by their several alliances and treaties.

Although the chain of measures unleashed through the assassination triggered the war, the war's origins go deeper, involving national politics, cultures, economics, and a intricate web of alliances and counterbalances that had urbanized flanked by the several European powers since, 1870. Some of the mainly significant extensive term or structural reasons are: the development of nationalism crossways Europe, unresolved territorial disputes, an complex organization of alliances, the perceived breakdown of the balance of power in Europe, convoluted and fragmented governance, the arms races of the previous decades, previous military scheduling, imperial and colonial rivalry for wealth, power and prestige, and economic and military rivalry in industry and deal - *e.g.*, the Pig War flanked by Austria and Serbia. Other reasons that came into play throughout the diplomatic crisis that preceded the war incorporated misperceptions of intent (*e.g.*, the German belief that the United Kingdom would remain neutral) and delays and misunderstandings in diplomatic communications.

The several categories of explanation for World War I correspond to dissimilar historians' overall ways. Mainly historians and popular commentators contain reasons from more than one category of explanation to give a rounded explanation of the reasons of the war. The deepest distinction in the middle of these accounts is flanked by stories that see it as the inevitable and predictable outcome of sure factors, and those that define it as an arbitrary and unfortunate mistake.

In attributing reasons for the war, historians and academics had to deal with an unprecedented flood of memoirs and official documents, released as each country involved tried to avoid blame for starting the war. Early releases of information through governments, particularly those released for use through the "Commission on the Responsibility of the Authors of the War" were shown to be partial and biased. In addition some documents, especially diplomatic cables flanked by Russia and France, were establish to have been doctored. Even in later decades though, when much more information had been released, historians from the similar civilization have been shown to approach to differing conclusions on the reasons of the war.

Backdrop

In November 1912, Russia was humiliated because of its inability to support Serbia throughout the Bosnian crisis of 1908 or the First Balkan War, and announced a biggest reconstruction of its military.

On November 28, German Foreign Secretary Gottlieb von Jagow told the Reichstag (the German parliament), that "If Austria is forced, for whatever cause, to fight for its location as a Great Power, then we necessity stand through her." As a result, British Foreign Secretary Sir Edward Grey responded through warning Prince Karl Lichnowsky, the German Ambassador in London, that if Germany offered Austria a "blank cheque" for war in the Balkans, then "the consequences of such a policy would be incalculable." To reinforce this point, R. B. Haldane, the Germanophile Lord Chancellor, met with Prince Lichnowsky to offer an explicit warning that if Germany were to attack France, Britain would intervene in France's favour.

With the recently announced Russian military reconstruction and sure British communications, the possibility of war was a leading topic at the German Imperial War Council of 8 December 1912 in Berlin, an informal meeting of some of Germany's top military leadership described on short notice through the Kaiser. Attending the conference were Kaiser Wilhelm II, Admiral Alfred von Tirpitz-the Naval State Secretary, Admiral Georg Alexander von Müller, the Chief of the German Imperial Naval Cabinet (Marinekabinett), Common von Moltke-the Army's Chief of Staff, Admiral August von Heeringen-the Chief of the Naval Common Staff and Common Moriz von Lyncker, the Chief of the German Imperial Military Cabinet. The attendance of the leaders of both the German Army and Navy at this War Council attests to its importance. Though, Chancellor Theobald von Bethmann-Hollweg and Common Josias von Heeringen, the Prussian Minister of War, were not invited.

Wilhelm II described British balance of power principles "idiocy," but agreed that Haldane's statement was a "desirable clarification" of British policy. His opinion was that Austria should attack Serbia that December, and if "Russia supports the Serbs, which she evidently does...then war would be unavoidable for us, too," and that would be bigger than going to war after Russia completed the huge modernization and expansion of their army that they had presently begun. Moltke agreed. In his professional military opinion "a war is unavoidable and the sooner the bigger". Moltke "wanted to launch an immediate attack".

Both Wilhelm II and the Army leadership agreed that if a war were necessary it were best launched soon. Admiral Tirpitz, though, asked for a "postponement of the great fight for one and a half years" because the Navy was not ready for a common war that incorporated Britain as an opponent.

He insisted that the completion of the construction of the U-boat foundation at Heligoland and the widening of the Kiel Canal were the Navy's prerequisites for war. As the British historian John Röhl has commented, the date for completion of the widening of the Kiel Canal was the summer of 1914. However Moltke objected to the postponement of the war as unacceptable, Wilhelm sided with Tirpitz. Moltke "agreed to a postponement only reluctantly."

Historians more sympathetic to the government of Wilhelm II often reject the importance of this War Council as only showing the thinking and recommendations of those present, with no decisions taken. They often cite the passage from Admiral Müller's diary, which states: "That was the end of the conference. The result amounted to nothing." Certainly the only decision taken was to do nothing.

Historians more sympathetic to the Entente, such as British historian John Röhl, sometimes rather ambitiously interpret these languages of Admiral Müller (an advocate of launching a war soon) as saying that "nothing" was decided for 1912-13, but that war was decided on for the summer of 1914. Röhl is on safer ground when he argues that even if this War Council did not reach a binding decision-which it clearly did not-it did non-etheless offer a clear view of their intentions, or at least their considerations, which were that if there was going to be a war, the German Army wanted it before the new Russian armaments programme began to bear fruit. Entente sympathetic historians such as Röhl see this conference, in which "The result amounted to nothing," as setting a clear deadline for a war to begin, namely the summer of 1914.

With the November 1912 announcement of the Russian Great Military Programme, the leadership of the German Army began clamoring even more strongly for a "preventive war" against Russia. Moltke declared that Germany could not win the arms race with France, Britain and Russia, which she herself had begun in 1911, because the financial structure of the German state, which gave the Reich government little power to tax, meant Germany would bankrupt herself in an arms race. As such, Moltke from late 1912 onwards was the leading advocate for a common war, and the sooner the bigger. During May and June 1914, Moltke occupied in an "approximately ultimative" demand for a German "preventive war" against Russia in 1914.

The German Foreign Secretary, Gottlieb von Jagow, accounted on a discussion with Moltke at the end of May 1914: "Moltke called to me his opinion of our military situation. The prospects of the future oppressed him heavily. In two or three years Russia would have completed her armaments. The military superiority of our enemies would then be therefore great that he did not know how he could overcome them. Today we would still be a match for them. In his opinion there was no alternative to creation preventive war in order to defeat the enemy while we still had a chance of victory. The Chief of the Common Staff so proposed that I should conduct a policy with the aim of provoking a war in the close to future."

The new French President Raymond Poincaré, who took office in 1913, was favourable to improving relations with Germany. In January 1914 Poincaré became the first French President to dine at the German Embassy in Paris. Poincaré was more interested in the thought of French expansion in the Transitional East than a war of revenge to regain Alsace-Lorraine. Had the Reich been interested in improved relations with France before August 1914, the opportunity was accessible, but the leadership of the Reich lacked such interests, and preferred a policy of war to destroy France. Because of France's smaller economy and population, through 1913 French leaders had mainly carried that France through itself could never defeat Germany.

In May 1914, Serbian politics were polarized flanked by two factions, one headed through the Prime Minister Nikola Paši?, and the other through the radical nationalist chief of Military

Intelligence, Colonel Dragutin Dimitrijevi?, recognized through his codename Apis. In that month, due to Colonel Dimitrigjevic's intrigues, King Peter dismissed Paši?'s government.

The Russian Minister in Belgrade intervened to have Paši?'s government restored. Paši?, however he often talked tough in public, knew that Serbia was close to-bankrupt and, having suffered heavy casualties in the Balkan Wars and in the suppression of a December 1913 Albanian revolt in Kosovo, needed peace. Since, Russia also favoured peace in the Balkans, from the Russian viewpoint it was desirable to stay Paši? in power. It was in the midst of this political crisis that politically powerful members of the Serbian military armed and trained three Bosnian students as assassins and sent them into Austria-Hungary.

DOMESTIC POLITICAL FACTORS

German Domestic Politics

Left-wing parties, especially the Social Democratic Party of Germany (SPD) made big gains in the 1912 German election. German government at the time was still dominated through the Prussian Junkers who feared the rise of these left-wing parties. Fritz Fischer famously argued that they deliberately sought an external war to distract the population and whip up patriotic support for the government. Russia was in the midst of a big-level military build-up and reform that they completed in 1916-17. Other authors argue that German conservatives were ambivalent in relation to the war, worrying that losing a war would have disastrous consequences, and even a successful war might alienate the population if it were lengthy or hard.

French Domestic Politics

The situation in France was quite dissimilar from that in Germany as going to war emerged to the majority of political and military leaders to be a potentially costly gamble. It is undeniable that forty years after the loss of Alsace-Lorraine a huge number of French were still angered through the territorial loss, as well as through the humiliation of being compelled to pay big reparation to Germany in 1870. The diplomatic alienation of France orchestrated through Germany prior to World War I caused further resentment in France. Nevertheless, the leaders of France established Germany's strong military advantage against them, as Germany had almost twice as much population and a bigger equipped army. At the similar time, the episodes of the Tangier Crisis in 1905 and the Agadir Crisis in 1911 had given France a strong indication that war with Germany could be inevitable if Germany sustained to oppose French colonial expansionism.

More than a century after the French Revolution, there was still a fierce thrash about flanked by the left-wing French government and its right-wing opponents, as socialists like Jean Jaurès pushed for peace against nationalists like Paul Déroulède who were inclined to go to war. Recent social reforms created a climate of insecurity which some right-wing politician's idea could be resolved through the nationalistic spirit of war. France in 1914 had never been therefore wealthy and influential in Europe since, 1870, nor its military therefore strong and confident in its leaders, emboldened through its success in North Africa and the overall pacification of its huge colonial empire. Indeed, if France had attempted for more than forty years to appease bellicose Germany, a majority of the Frenchmen now whispered it could face the German threat with more tranquility than before. The Entente Cordiale with Great Britain signed in 1904 seemed to last, being aided through mutual interests abroad and strong economic ties. Russia had fled the triple crown alliance with Germany and Austria-Hungary because of disagreements with Austria-Hungary in excess of policy in the Balkans. Russia also hoped that big French investments in its industry and infrastructures coupled with a significant military partnership would prove themselves profitable and durable.

France ultimately perceived it could fight Germany and effort to gain back the German-speaking provinces of Alsace-Lorraine. It is significant to note though, that France never could have permitted itself to initiate a war with Germany, as its military pact with Great-Britain was only purely suspicious. The misperception that Germany wouldn't, as prepared through the Schlieffen Plan invade neutral Belgium, would discover itself lethal to the suspicious French military doctrine on the eve of the first worldwide clash.

Changes in Austria

In 1867, the Austrian Empire fundamentally changed its governmental structure, becoming the Dual Monarchy of Austria-Hungary. For hundreds of years, the empire had been run in an essentially feudal manner with a German-speaking aristocracy at its head. Though, with the threat represented through an emergence of nationalism within the empire's several component ethnicities, some elements, including Emperor Franz Joseph, decided that a compromise was required to preserve the power of the German aristocracy. In 1867, the Ausgleich was agreed on, which made the Magyar (Hungarian) elite in Hungary approximately equal partners in the government of Austria-Hungary.

This arrangement fostered a tremendous degree of dissatisfaction amongst several in the traditional German ruling classes. Some of them measured the Ausgleich to have been a calamity because it often frustrated their intentions in the governance of Austria-Hungary. For instance, it was very hard for Austria-Hungary to form a coherent foreign policy that suited the interests of both the German and Magyar elite.

During the fifty years from 1867 to 1914, it proved hard to reach adequate compromises in the governance of Austria-Hungary, leading several to search for non-diplomatic solutions. At the similar time, a form of social Darwinism became popular in the middle of several in the Austrian half of the government. This thinking emphasized the primacy of armed thrash about flanked by nations, and require for nations to arm themselves for an ultimate thrash about for survival.

As a result, at least two separate strains of idea advocated war with Serbia, often unified in the similar people. Some reasoned that relation with political deadlock required that more Slavs be brought into Austria-Hungary to dilute the power of the Magyar elite. With more Slavs, the South Slavs of Austria-Hungary could force a new political compromise in which the Germans could play the Magyars against the South Slavs. Other variations on this theme lived, but the essential thought was to cure internal stagnation by external conquest.

Another fear was that the South Slavs, primarily under the leadership of Serbia, were organizing for a war against Austria-Hungary, and even all of Germanic culture. Some leaders, such as Conrad von Hötzendorf, argued that Serbia necessity be dealt with before it became too powerful to defeat militarily. A powerful contingent within the Austro-Hungarian government was motivated through these considerations and advocated war with Serbia extensive before the war began. Prominent members of this group incorporated Leopold von Berchtold, Alexander von Hoyos, and Johann von Forgách. Although several other members of the government, notably Franz Ferdinand, Franz Joseph, and several Hungarian politicians did not consider that a violent thrash about with Serbia would necessarily solve any of Austria-Hungary's troubles, the hawkish elements did exert a strong power on government policy, holding key positions.

Samuel R. Williamson has accentuated the role of Austria-Hungary in starting the war. Influenced Serbian nationalism and Russian Balkan ambitions were disintegrating the Empire, Austria-Hungary hoped for a limited war against Serbia and that strong German support would force Russia to stay out of the war and weaken its Balkan prestige.

PEACE INITIATIVES OF THE BOLSHEVIK GOVERNMENT

The Decree on Peace, one of the first biggest acts of the new Soviet State, proclaimed the abolition of secret diplomacy and in accordance with this law, the Soviet foreign ministry published the previous secret treaties signed through the Tsarist state (Russian emperors were described Tsars), including the Anglo-Russian secret treaty and convention of 1907 on "demarcation" of spheres of interests of both the Powers England and Russia in. the Transitional East; agreement to carve up Turkey flanked by the above two and France concluded in 1916 *etc.*

The refusal of the Entente Powers (the ultimate victorious powers in the First World War) to negotiate a common peace resolution, forced Soviet Russia to enter into peace talks with Germany, Austria, Hungary, Turkey and Bulgaria (the other camp in the war). The Soviet proposal incorporated six points: no forcible, annexation of territories engaged throughout the war; restoration of political independence to nations vanquished throughout the war, freedom of choice to the national minorities to either remain within a state or become self-governing by a referendum; safeguarding of the rights of the national minorities in a state through special legislation protecting their national civilization and whenever possible, administrative autonomy; renunciation of war indemnities; and solution of colonial troubles in accordance with the first four principles. However imperialist Germany rejected the Soviet proposals and imposed humiliating peace conditions on the latter, Lenin still agreed to sign the Peace Treaty of Breast-Litovsk on Germany's conditions despite strong opposition within the Bolshevik party and government. Lenin firmly whispered that war is detrimental to the interests of the toiling people.

Bolshevik Renunciation of Special Privileges in the Neighbouring Countries

The thought of national sovereignty and excellence ran by the theory and practice of Soviet foreign policy, which aimed at reshaping international relations on democratic principles. The emergence of the first socialist state inspired formally self-governing small states, colonies and semi-colonies to thrash about for and defend their sovereignty against depression and encroachment through imperialist powers. In the procedure of evolving a new organization of international relations, the Soviets attached special significance to relations with the Eastern Countries based on the principles of equality, mutual respect and friendship. The Soviet state was willing to provide them friendly assistance in their thrash about against 'imperialism. Despite its hard economic situation, the new socialist state rendered not only political and moral but also $eat material support to countries such as Turkey, Afghanistan, Iran and others. In June 1919, the Soviet government abolished all special privileges for Russian nationals in Iran, renounced all concessions and manage in excess of Iran's state revenue, and handed in excess of to Iran without challenging any compensation, the banks, the railways, highways and port facilities on Iran's Caspian coast and other property which had belonged to Tsarist Russia. A treaty of friendship with Iran was signed in February, 1921 (the first equal treaty flanked by Iran and a European power), guaranteeing Iran's independence and security of her borders with the Soviet state. Likewise, a treaty of friendship and alliance was signed with Turkey, which received generous, economic, financial and military aid from the Soviet state. A Soviet Afghan treaty was signed in Spring 1921 through which interest-free loans were given to the latter and Soviet specialists were assigned to work there.

Rise and Development of Communist and Worker's Movement

The October revolution not only had a great impact on the liberation movements in the colonies, it also paved the method for the rise and development of the communist and workers' movement in the East. To unite several communist groups, parties and movements, to popularize Marxist-Leninist theory and to talk about the debate strategies and tactics of uniting with other nationalist non-communist forces against imperialism, a Communist International was shaped in Moscow in 1919. The ideal that was embodied in the formation of the International was the unity of the working class in the urbanized West and the oppressed peoples of the colonies in their general thrash about against imperialism. The Communist International became the coordinating centre of revolutionaries the world in excess of. The problem of a united anti-imperialist front engaged a central lay in the Comintern's theoretical and practical activities on the national and colonial question. The thought of the unity of all the anti-imperialist forces, in other languages the unity flanked by forces of socialism and the national libration movement crystallized at the second congress of the Comintern in 1920.

Given the repressive nature of the colonial regimes, several communist parties of the Eastern countries were famed in the Soviet Russia under the auspices of the Comintern. Turkish communists were the first to organize a communist party in Soviet Russia, followed through Iranian, Chinese and the, Koreans. The first group of Indian communists, was shaped in October 1920 following the arrival in Tashkent of Indians who had attended the second congress of the Comintern. On the initiative of M.N. Roy and H. Mukherjee this group of seven people proclaimed itself the Communist party of India.

STRATEGY IN WORLD WAR I

At the start of World War I strategy was dominated by the offensive thinking that had been in vogue since 1870, despite the more recent experiences of the Second Boer War (1899-1902) and RussoJapanese War (1904-05), where the machine gun demonstrated its defensive capabilities. By the end of 1914, the Western Front was a stalemate and all ability to manoeuver strategically was lost. The combatants resorted to a "strategy of attrition". The German battle at Verdun, the British on the Somme and at Passchendaele were among the first widescale battles intended to wear down the enemy. Attrition was timeconsuming so the duration of World War I battles often stretched to weeks and months. The problem with attrition was that the use of fortified defenses in depth generally required a ratio of ten attackers to one defender, or a level of artillery support which was simply not feasible until late 1917, for any reasonable chance of victory. The ability of the defender to move troops using interior lines prevented the possibility of fully exploiting any breakthrough with the level of technology then attainable.

Perhaps the most controversial aspect of strategy in World War I was the difference among the British between the "Western" viewpoint (held by Field Marshal Haig) and the "Eastern"; the former being that all effort should be directed against the German Army, the latter that more useful work could be done by attacking Germany's allies. The term "Knocking away the props" was used, perhaps an unfortunate consequence of the fact that all of Germany's allies lay south of (i.e. 'beneath') her on the map. Apologists and defenders of the Western viewpoint make the valid point that Germany's allies were more than once rescued from disaster or rendered capable of holding their own or making substantial gains by the provision of German troops, arms or military advisers, whereas those allies did not at any time provide a similar function for Germany. That is, it was Germany which was the prop, and her allies (particularly Bulgaria and AustriaHungary) did not suffer significant reverses until Germany's ability to come to their aid was grossly impaired.

On other fronts, there was still room for the use of strategy of manoeuver. The Germans executed a perfect battle of annihilation against the Russians at the Battle of Tannenberg (1914). In 1915 Britain and France launched the well-intentioned but poorly conceived and ultimately fruitless Dardanelles Campaign, combining naval power and an amphibious landing, in an effort to aid their Russian ally and knock the Ottoman Empire out of the war. The Palestine campaign was dominated by cavalry, which flourished in the local terrain, and the British achieved two breakthrough victories at Gaza (1917) and Megiddo (1918). Colonel T.E. Lawrence and other British officers led Arab irregulars on a guerrilla campaign against the Ottomans, using strategy and tactics developed during the Boer Wars.

World War I saw armies on a scale never before experienced. The British, who had always relied on a strong navy and a small regular army, were forced to undertake a rapid expansion of the army. This outpaced the rate of training of generals and staff officers able to handle such a mammoth force, and overwhelmed the ability of British industry to equip it with the necessary weapons and adequate highquality munitions until late in the war. Technological advances also had a huge influence on strategy: aerial reconnaissance, artillery techniques, poison gas, the automobile and tank (though the latter was, even at the end of the war, still in its infancy), telephone and radio telegraphy.

More so than in previous wars, military strategy in World War I was directed by the grand strategy of a coalition of nations; the Entente on one side and the Central Powers on the other. Society and economy were mobilized for total war. Attacks on the enemy's economy included Britain's use of a naval blockade and Germany employing submarine warfare against merchant shipping.

Unity of command became a question when the various nation states began coordinating assaults and defenses. Under the pressure of horrendously destructive German attacks beginning on March

21, 1918, the Entente eventually settled under Field Marshal Foch. The Germans generally led the Central Powers, though German authority diminished and lines of command became confused at the end of the war. World War I strategy was dominated by the "Spirit of the Offensive" where generals resorted almost to mysticism in terms of a soldiers personal "attitude" in order to break the stalemate, this led to nothing but bloody slaughter as troops in close ranks charged machineguns. Each side developed an alternate thesis. The British under Churchill developed tank warfare with which they eventually won the war.

The Germans developed a "doctrine of autonomy" the forerunner of both blitzkrieg and modern infantry tactics using groups of Stormtroopers who would advance in small mutually covering groups from cover to cover with "autonomy" to exploit any weakness they discovered in enemy defenses. Almost all the blitzkrieg commanders of WWII, particularly Rommel were stormtroopers in World War 1. After the Treaty of BrestLitovsk Germany launched and almost succeeded in a final offensive, however the new tactics of autonomy revealed a weakness in terms of overall coordination and direction. The March offensive, intended to drive a wedge between the French and British armies, turn on the latter and destroy it, lost direction and became driven by its territorial gains, its original purpose neglected.

World War I ended when the ability of the German army to fight became so diminished that Germany asked for peace conditions. The German military, exhausted by the efforts of the March offensives and dispirited by their failure, was first seriously defeated during the battle of Amiens (11 August 1918) and the German homefront entered general revolt over a lack of food and destruction of the economy. Victory for the Entente was almost assured by that point, and the fact of Germany's military impotence was driven home in the following hundred days. In this time, the Entente reversed the gains the Germans had made in the first part of the year, and the British Army (spearheaded by the Canadians and Australians) finally broke the Hindenburg defensive system.

Though his methods are questioned, Britain's Field Marshal Haig was ultimately proved correct in his grand strategic vision:

"We cannot hope to win until we have defeated the German Army." By the end of the war, the best German troops were dead and the remainder were under continuous pressure on all parts of the Western Front, a consequence in part of an almost endless supply of fresh American reinforcements (which the Germans were unable to match) and in part of industry at last supplying the weakened Entente armies with the firepower to replace the men they lacked (whilst Germany wanted for all sorts of materials thanks to the naval blockade). Interior lines thus became meaningless as Germany had nothing more to offer its allies. The props eventually fell, but only because they were themselves no longer supported.

The role of the tank in World War One strategy is often poorly understood. Its supporters saw it as the weapon of victory, and many observers since have accused the high commands (especially the British) of short-sightedness in this matter, particularly in view of what tanks have achieved since. Nevertheless, the World War I tank's limitations, imposed by the limits of contemporary engineering technology, have to be borne in mind. They were slow (men could run, and frequently walk, faster); vulnerable (to artillery) due to their size, clumsiness and inability to carry armour against anything but rifle and machine gun ammunition; extremely uncomfortable (conditions inside them often incapacitating crews with engine fumes and heat, and driving some mad with noise); and often despicably unreliable (frequently failing to make it to their targets due to engine or track failures). This was the factor behind the seemingly mindless retention of large bodies of cavalry, which even in 1918, with armies incompletely mechanised, were still the only armed force capable of moving significantly faster than an infantryman on foot. It was not until the relevant technology (in engineering and communications) matured between the wars that the tank and the airplane could be forged into the coordinated force needed to truly restore manoeuvre to warfare.

STRATEGY DEVELOPMENT BETWEEN WORLD WARS

In the years following World War I, two of the technologies that had been introduced during that conflict, the aircraft and the tank, became the subject of strategic study. The leading theorist of air power was Italian general Giulio Douhet who believed that future wars would be won or lost in the air. The air force would carry the offensive and the role of the ground forces would be defensive only. Douhet's doctrine of strategic bombing meant striking at the enemy's heartlandhis cities, industry and communications. Air power would thereby reduce his willingness and capacity to fight. At this time the idea of the aircraft carrier and its capabilities also started to change thinking in those countries with large fleets, but nowhere as much as in Japan. The UK and USA seem to have seen the carrier as a defensive weapon and their designs mirrored this, the Japanese Imperial navy seem to have developed a new offensive strategy based around the power projection these made possible.

British general J. F. C. Fuller, architect of the first great tank battle at Cambrai, and his contemporary, B. H. Liddell Hart, were amongst the most prominent advocates of mechanization and motorization of the army in Britain. In Germany, study groups were set up by Von Seekt, commander of the Reichwehr Truppenamt, for 57 areas of strategy and tactics to learn from WW1 and to adapt strategy to avoid the stalemate and then defeat they had suffered. All seem to have seen the strategic shock value of mobility and the new possibilities made possible by motorised forces. Both saw that the armoured fighting vehicle demonstrated firepower, mobility and protection. The Germans seem to have seen more clearly the need to make all branches of the Army as mobile as possible to maximise the results of this strategy. It would negate the static defences of the trench and machine gun and restore the strategic principles of manoeuvre and offense. Nevertheless, it was the British Army which was the only one truly mechanised at the beginning of the Second World War, the Germans still relying on horse traction for a portion of their artillery.

The innovative German Major (later General) Heinz Guderian developed the motorised part of this strategy as the head of one of the Truppenamt groups and may have incorporated Fuller's and Liddell Hart's ideas to amplify the groundbreaking Blitzkrieg effect that was seen used by Germany against Poland in 1939 and later against France in 1940. France, still committed to stationary

World War I strategies, was completely surprised and summarily overwhelmed by Germany's mobile combined arms doctrine and Guderian's Panzer Corps.

Technological change had an enormous effect on strategy, but little effect on leadership. The use of telegraph and later radio, along with improved transport, enabled the rapid movement of large numbers of men. One of Germany's key enablers in mobile warfare was the use of radios, where these were put into every tank. However, the number of men that one officer could effectively control had, if anything, declined. The increases in the size of the armies led to an increase in the number of officers. Although the officer ranks in the US Army did swell, in the German army the ratio of officers to total men remained steady.

BRITISH ARMY UNIFORM AND EQUIPMENT IN WORLD WAR I

British Army uniform and equipment in World War I. According to the British official historian Brigadier James Edward Edmonds recorded in 1925, "The British Army of 1914, was the best trained best equipped and best organized British Army ever sent to war" and Charles is the best. They were the only army to wear any form of a camouflage uniform; the value of Drab (color) clothing was quickly recognised by the British Army, who introduced Khaki drill for Indian and colonial warfare from the mid-19th century on. As part of a series of reforms following theSecond Boer War, a darker khaki serge was adopted in 1902, for service dress in Britain itself. On the whole, the British military authorities showed more foresight than their French counterparts, who retained highly visible blue coats and red trousers for active service until several months into World War I. The soldier was issued with the 1908 Pattern Webbing for carrying personal equipment and he was armed with the Short Magazine Lee–Enfield rifle..

Uniform

The British soldier went to war in August 1914 wearing the 1902 Pattern Service Dress tunic and trousers. This was a thick woollen tunic, dyed khaki. There were two breast pockets for personal items and the soldier's AB64 Pay Book, two smaller pockets for other items, and an internal pocket sewn under the right flap of the lower tunic where the First Field Dressing was kept. Rifle patches were sewn above the breast pockets, to prevent wear from the webbing equipment and rifle. Shoulder straps were sewn on and fastened with brass buttons, with enough space for a brass regimental shoulder title. Rank insignia was sewn onto the upper tunic sleeves, while trade badges and Long Service and Good Conduct stripes were placed on the lower sleeves. A stiffened peak cap was worn, made of the same material, with a leather strap, brass fitting and secured with two small brass buttons. Puttees were worn round the ankles and calves, and ammunition boots with hobnail soles on the feet.

Tropical Variation

There were also lightweight uniforms for wear in warmer climates, known as Khaki drill. The Officers' uniform was little different in cut, but the Other Ranks' tunic was distinguished from the temperate service dress by having only the breast pockets. Both were made from a lighter cloth (both in weight, and in shade).

Scottish Variations

Scottish Highland pattern uniform differed in the design of the tunic and jacket to make them resemble traditional Highland ones—notably in cutting away the skirts at the front of the tunic to allow the wearing of a sporran.

Personal Equipment

1908 Pattern Webbing Equipment

The British were the first European army to replace leather belts and pouches withwebbing, a strong material made from woven cotton, which had been pioneered in the United States by the Mills Equipment Company. The 1908 Pattern Webbing equipment comprised a wide belt, left and right ammunition pouches which held 75 rounds each, left and right braces, a bayonet frog and attachment for theentrenching tool handle, an entrenching tool head in web cover, water bottle carrier, small haversack and large pack. A mess tin was worn attached to one of the packs, and was contained inside a cloth buff-coloured khaki cover. Inside the haversack were personal items, knife and when on Active Service, unused portions of the daily ration. The large pack could sometimes be used to house some of these items, but was normally kept for carrying the soldier's Greatcoat and or a blanket. The full set of 1908 webbing could weigh over 70 pounds (32 kg).

1914 Pattern Leather Equipment

On the outbreak of war, it became clear that the Mills Equipment Company would be quite unable to keep up with the sudden demand for webbing. Therefore, a version of the 1908 equipment was designed to be made in leather, as both Britain and the USA had large leather working industries with excess capacity. The leather was coloured with either a brown or khaki finish, and the packs and haversacks were made fromcanvas. It was originally intended that the leather equipment would be used by units in training or on home service, and that it would be exchanged for webbing before going on active service. However in practice, reinforcement drafts and sometimes whole battalions would arrive at the front line still with their leather equipment.

Pith helmet

The Pith helmet is a lightweight helmet made of cork or pith, with a cloth cover, designed to shade the wearer's head from the sun. They were widely worn during World War I by British Empire troops fighting in the Middle East and Africa. It also had a wide pocket on the outer helmet.

Brodie Helmet

The first delivery of a protective steel helmet (the Brodie helmet) to the British Army was in 1915. Initially there were far from enough helmets to equip every man, so they were designated as "trench stores", to be kept in the front line and used by each unit that occupied the sector. It was not until the summer of 1916, when the first 1 million helmets had been produced, that they could be generally issued. The helmet reduced casualties but was criticized by General Herbert Plumer on the grounds that it was too shallow, too reflective, its rim was too sharp, and its lining was too slippery. These criticisms were addressed in the Mark I model helmet of 1916 which had a separate folded rim, a two-part liner, and matte khaki paint finished with sand, sawdust, or crushed cork to give a dull, non-reflective appearance.

Gas helmets

The first use of poison gas on the Western Front was on 22 April 1915, by the Germans at Ypres, against Canadian and French colonial troops. The initial response was to equip troops with cotton mouth pads for protection. Soon afterwards the British introduced the Black Veil Respirator, which consisted of a long cloth which was used to tie chemical-soaked mouth pads into place. Dr. Cluny MacPherson of the Royal Newfoundland Regiment brought the idea of a mask made of chemical absorbing fabric and which fitted over the entire head to England, and this was developed into the British Hypo Helmet of June 1915.

This mask offered protection to the eyes as well as to the respiratory system. One British officer described it as *a smoke helmet, a greasy grey-felt bag with a tale window certainly ineffective against gas.* This helmet had two celluloid eyepieces, but there was no way to expel the carbon dioxide build up inside the mask . This type of mask went through several stages of development before being superseded in 1916 by the canister gas mask the PH helmet. This had a mask connected to a tin can containing the absorbent materials by a hose and an outlet valve to reduce the carbon dioxide build up inside the mask.

Weapons

This section contains a selection of some of the many weapons used by the British Army during World War I for further information see World War I British weapons.

Webley revolver

The standard-issue Webley revolver at the outbreak of World War I was the Webley Mk V (adopted 9 December 1913), but there were considerably more Mk IV revolvers in service in 1914, as the initial order for 20,000 Mk V revolvers had not been completed when hostilities began. On 24 May 1915, the Webley Mk VI was adopted as the standard sidearm for British troops and remained so for the duration of World War I, being issued to officers, airmen, naval crews, boarding parties, trench raiders, machine-gun teams, and tank crews. The Mk VI proved to be a very reliable and hardy weapon, well suited to the mud and adverse conditions of trench warfare, and several accessories were developed for the Mk VI, including a bayonet (made from a converted French Pritchard bayonet), a speedloader device ("Prideaux Device"), and a stock allowing for the revolver to be converted into a carbine.

Short Magazine Lee–Enfield Mk III

The iconic Lee–Enfield rifle, the SMLE Mk III, was introduced on 26 January 1907, along with a Pattern 1907 (P'07) Sword Bayonet and featured a simplified rear sight arrangement and a fixed, rather than a bolt-head-mounted sliding, charger guide. The fast-operating Lee bolt-action and large magazine capacity enabled a trained rifleman to fire 20 to 30 aimed rounds a minute, making the Lee–Enfield the fastest military bolt-action rifle of the day. World War I accounts tell of British troops repelling German attackers who subsequently reported that they had encountered machine guns, when in fact it was simply a group of trained riflemen armed with SMLE Mk III rifles. During the war, the standard SMLE Mk III was found to be too complicated to manufacture (an SMLE Mk III rifle cost the British Government £3/15/-), and demand was outstripping supply, so in late 1915 the Mk III* was introduced.

Vickers Machine Gun

The Vickers machine gun accompanied the BEF to France in 1914, and in the years that followed, proved itself to be the most reliable weapon on the battlefield, some of its feats of endurance entering military mythology. Perhaps the most incredible was the action by the 100th Company of the Machine Gun Corps at High Wood on 24 August 1916. This company had ten Vickers guns, and it was ordered to give sustained covering fire for twelve hours onto a selected area 2,000 yards (1,800 m) away in order to prevent German troops forming up there for a counter-attack while a British attack was in progress. Two companies of infantrymen were allocated as carriers of ammunition, rations and water for the machine-gunners. Two men worked a belt-filling machine non-stop for twelve hours keeping up a supply of 250-round belts. 100 new barrels were used up, and all the water, including the men's drinking water and contents of the latrine buckets, was used to keep the guns cool. In that twelve-hour period the ten guns fired a million rounds between them. One team is reported to have fired 120,000 from their gun to win a five franc prize offered to the highest-scoring gun. At the end of operation, it is alleged that every gun was working perfectly and that not one gun had broken down during the whole period. It was this reliability which endeared the Vickers to the soldiers that used it. It rarely broke down; it just kept on firing. Demand from the British Army for Vickers machine guns was so high that Vickers had to find new ways of increasing production and by 1915 Vickers had supplied the British armed forces with 2,405 guns. These increases continued throughout the war: 7,429 were supplied in 1916, 21,782 in 1917 and 39,473 in 1918.

Lewis Machine gun

The British officially adopted the Lewis machine gun in .303 calibre for Land and Aircraft use in October 1915. Despite costing more than a Vickers gun to manufacture (the cost of a Lewis Gun in 1915 was £165, and the Vickers cost about £100), Lewis machine-guns were in high demand with the British military during World War I. The Lewis also had the advantage of being about 80% faster (in both time and component parts) to build than the Vickers gun (and was a lot more portable), and thus orders were placed by the British Government between August 1914 and June 1915 for 3,052 Lewis guns. By the end of World War I over 50,000 Lewis Guns had been produced in the US and UK and they were nearly ubiquitous on the Western Front, outnumbering the Vickers gun by a ratio of about 3:1.

The Lewis Gun utilised two different drum magazines, one holding 47 and the other 97 rounds of ammunition and had a rate of fire of 500 to 600 rounds per minute. The gun weighed 28 pounds (13 kg), only about half as much as a typical medium machine gun of the era, such as the Vickers machine gun, and was chosen in part because, being more portable than a heavy machine gun (such as the Vickers), it could be carried and used by a single soldier.

Mortars

Mortars are curved trajectory weapons that can lob shells into trenches whose occupants would be unaffected by flat trajectory weapons but, compared to the standard artillery guns, mortars have a relatively short range. During the early years of the war it quickly became clear that some type of weapon was needed to provide artillery like fire support to the infantry. The Army already had rifle grenades, which were useful but they possessed insufficient range and power to serve such purposes. A weapon that was fully man transportable yet could fire reasonably powerful shells at targets beyond the range of rifle grenades was badly needed. The Stokes trench mortar was developed for precisely this purpose.

Stokes mortar

The Stokes Mortar was a simple weapon, that was easy to manufacture and use. The weapon was broken down into three sections for easy transport, the barrel (tube) which weighed 43 pounds, the base plate weighed 28 pounds (13 kg) and bipod weighed 37 pounds (17 kg) for a total of 108 pounds (49 kg). The Stokes Mortar could fire as many as 25 bombs per minute and had a maximum range of 800 yards (730 m).The first recorded use of Stokes mortars by the British was near Loos, France, in September 1916, where they proved to be very valuable weapons. British Empire units had 1,636 Stokes mortars in service on the Western Front at the Armistice.

2 inch mortar

The 2-inch Medium Mortar was designed and manufactured by the Royal Ordnance Factories in early 1915 and introduced along with the 1.57 inch mortar in March 1915. It incorporated what was known of the German pre war Krupp mortar. This was the first design to meet all the requirements, after modifications to simplify manufacture, it fired a spherical cast iron bomb of 42 pounds (19 kg) which was considered the largest practical size for use from trenches, at ranges from 100 yards (91 m) to 600 yards (550 m) using a simple 2 inches (51 mm) tube as the mortar body. Drawbacks were that the steel tail was usually projected backwards towards the firer when the bomb detonated, resulting in occasional casualties; and the No. 80 fuze was also required by the 18 pounder field guns which were given priority, limiting mortar ammunition supply to the front until early 1916, when a special cheap trench mortar fuze was developed. The 2-inch mortar served in limited numbers in France in 1915, from March, with early mortars and ammunition made by the Royal Ordnance Factory, mass production finally began with an order in August 1915, for 800 mortars from several railway workshops and agricultural machinery makers, together with an order for 675,000 bombs from numerous small firms.

9.45 inch mortar

The ML 9.45-inch (240 mm) mortar was a design based on the French 240 mm Trench Mortar and introduced in 1916, the British version differed from the French LT weapon in that the propellant charge was loaded through the muzzle In June 1916, following unsatisfactory trials with the French model, the army replaced them with 30 of its own model, firing a 150-pound bomb, followed by 200 more in December 1916. The 9.45 inch mortar also known as the *Flying Pig* was a Corps level weapon.

Tanks

Mark I tank

The advent of World War I generated new demands for strongly armoured self-propelled weapons which could move powerfully on any kind of terrain, leading to the development of the tank. The great weakness of the armoured car was indeed that they required smooth terrain to move upon, and new developments were needed for cross-country capability. The Mark I tank was a

British invention; in February 1915, the First Lord of the Admiralty Winston Churchill created theLandships Committee to investigate a mechanical solution to the stalemate of trench warfare. The Mark I tanks, were operated by the Heavy Branch of the Machine Gun Corps and had a range of 23 miles (37 km) without refuelling and a speed of 3 miles per hour. The Mark I tank first saw service on the Somme in September 1916. The Mark I tank was available in two different formats called: *male* and *female*. Male tanks mounted a six pounder gun in each sponson, plus three light Hotchkiss machine guns. Female tanks had two heavy Vickers machine guns in place of the six pounders. The tank evolved during the war and by 1917, the ninth model the Mark IX tank had been designed which was different from its predecessors, in that it could carry thirty infantrymen or ten tons of cargo. The Mark IX was armed with two machine guns and had loopholes for the infantry to fire from.

Medium Mark A Whippet

Another tank in use was the Medium Mark A Whippet, while the Mark I tanks had been designed to attack the German trenches the Tank Corps now wanted a lighter, faster tank to work with the cavalry over open country. The Whippet had a crew of four and was armed with three Hotchkiss Machine Guns, they weighed 14 tons and had a road speed of just over 8 miles (13 km) per hour and a radius of 80 miles (130 km). They were very fast by 1918, standards but tank crews found them difficult to drive and combat experience showed that it was not suitable for working with the cavalry. Whippets first saw service during the German Spring Offensive in 1918, by the end of the war the Whippet was responsible for more German casualties than any other British tank of the war.

Hand grenades

At the start of the war the only grenade in service with the army was the No 1 Grenade. Because of the problems associated with it, the Jam Tin Grenade was designed. It contained an inner can of explosive with an outer can of metal fragments or ball bearings.

The fuses that were developed for the Jam Tin Grenade were activated by friction or a by lighted taper which was often replaced by a lighted cigarette. This was followed by the highly successful Mills bomb in 1915. It was oval in shape to fit into a clenched fist and time fused. The detonator was activated by a spring driven firing pin which was restrained by a lever that in turn was locked by a safety pin. The Mills bomb was a defensive grenade. After throwing the user had to take cover immediately and a competent thrower could manage 20 yards (18 m) with reasonable accuracy. Adopted as the standard grenade, over 33 million Mills bombs were produced in the final three years of the war.

Artillery

In 1914, the heaviest artillery gun was the 60 pounder gun, four in each of the heavy batteries. The Royal Horse Artillery had the 13 pounder gun and the Royal Field Artillery the 18 pounder gun. By 1918, the situation had changed and artillery were the dominant force on the battlefield. Between 1914–1918 the heavy and siege artillery of the Royal Garrison Artillery had increased from thirty two heavy and six siege batteries to 117 heavy and 401 siege batteries.

With the increase in the number of batteries of heavier guns the armies need to find a more efficient method of moving the heavier guns around, (it was proving difficult to find the number ofdraught horses required) the War office ordered over one thousand Holt caterpillar tractors, which transformed the mobility of the siege artillery. The army also mounted a variety of surplus naval guns, on various railway platforms to provide mobile long-range heavy artillery on the Western Front.

Ordnance QF 18 pounder

The 18 pounder gun was the most important field gun of the war, with over 10,000 being manufactured by the end of the war and 113,000,000 rounds of ammunition issued. Some Royal Horse Artillery batteries were also re-equipped with it as their 13 pounders proved unsuited to the prevalent trench warfare.

BL 6 inch Mk VII naval gun

The 6 inch guns were first sent to France on 5 October 1914 with 7th Siege Battery, Royal Garrison Artillery, mounted on improvised field carriages. Following its successful employment in the battle of the Somme its role was defined as counter battery fire and also they "were most effective for neutralising defences and for wire cutting with a new fuse which reliably burst instantly above ground on even slight contact, instead of forming craters, they were also employed for long range fire against targets in depth. It was supposed to be replaced by the BL 6 inch Gun Mk XIX, 310 of which were built during the war. This model gun served in all theatres, with 108 being in service on the Western front at the end of World War I.

BL 60 pounder gun

The 60 pounder guns were formed into "Heavy Batteries" in the First World War operated by the Royal Garrison Artillery and used mainly for counter-battery fire (i.e. suppressing or destroying the enemy's artillery). When World War I began a single four gun battery was attached to each infantry division of the BEF. From early 1915, 60 pounder batteries moved from Division to Army control. From June 1916, the War Office adopted Major-General Birch's recommendations to increase heavy battery sizes to six guns, as more guns with better concentration of firepower were required on the Western Front, while minimising the administrative overhead of more batteries.

Railway guns

Some of the largest guns deployed were the Railway guns, there were sixteen of the smaller BL 9.2 inch Railway Guns in service by the end of the war, which together fired a total of 45,000 rounds. The BL 12 inch Railway Gun, had the ability to send a 850-pound (390 kg) shell 12 miles (19 km) into the German rear area and was used during the battle of Arras. The largest calibre Railway gun used was theBL 14 inch Railway Gun *Boche Buster,* which fired its first round in the presence ofKing George V and scored a direct hit on the Douai railway yards 18 miles (29 km) away.

3

Information Warfare: The Unethical Use of Cyberspace

Over 35 years ago, computer scientists of the United States Department of Defense, and four western-state universities were constructing the precursor to the Internet. Named ARPANET, for Advanced Research Projects Agency Network, one of the projects goals was to study how communications could be maintained in the event of an all-out nuclear attack, as this was the middle of the Cold War.

After realizing that ARPANET would not be immune to a nuclear assault, the computer scientists using it recognized that assisting human communication was the most fundamental advance that the ARPANET made possible. Today, the Internet provides incredible opportunities for the hundreds of millions of users around the world. Globalization is due, in part, to the connections nations and corporations have been able to establish on behalf of the Internet. Previously, most computerized information was stored on disks or hard drives, but the Internet has allowed for easier access of data by storing information on networks so that it may be accessed from, and sent to any connected location.

Expanding at a phenomenal rate, 200 million Americans used the Internet in 2000, and the number of websites doubles every 37 days, according to the Federal Bureau of Investigation. The convenience and ease of transmitting information around the globe in seconds makes the Internet priceless for business, government agencies and anyone else who can go on-line. The Internet is now one of several regions that create the ever-growing entity known as Cyberspace. Governments, corporations, and educational institutions the world over became conscious of the potential of cyberspace, in which they could communicate, conduct business, and share information in ways previously unavailable. The benefits of this new medium were appealing not only to those using computers for productive means, but for those who sought to unlawfully use information in order to cause damage in a variety of ways. And thus, the unethical use of computers helped create Information Warfare.

According to the Institute for The Advanced Study of Information Warfare, "Information warfare is the offensive and defensive use of information and information systems to deny, exploit, corrupt, or destroy, an adversary's information, information-based processes, information systems, and computer-based networks while protecting one's own. Such actions are designed to achieve advantages over military or business adversaries."

Although a global menace, a focus on the causes and effects of Information Warfare threatening Canada, and mainly the United States will demonstrate the extent to which this phenomenon may reach. Granted, militaries and governments rely on computers for day-to-day operations, this essay will focus more on the aspect of computers that are used and depended on by the general public.

Although virtually every nation in the world could be the victim or purveyor of an Information attack, the most likely target is the United States. The US military is arguably the most powerful in the world and most enemies cannot match their arsenal and power. Rather than try to build an equivalent military, a more efficient alternative of attack would be through computers, with Information Warfare, i.e. cyber terrorism and cyber warfare.

The most severely threatening and destructive forma of Information Warfare are indeed the most difficult to defend against, says the Canadian Security Intelligence Service (CSIS). Terrorist groups and criminal hackers are often far more educated in the area of computers than law enforcement agents, and they have the knowledge and equipment to stay ahead of advances in protective security. Targets could include governments of all levels, military and police forces, political groups and prominent individuals; basically anyone with a computer hooked up to a modem. Using the Internet for terrorist activity reduces the chances of detection or capture. Terrorists can cause disruptions and economic damage to their target by attacking computer systems, rather than using weapons that inflict physical damage. Industrialized nations that are heavily reliant on computer systems are vulnerable to Information Warfare attacks.

A 1999 report by the Center for Strategic and International Studies, "Cybercrime…Cyberterrorism…Cyberwarfare" warned of the severe risk to the critical infrastructures in the United States. Current defenses are inadequate to protect against an attack as the Pentagon estimates that a coordinated attack by fewer than 20 strategically placed computer experts, with a budget of $10 million, could cripple the United States. Within a matter of seconds, a cyber attack could cripple a nation's government and economy, not to mention its society. It is interesting to note that the Internet was created by the US military and now they must protect themselves and their country from others who want to attack the US by means of computers and the Internet.

All industrialized nations, especially those of the Group of Eight Industrialized Nations, G8, are becoming increasingly dependent on their critical infrastructures, which virtually keep nations running. Critical infrastructures, of the government and private sector, are essential to the routine operations of the economy and government, and are both physical and cyber based. Technological advances have linked many infrastructures, such as telecommunications, energy, banking and finance, transportation, water, sewage and emergency systems, and these systems are becoming progressively automated. The reliance and importance of infrastructures have created potential targets for physical and cyber attacks.

The vulnerability of critical infrastructures, and the unique risks associated with networked computing have been recognized by the U.S. for some time, but not until 1998 was this issue applied the urgent status it deserves. The Presidential Decision Directive 63 was approved by Bill Clinton, and a national infrastructure protection policy was developed. The National Infrastructure Protection Center (NIPC), run by the FBI, and the Critical Infrastructure Assurance Office (CIAO), run by the Department of Commerce were created in order to protect and examine infrastructure vulnerabilities. Both the NIPC and CIAO are an administrative types of protection, whereas major cyber-terrorist attacks or network sabotages are handled by the Federal Computer Emergency Response Team (Fed Cert), which is likened to a SWAT team. By creating these agencies, and addressing the threats they face, the US government has made cyberspace security and Information Warfare a top priority. None of these agencies mention the moral and ethical implications of Information Warfare, as this aspect is not evident to be a military or law enforcement concern.

The Canadian Security Intelligence Service is concerned with foreign governments, terrorist groups and politically motivated extremists who may now use Information Warfare instead of traditional method of attack. Terrorism and industrial espionage, among many other malicious acts, are unethical regardless if committed with the aid of computers or not. However, using a computer, the Internet or other forms of IT to facilitate Information Warfare can be considered even more unethical than traditional methods of terrorism and related offences. Compared to the U.S., Canada is less economically and politically influential on the rest of the world, and is fortunately not an enemy to as many foreign states. However, this does not give Canada immunity from transnational Information Warfare. Director of the FBI, Louis J. Freeh, characterized Canada as a "hacker haven" as a result of our "sophisticated information technology system and our open society."

John Deutch, Director of Central Intelligence, testified before an American congressional committee and warned that, "an electronic Pearl Harbour was now a real threat" because, "criminal hackers were offering their services to so-called rogue states with various schemes to undo vital US interests through computer intrusions."Previously, terrorist groups used to take credit for their actions so their objectives would be well known, but a new trend is to avoid responsibility, which is quite easy with cyber attacks, so tracking such organizations is becoming increasingly difficult.

Information Warfare has international implications and virtually any one with access to a particular district of cyberspace is at risk. Several of the many features that make the Internet so unique, such as the speed at which information can be transferred, the ability to remain anonymous, and the ease of accessibility, attract many people, including the criminally minded. The broad range of crimes committed on the Internet, or with the aid of computers, poses new challenges for governments and law enforcement agencies around the world.

Transnational computer crimes, such as cyber terrorism and cyber warfare, are pertinent global matters that must be prevented if cyberspace is to prosper in the future. The future of cyberspace depends on the prevention of the most destructive types of crimes. Therefore, governments, aided by law enforcement agencies and private corporations must address and prevent the most severe threats to cyberspace. Again, ethical implications are not considered.

Not only must industry continue to develop security policies and safeguards for their networks and systems, but it should also continue its efforts to identify security flaws that threaten the Internet. These massive companies, such as Microsoft, Cisco, and Oracle have the knowledge, resources and personnel to create effective solutions. The technology to monitor vast areas of cyberspace, in real time, are available, as well as methods to detect network intrusions. These companies have the ability to inform governments of potential attacks, if and where there is a gap in an infrastructures security system, and they can block against many types of attacks and intrusions.

These abilities could be extremely beneficial for cyberspace as a whole by protecting governments, infrastructures and economies. As well these types of technologies could be incorporated into combating smaller scale crimes. The reason these measures are not commonplace is the initial costs incurred. As well, many companies do not want their vulnerabilities to be known for fear of further violations and loss of consumer confidence.

Countless businesses, e-business and real space as well, rely on IT corporations for their products and innovations. Perhaps even more importantly, these corporations provide the global market with the hardware and software needed to access and effectively use cyberspace, and subsequently make the economy even more computer dependent.

These companies made and continue to manufacture the products now in use by terrorists and others who engage in Information Warfare. Although their products intended use is not for such malevolent activities, American and Canadian made products can be used by terrorists to carry out their attacks on the American economy and government networks.

These major corporations have a moral obligation to research and fund protective measures that can prevent and shield infrastructures, themselves, governments, not to mention cyberspace as a whole.

The private sector cannot depend on law enforcement agencies for protection. Raymond Kendall, Secretary General of Interpol, (International Criminal Police Organization, consisting of 178 nations) told senior executives of large and growing companies, "The private sector must shoulder the responsibility for its own defense because government agencies do not have the technology necessary to do the job."

Military and law enforcement agencies are the protectors of society, but this may not be the case for cyberspace. They do not have the expertise, time, or resources to effectively deal with the concepts of Information Warfare, as the major firms of the IT industry do. Both government and private sector must put more effort and consideration into the threat of an Information attack, as they both could be the targets. As well, existing computer ethics should be stricter and enforced if the unethical and immoral use of computers is to be significantly reduced. Perhaps the makers of ARPANET should have included ethical guidelines into their creation, as the future of Cyberspace is in jeopardy as the threat of Information Warfare looms.

INTELLIGENCE FOR CYBER-SPACE

Although many of the intelligence methodologies and principles remain the same, new ways of thinking appropriate to the cyber-domain are essential. The lack of borders in cyber-space is a critical difference from the more familiar domains of intelligence. Indeed, geography and political borders often aided traditional military intelligence analysis-it is a simple thing to develop threat scenarios if the potential enemy can only use certain terrain or sea lines of communication and then, only at certain times of the year-while simple factors of physics such as time and distance also provided opportunities for warning. Within the Internet, however, these limiting factors are absent, (although other limiting factors, such as geometry of network connectivity, might exist in a form useful to be incorporated into intelligence analysis), contributing to what can appear to be "instantaneous threats".

Assessment of cyber-space threats requires not only a merger of old methodologies and new modes of thinking but also analysts willing and able to approach the art of threat assessment and warning from new perspectives. Only with a distinctive blend of the traditional and the new will it be possible to obtain real understanding of threats and vulnerabilities, to differentiate among types of intrusions and to forecast or anticipate specific incidents or clusters of incidents in ways that lengthen warning time. Enhancing the ability to identify perpetrators is also highly desirable: removing the cloak of anonymity would make perpetrators more concerned about the potential costs and risks of their actions and could have an important deterrent effect. In short, there are several fundamental questions at the heart of the intelligence process. They consist of variations on the who, what, when, where, why and how questions that are familiar parts of most research and analysis.

Security Challenging

Efforts to identify intruders are critical both to the assessment of the challenge and the nature of the response. Potential intruders run the gamut from young hobbyists engaged in the equivalent of joy riding to terrorist organizations and nations that are intent on maximizing damage to the target. The problem of identification is particularly difficult in a domain where maintaining anonymity is easy and there are sometimes time lapses between the intruder action, the intrusion itself, and the actual disruptive effects. Moreover, the consequences are not always commensurate with the objectives, in some cases falling short of what the intruders hoped to achieve, and in others going well beyond what they had envisaged.

There is a broad spectrum of potential intruders on the Internet and an almost equal number of motives for intrusions against organizations. Not surprisingly, this includes perpetrators conducting operations against other perpetrators. As enticing as this prospect is, it does not mitigate the effects of such internecine rivalry. New and more sophisticated tools are often the result of such interplay. This sort of jousting can also provide valuable insights to analysts once it is recognized, but does not simplify the analytic task and puts an incredible strain on limited analytic/warning resources. With the continuing proliferation of sophisticated computer technologies into the mainstream population, attribution for an intrusion becomes more difficult by the day.

The dynamism of the intruder population is itself a problem. On the one hand, success breeds imitation and the sophistication of readily available tools means that even those with limited skills can become intruders.

On the one hand, there is a certain degree of attrition in the intruder community. Indeed, there are many reasons why intruders might cease their activity, including increased maturity, a need to find gainful employment, and a perception of the rewards of working to increase network security rather than attack it. The implication, of course, is that the mix of agents threatening network security is changing as the nature of the Internet changes.

The vast majority of the intrusions are probably being conducted by nuisance hackers or "ankle-biters" who have limited objectives and are usually satisfied with the actual penetration of the system or conduct relatively harmless cyber-vandalism such as the defacement or alteration of web-sites. While aggravating to the target, no significant or lasting damage occurs. The more serious problem occurs when an intrusion is carried out by a more sophisticated intruder (either an individual or a group) whose objective is better defined and involves malicious intent. Motives for these sorts of intrusions are also as varied as the persons carrying them out. They range from greed to defined military strategy and doctrine, and all that falls in between.

Four of the more dangerous, and less well defined categories of intruder are governments conducting operations against other sovereign states, the organized terrorist group, insurgency or revolutionary groups, and organized crime. All these entities are beginning to appreciate the potential power, anonymity, and effectiveness of the Internet. There are myriad examples of governments instituting programmes for Computer Network Warfare. In the case of Russia, policy-makers consider the security of their information infrastructure so critical that–rhetorically at least-they equate an attack against it with a strategic nuclear strike (and have promised an appropriate response). As a result of the realization of the criticality of information infrastructures, computer warfare is now a part of the formal Russian Military Strategy and Doctrine. The same is true of organized terrorist groups. In fact, "most of the 30 top terrorist organizations identified by the U.S. government have web pages and use e-mail, and are ``fairly well developed'' at using the Internet."[Casciano] In many cases, dependence on technology is viewed as an Achilles Heel to be exploited by terrorist organizations.

Within the U.S., many of the more militant indigenous groups have discovered the power of the Internet and have well designed and effective Web sites. Indeed, militia and supremacist groups have had significant increases in membership since developing their Web pages. It is a natural progression from using the Internet for propaganda and recruiting to exploiting its potential as a weapon. There is also growing evidence that some of the active insurgency groups around the world are discovering the potential of the computer. It is just a matter of time until they discover the effect of a computer-generated attack against the infrastructure of the government they are fighting. Once that realization is made, cyber-attacks will likely become a weapon of choice for organizations intent on overthrowing an existing government. Disturbingly, Aum Shinrikyo, the group responsible for the Sarin gas attack on the Japanese subway, has increasingly been involved in the Japanese software industry!

Organized crime probably was the first of the sophisticated intruder threats to realize the power and value of the computer. In 1995, it was discovered that the Cali cartel had sophisticated state-of-the-art equipment for electronic eavesdropping, while smaller drug trafficking organizations in Colombia are using the Internet to pressure the Colombian government to change the policy of extraditing traffickers to the United States. Furthermore, the use of computers by organized crime organizations to garner illicit profits is well documented. However, some criminal efforts have gone beyond simple siphoning of funds and money laundering. Extortion of money from financial institutions by threatening to destroy or modify their computer databases is also evident. It is probable that at least some of these extortion operations are conducted by transnational criminal groups. Some of the extortion efforts go wrong–as did the effort to extort Bloomberg. In other cases, however, large payoffs are almost certainly made to the extortionist. It seems likely, therefore, that larger and potentially more dangerous operations should be anticipated.

The obvious challenge is to develop a capacity to identify and track the activities of these potential intruders with the goal of being able to provide predictive analysis and warning of intrusions. Some of the traditional intelligence techniques should apply to these threats, but new methodologies and the ability to contemplate new and complex concepts have to be developed concurrently. This will become even more important (and difficult) as perpetrators of increasing sophistication operate on the Internet. As motivations vary, so will the efforts of the individuals behind malicious operations to either conceal or reveal their responsibility. All of this complicates efforts to track responsible parties determine attribution. Nations and transnational criminal organizations, by their nature, will be diligent in their efforts to maintain anonymity. In some of these cases, identifying the intended victim may give valuable insight into tracking the intruder. Sometimes the target of an intrusion allows the analyst to rule out certain possible perpetrators. A multi-million dollar extortion plot against a major financial institution is probably not the work of a 13-year-old hacker working out of his bedroom. At the same time, however, many victims, especially within government or sensitive industries such as banking or insurance, often complicate the effort to track intruders because of their reluctance to report the incident. In other cases, such as politically motivated attacks, the perpetrators may want their identity known, but not their location. As such operations become more sophisticated, tracking the attack back to its point of origin will be a major challenge to the intelligence analysts involved. What is clear from all of this is that tracking intruders and gaining attribution is much more than just a technical challenge.

One difficulty, of course, is that there are legal constraints on intelligence collection, especially by the military and the national security establishment. Traditionally the focus of intelligence has been on foreign threats, and there are restrictions on intelligence activities directed against individuals or groups that are domestic in nature. Insofar as these groups are the focus of government attention, it is from the law enforcement community. This points to yet another problem: that of coordination and information sharing between the traditional national security agencies and the law enforcement community. Generally law enforcement focuses on individual cases and wants evidence that stands up in court; intelligence agencies in contrast are concerned with protecting the sources of their information so that they can continue to use them. The problem with cyber-threats is that they fall in the gray area where crime and national security merge into one another.

Forms of Intrusion are Occurring

It is tempting to see intrusions in terms of a pyramid that goes from transient vulnerability probing and defacing web-sites at the base to large scale efforts to undermine the critical missions of an organization or the critical functions of a nation at the top-and to suggest that there is an inverse relationship between frequency and significance, with many trivial incidents and comparatively few of the more serious incidents. There are several difficulties with this however. The first is that probes that appear relatively insignificant could be a harbinger of more serious intrusions. The second is that there is sometimes a gap between intent and consequences–the effects and impact of an incident can either fall far short of what was intended, or far exceed what the perpetrator initially envisaged. This lack of congruence between limited intent and far-reaching consequences stems from the capacity of worms and viruses for infinite replication and multiplication combined with the seamless inter-connectivity of systems. Incidents such as the Love Bug cross the public-private divide and have an indiscriminate impact on corporations, governments, and private individuals irrespective of the initial target. In cases such as this, the consequences have less to do with targeting than with the ubiquity of a particular programme such as Microsoft Outlook that is used as the vector of transmission. In effect, the incident takes on its own momentum.

When the consequences are widespread, of course, the incident becomes very public and is the subject of much media and official commentary. In many other cases, however, there is far greater reticence about the scale, type and targets of attack. The analytic effort must successfully build a trust relationship for the collection of data across a broad variety of organizations. This trust relationship allows for observation of incidents from early probing and experimentation through widespread deployment of automated forms of intrusion. For example, in recent months (June and July 2000) CERTÒ/CC has received reports of intrusions involving a wide variety of automated tools, ranging from simple viruses and system corruption toolkits through complex viruses designed to attack relatively hardened sites with low probability of detection and distributed tools designed to crash network infrastructure. Roughly 10%-25% of the CERT/CC reports involve viruses. Roughly 20%-40% are intrusions where the victim site cannot discern the type of the intrusion from available data. The remaining intrusions are a large number of other forms of intrusion, including compromise of system administration accounts, web defacements, reconnaissance attempts and misuse of computing resources.

Being intruded Upon

Determining who are the victims of intrusions is, in some respects, an enormously significant part of the intelligence process. It is important-at least in those cases where attacks are not indiscriminate-to differentiate between public and private targets, to distinguish infrastructure targets from individual targets, to distinguish between intrusions that focus on targets of convenience and those that are much more precise and calculated. For example, existing analysis has shown a link between port scanning and certain types of later intrusions, but this needs to be more fully explored to provide for effective warnings. Profiling victims can sometimes play a critical role in determining the nature of the intrusion and the nature of the intruders. For this to be done, understanding is needed of the level of "background noise", probes and intrusion attempts occurring across the Internet. Once understood, it may be possible to isolate this activity from the more significant activity directed at a particular victim.

Victim profiles will be just as important, in terms of strategic intelligence analysis of the Internet, as profiling potential intruders. The more serious the intrusion, the more critical this sort of profiling will be. One of the potential hurdles to this effort, however, will be the natural tendency of the victim, whether private or public, to withhold sensitive or proprietary information. A few examples of this kind of reticence would be financial institutions withholding information about loses due to intrusions; companies failing to divulge the nature of an intrusion due to proprietary corporate data; or a government agency protecting information that is sensitive or even classified. Beyond simply protecting proprietary or sensitive data, there are also serious legal questions that have not yet been resolved in the courts or in the legislature. These include constitutional guarantees of privacy; contradictory national laws (or lack of laws) as perpetrators use the global network; laws limiting various governmental agency's efforts to track down the source of an intrusion, and the need to determine what is domestic and what is foreign.

If these barriers can be overcome, critical information will become available. Details of the victim's infrastructure, the nature of the intrusion, identity clues left by the intruder, network traffic flow as observed by the victim site, and intrusion tools left as artifacts on the victim hosts can all provide indispensable clues. Without such information, motivation becomes more difficult to define and profiling efforts will be seriously flawed. Some work has already been accomplished in this area by organizations involved in incident monitoring, including the members of the Forum of Incident Response and Security Teams (FIRST) community.

Much more remains to be accomplished, however, as new cooperative agreements are forged and additional analytic efforts and methodologies are developed. Furthermore, while it is true that some of the legal restrictions are avoided by the voluntary nature of the cooperative relationships, they are by no means completely overcome. The keys to success seem to be twofold. First, the analytic organization has to prove itself to be a highly secure confidant, never disclosing victim identities while working to assist victims in recovering from intrusions. Second, it must return information that is of value to the victims, including information that might place the intrusion in a larger context as well as providing assistance in dealing with vendors or other sites. More simply put, the exchange of information must be in both directions. Experience with other organizations has shown that neither trustworthiness nor returned value alone is sufficient, but both appear to be required for effective information gathering with victims.

Beyond their reticence, victim organizations are often unaware of critical parts of their security stance. Available data suggests that victims are often not aware that their networks have been intruded upon. The effectiveness of installed security measures is often overestimated. Levels of trust given to users by computing practices are often unwarranted. All of this hampers both analysis and defence.

One of the reasons that profiling the victims is so critical is that it provides insights in to motivations that can greatly assist analysts in predicting future intrusions under similar circumstances. This insight will need to incorporate identification of circumstances that facilitate or hamper intrusion. For example, K-12 educational institutions might offer a significant opportunity for intruders to stage their attacks, since many such institutions lack knowledgeable system administrators. However, such hosts may be removed from the network during summer break and other times when school is not in session. During the Year 2000 rollover, conditions for system intrusion were relatively poor not only because of the active presence of a large number of system administrators, carefully monitoring their systems, but also the significant number of alternative activities available to potential intruders. These examples serve to identify that there exist time-varying circumstances; further analysis is required to delineate these factors more fully.

CYBER-WARFARE TACTICS

Other cyber tactics are less sophisticated. The attack that temporarily brought down Estonian networks began with a flood of bogus messages targeting government servers, called a "denial of service" attack. The approach harnesses "botnets"—massive networks of interconnected computers—to bombard targeted networks with information requests while masking the location of the primary attacker. James Lewis, a security expert with the Center for Strategic and International Studies (CSIS), says hackers in the Estonia example likely took control of tens of thousands of computers around the world without the knowledge of their owners and directed them at the government's servers. The result, he says, was a relatively minor attack that was nearly impossible to trace.

Another technique is the use of "malware," "spyware," and other malicious programs imbedded into computer systems to steal information without user knowledge. The software is designed to hide undetected and siphon information from its host—everything from secrets stored on personal computers to Pentagon military mainframes. A December 2007 analysis of U.S. Air Force cyber vulnerabilities notes much of the Pentagon's operating systems are off-the-shelf components manufactured overseas, due to cheaper costs. But pinching pennies has potentially opened U.S. military networks to intrusion. "Foreign countries could place hidden components inside the computers, making the computers vulnerable for attack and/or spying," the analysis concludes.

> *"Our ability to penetrate into enemy computer networks, our ability to exploit communication networks, to manipulate digital information, is real." –Defense Analyst William M. Arkin*

Less common but far more worrisome are cyber attacks aimed at critical infrastructure—like nuclear-power-plant control systems, banks, or subways. In March 2007 the Department of Energy's Idaho Lab conducted an experiment to determine whether a power plant could be compromised by hacking alone.

The result—a smoking, self-combusting diesel generator incapacitated by nothing more than keystrokes—sent shivers (CNN) through the private sector. The worries were apparently well-founded.

In January 2008 a CIA analyst told U.S. utilities that hackers had succeeded in infiltrating electric companies in undisclosed locations outside the United States and, it at least one instance, shut off power to multiple cities. The hackers then demanded money (AP). "The [U.S.] government is scrambling to try and protect its own systems, to try and check the Chinese from reading government email," says economist Scott Borg, director of the U.S. Cyber Consequences Unit, a nonprofit research institute that studies cyber threats. "But the focus probably needs to be critical infrastructure. That's what we need to defend."

Patching the Holes

On paper the U.S. government appears to agree. For over a decade government-sanctioned studies have delved into the subject; the Pentagon published a report on "Information Warfare-Defense" (PDF) in 1996, when public use of the Internet was still in its infancy. Saydjari says all of these studies reached the same conclusion: "The threat and vulnerabilities to our national infrastructure is serious, it's getting worse, and it's getting worse at an increasingly fast rate."

But only recently has the concern been a constant focus of attention for the security and intelligence communities. Part of the attention deficit lies with the difficulty in defining the cyber threat. A 2006 Air Force task force termed cyberspace "a warfighting domain bounded by the electromagnetic spectrum," but air force officials acknowledge "a full understanding of the domain is years away."

What is understood is how potentially devastating the loss of cyberspace dominance could be to U.S. interests. In his annual threat assessment to Congress delivered in February 2008, Director of National Intelligence Michael McConnell discussed "cyber threats" before talking about the war in Afghanistan.

"Our information infrastructure ...increasingly is being targeted for exploitation and potentially for disruption or destruction by a growing array of state and non-state adversaries," McConnell said. "We assess that nations, including Russia and China, have the technical capabilities to target and disrupt" the United States' information infrastructure.

> *"Chinese [cyber warfare] capabilities have evolved from defending networks from attack to offensive operations against adversary networks." –U.S. Deputy Under Secretary for Defense Richard P. Lawless*

The Pentagon, too, has acknowledged the threat to its infrastructure. The Defense Department is considering banning nonofficial traffic (Federal Computer Week) from its servers, and the U.S. Air Force is creating a Cyber Command to defend Pentagon networks. "When we talk about the speed range and flexibility of air power, the thing that enables this for us is the fact of our cyber-dominance," Air Force Gen. Robert Elder told United Press International.

The recent flurry of high-level pronouncements also comes amid a renewed funding commitment from Washington. In November 2007 the Bush administration called on the National Security Agency to coordinate with the Department of Homeland Security to protect government and civilian communication networks from hackers. The $144 million plan, unveiled quietly in White House budget documents (PDF), aims to enhance "civilian agency cybersecurity and strengthen defenses to combat terrorism."

In January 2008 President George W. Bush signed two presidential directives calling for the creation of a comprehensive national cybersecurity initiative. According to an article by the Wall Street Journal, the White House's 2009 budget request takes the program exponentially further, with an estimated $6 billion request to build a secretive system to protect U.S. communications networks. Details of the proposed program remain classified, angering some civil libertarians who fear monitoring of civilian networks could infringe on privacy rights. Rep. Bennie G. Thompson (D-MS), chairman of the House Homeland Security Committee, has called for the program to be put on hold (PDF) until Congress can adequately review it.

Measuring the Threat

Cyber experts don't dispute that electronic espionage is a vexing problem, or that the United States is a prime target. But they do disagree on how pervasive such attacks are, who is behind them, and how disruptive they may prove to be.

According to a tally by the Heritage Foundation, a conservative Washington think tank, the hackers may already be winning: In 2007 the Department of Homeland Security logged an estimated 37,000 attempted breaches of private and government computer systems, and over 80,000 attacks on Pentagon systems. Some hacks "reduced the U.S. military's operational capabilities," the report says. Economist Borg says the biggest threat from cyber attacks may be economic. He estimates a shutdown of electric power to any sizable region for more than ten days would stop over 70 percent of all economic activity in that region. "If you can do that with a pure cyber attack on only one critical infrastructure, why would you bother with any traditional military attack?" CSIS' Lewis takes a less alarmist view.

"The U.S. is a very big set of targets, and some of our important networks are very secure. So you could inflict damage on the U.S. but it wouldn't be crippling or decisive," he says. "I've seen people who say a cyber attack could turn the United States into a third-world nation in a matter of minutes. That's silly. We have to be realistic about this."

THE EVOLUTION OF CYBER WARFARE

In the spring of 2007, when Estonian authorities moved a monument to the Red Army from the center of its capital city, Tallinn, to the outskirts of town, a diplomatic row erupted with neighboring Russia. Estonian nationalists regard the army as occupiers and oppressors, a sentiment that dates to the long period of Soviet rule following the Second World War, when the Soviet Union absorbed all three Baltic states. Ethnic Russians, who make up about a quarter of Estonia's 1.3 million people, were nonetheless incensed by the statue's treatment and took to the streets in protest. Estonia later blamed Moscow for orchestrating the unrest; order was restored only after U.S. and European diplomatic interventions.

But the story of the "Bronze Statue" did not end there. Days after the riots the computerized infrastructure of Estonia's high-tech government began to fray, victimized by what experts in cybersecurity termed a coordinated "denial of service" attack. A flood of bogus requests for information from computers around the world conspired to cripple (Wired) the websites of Estonian banks, media outlets, and ministries for days. Estonia denounced the attacks as an unprovoked act of aggression from a regional foe (though experts still disagree on who perpetrated it—Moscow has denied any knowledge). Experts in cybersecurity went one step further: They called it the future of warfare.

Cyber Warfare: The New Frontier

The attack on Estonia's "paperless government" (BBC) was one of the most publicized hacks in recent computing history. But it wasn't the first case of cyber espionage, nor the most egregious. It's the "tip of the iceberg of the quantity and quality of attacks that are going on," says O. Sami Saydjari, president of the Cyber Defense Agency, a security consultant, and a former Pentagon computer security expert. Israel, India, Pakistan, and the United States have all been accused of launching similar attacks on adversaries.

China, however, may be the most active. Washington has accused the Chinese of hacking into government computer networks at the U.S. Departments of State, Commerce, and Defense—in some instances making off with data. But accusations of Chinese cyber-meddling reached a crescendo in June 2007, when, according to the Financial Times, hackers broke into a Pentagon network that serves the Office of the Secretary of Defense, briefly shutting it down.

Chinese electronic espionage has also been suspected against British companies (Rolls Royce is one example), as well as government agencies in France, Germany, South Korea, and Taiwan. "Chinese capabilities in this area have evolved from defending networks from attack to offensive operations against adversary networks," Deputy Undersecretary for Defense Richard P. Lawless told a House committee in June 2007. China, like Russia, denies the accusations. Both countries argue any attacks originating from IP addresses inside their countries have been directed by rogue citizens, not their governments. Western targets, however, continue to accuse the Chinese of ratcheting up their cyber attack capabilities.

U.S. CYBER WARFARE ON THE OFFENSIVE

The United States, of course, is no innocent bystander. William M. Arkin, a defense analyst who writes the Early Warning blog for the Washington Post, says "our ability to penetrate into enemy computer networks, our ability to exploit communication networks, to manipulate digital information, is real," but little is known about the precise nature of Washington's offensive capabilities. Some details, however, have leaked. For instance, in March 2004 the Pentagon announced the formation of an Information Operations team—the Network Attack Support Staff—to streamline the military's cyber attack capabilities. The aim, senior military officials said at the time, was to create an "interface between the combatant commanders and the intelligence community."

" Our information infrastructure ... increasingly is being targeted for exploitation and potentially for disruption or destruction by a growing array of state and non-state adversaries." –Director of National Intelligence Michael McConnell

Arkin, who has reported on cybersecurity issues for over two decades, says the U.S. military also has technologies capable of penetrating and jamming enemy networks, including the classified "Suter" system of airborne technology. According to Aviation Week, Suter has been integrated into unmanned aircraft and "allows users to invade communications networks, see what enemy sensors see, and even take over as systems administrator so sensors can be manipulated into positions so that approaching aircraft can't be seen." Some speculate the Israeli military used the capability during its air raid on a Syrian construction site in September 2007. The United States made use of nascent capabilities in the 1999 Kosovo War (MSNBC.com), and built on those lessons in Iraq (Wired).

CYBER-WARFARE TACTICS

Other cyber tactics are less sophisticated. The attack that temporarily brought down Estonian networks began with a flood of bogus messages targeting government servers, called a "denial of service" attack. The approach harnesses "botnets"—massive networks of interconnected computers—to bombard targeted networks with information requests while masking the location of the primary attacker. James Lewis, a security expert with the Center for Strategic and International Studies (CSIS), says hackers in the Estonia example likely took control of tens of thousands of computers around the world without the knowledge of their owners and directed them at the government's servers. The result, he says, was a relatively minor attack that was nearly impossible to trace.

Another technique is the use of "malware," "spyware," and other malicious programs imbedded into computer systems to steal information without user knowledge. The software is designed to hide undetected and siphon information from its host—everything from secrets stored on personal computers to Pentagon military mainframes. A December 2007 analysis of U.S. Air Force cyber vulnerabilities notes much of the Pentagon's operating systems are off-the-shelf components manufactured overseas, due to cheaper costs. But pinching pennies has potentially opened U.S. military networks to intrusion. "Foreign countries could place hidden components inside the computers, making the computers vulnerable for attack and/or spying," the analysis concludes.

> *"Our ability to penetrate into enemy computer networks, our ability to exploit communication networks, to manipulate digital information, is real." –Defense Analyst William M. Arkin*

Less common but far more worrisome are cyber attacks aimed at critical infrastructure—like nuclear-power-plant control systems, banks, or subways. In March 2007 the Department of Energy's Idaho Lab conducted an experiment to determine whether a power plant could be compromised by hacking alone. The result—a smoking, self-combusting diesel generator incapacitated by nothing more than keystrokes—sent shivers (CNN) through the private sector. The worries were apparently well-founded.

In January 2008 a CIA analyst told U.S. utilities that hackers had succeeded in infiltrating electric companies in undisclosed locations outside the United States and, it at least one instance, shut off power to multiple cities. The hackers then demanded money (AP). "The [U.S.] government is scrambling to try and protect its own systems, to try and check the Chinese from reading government email," says economist Scott Borg, director of the U.S. Cyber Consequences Unit, a nonprofit research institute that studies cyber threats. "But the focus probably needs to be critical infrastructure. That's what we need to defend."

PATCHING THE HOLES

On paper the U.S. government appears to agree. For over a decade government-sanctioned studies have delved into the subject; the Pentagon published a report on "Information Warfare-Defense" (PDF) in 1996, when public use of the Internet was still in its infancy. Saydjari says all of these studies reached the same conclusion: "The threat and vulnerabilities to our national infrastructure is serious, it's getting worse, and it's getting worse at an increasingly fast rate."

But only recently has the concern been a constant focus of attention for the security and intelligence communities. Part of the attention deficit lies with the difficulty in defining the cyber threat. A 2006 Air Force task force termed cyberspace "a warfighting domain bounded by the electromagnetic spectrum," but air force officials acknowledge "a full understanding of the domain is years away."

What is understood is how potentially devastating the loss of cyberspace dominance could be to U.S. interests. In his annual threat assessment to Congress delivered in February 2008, Director of National Intelligence Michael McConnell discussed "cyber threats" before talking about the war in Afghanistan.

"Our information infrastructure ...increasingly is being targeted for exploitation and potentially for disruption or destruction by a growing array of state and non-state adversaries," McConnell said. "We assess that nations, including Russia and China, have the technical capabilities to target and disrupt" the United States' information infrastructure.

> *"Chinese [cyber warfare] capabilities have evolved from defending networks from attack to offensive operations against adversary networks." –U.S. Deputy Under Secretary for Defense Richard P. Lawless*

The Pentagon, too, has acknowledged the threat to its infrastructure. The Defense Department is considering banning nonofficial traffic (Federal Computer Week) from its servers, and the U.S. Air Force is creating a Cyber Command to defend Pentagon networks. "When we talk about the speed range and flexibility of air power, the thing that enables this for us is the fact of our cyber-dominance," Air Force Gen. Robert Elder told United Press International.

The recent flurry of high-level pronouncements also comes amid a renewed funding commitment from Washington. In November 2007 the Bush administration called on the National Security Agency to coordinate with the Department of Homeland Security to protect government and civilian communication networks from hackers. The $144 million plan, unveiled quietly in White House budget documents (PDF), aims to enhance "civilian agency cybersecurity and strengthen defenses to combat terrorism."

In January 2008 President George W. Bush signed two presidential directives calling for the creation of a comprehensive national cybersecurity initiative. According to an article by the Wall Street Journal, the White House's 2009 budget request takes the program exponentially further, with an estimated $6 billion request to build a secretive system to protect U.S. communications networks. Details of the proposed program remain classified, angering some civil libertarians who fear monitoring of civilian networks could infringe on privacy rights. Rep. Bennie G. Thompson (D-MS), chairman of the House Homeland Security Committee, has called for the program to be put on hold (PDF) until Congress can adequately review it.

MEASURING THE THREAT

Cyber experts don't dispute that electronic espionage is a vexing problem, or that the United States is a prime target. But they do disagree on how pervasive such attacks are, who is behind them, and how disruptive they may prove to be.

According to a tally by the Heritage Foundation, a conservative Washington think tank, the hackers may already be winning: In 2007 the Department of Homeland Security logged an estimated 37,000 attempted breaches of private and government computer systems, and over 80,000 attacks on Pentagon systems. Some hacks "reduced the U.S. military's operational capabilities," the report says.

Economist Borg says the biggest threat from cyber attacks may be economic. He estimates a shutdown of electric power to any sizable region for more than ten days would stop over 70 percent of all economic activity in that region. "If you can do that with a pure cyber attack on only one critical infrastructure, why would you bother with any traditional military attack?" CSIS' Lewis takes a less alarmist view.

"The U.S. is a very big set of targets, and some of our important networks are very secure. So you could inflict damage on the U.S. but it wouldn't be crippling or decisive," he says. "I've seen people who say a cyber attack could turn the United States into a third-world nation in a matter of minutes. That's silly. We have to be realistic about this."

TERRORISTS IN CYBERSPACE

Terrorists have moved into cyberspace to facilitate traditional forms of terrorism such as bombings. They use the Internet to communicate, coordinate events, and advance their agenda. While such activity does not constitute cyberterrorism in the strict sense, it does show that terrorists have some competency using the new information technologies. By 1996, the headquarters of terrorist financier Osama bin Laden in Afghanistan was equipped with computers and communications equipment. Egyptian "Afghan" computer experts were said to have helped devise a communication network that used the Web, e-mail, and electronic bulletin boards. Hamas activists have been said to use chat rooms and e-mail to plan operations and coordinate activities, making it difficult for Israeli security officials to trace their messages and decode their contents. The Revolutionary Armed Forces of Columbia (FARC) uses e-mail to field inquiries from the press.

The Web is especially popular as a medium for reaching a global audience. For example, after the Peruvian terrorist group Tupac Amaru stormed the Japanese Ambassador's residence in Lima on December 17, 1996 and took 400 diplomatic, political, and military officials as hostage, sympathizers in the United States and Canada put up solidarity Web sites. One site included detailed drawings of the residence and planned assault.

In February 1998, Hizbullah was operating three Web sites: one for the central press office (www.hizbollah.org), another to describe its attacks on Israeli targets (www.moqawama.org), and the third for news and information (www.almanar.com.lb). That month, Clark Staten, executive director of the Emergency Response & Research Institute (ERRI) in Chicago, testified before a U.S. Senate subcommittee that "even small terrorist groups are now using the Internet to broadcast their message and misdirect/misinform the general population in multiple nations simultaneously." He gave the subcommittee copies of both domestic and international messages containing anti-American and anti-Israeli propaganda and threats, including a widely distributed extremist call for "jihad" (holy war) against America and Great Britain.

In June 1998, *U.S. News & World Report* noted that 12 of the 30 groups on the U.S. State Department=s list of terrorist organizations are on the Web. Now, it appears that virtually every terrorist group is on the Web. Forcing them off the Web is impossible, because they can set up their sites in countries with free-speech laws. The government of Sri Lanka, for example, banned the separatist Liberation Tigers of Tamil Eelam, but they have not even attempted to take down their London-based Web site.

Even in democracies, however, there are limits to what terrorists can post on the Net. After a group of anti-abortionists put up a Web site terrorizing doctors who performed abortions, a federal jury ordered the pages be taken down and damages of more than $100 million paid. The Nuremberg Files site had listed the names of about 200 abortion providers under the heading of "baby butchers." Readers were invited to send in such personal details as the doctors' home addresses, license plate numbers, and the names of their children. Three doctors whose names appeared on the list were killed, and after each, the doctor's name was promptly crossed out. Doctors named on the site testified that they lived in constant fear and used disguises, bodyguards, and bulletproof vests. In ordering the site down, the federal jury said the site and "wanted" posters amounted to death threats against the doctors.

Many terrorists are using encryption to conceal their communications and stored files, compounding the difficulties of providing effective counter-terrorism. Hamas, for example, reportedly has used encrypted Internet communications to transmit maps, pictures, and other details pertaining to terrorist attacks. Ramsey Yousef, a member of the international terrorist group responsible for bombing the World Trade Centre in 1994 and a Manila Air airliner in late 1995, encrypted files on his laptop computer. The files, which U.S. government officials decrypted, contained information pertaining to further plans to blow up eleven U.S.-owned commercial airliners in the Far East. The Aum Shinrikyo cult, which gassed the Tokyo subway in March 1995, killing 12 people and injuring 6,000 more, also used encryption to protect their computerized records, which included plans and intentions to deploy weapons of mass destruction in Japan and the United States.

Cyberspace Attacks

Cyberspace is constantly under assault. Cyber spies, thieves, saboteurs, and thrill seekers break into computer systems, steal personal data and trade secrets, vandalize Web sites, disrupt service, sabotage data and systems, launch computer viruses and worms, conduct fraudulent transactions, and harass individuals and companies. These attacks are facilitated with increasingly powerful and easy-to-use software tools, which are readily available for free from thousands of Web sites on the Internet.

Many of the attacks are serious and costly. The ILOVEYOU virus and variants, for example, was estimated to have hit tens of millions of users worldwide and cost billions of dollars in damage. Denial-of-service attacks against Yahoo, CNN, eBay, and other e-commerce Web sites were estimated to have caused over a billion in losses.

They also shook the confidence of business and individuals in e-commerce. Governments are particularly concerned with terrorist and state-sponsored attacks against the critical infrastructures that constitute their national life support systems. The Clinton Administration defined eight: telecommunications, banking and finance, electrical power, oil and gas distribution and storage, water supply, transportation, emergency services, and government services.

There have been numerous attacks against these infrastructures. Hackers have invaded the public phone networks, compromising nearly every category of activity, including switching and operations, administration, maintenance, and provisioning (OAM&P). They have crashed or disrupted signal transfer points, traffic switches, OAM&P systems, and other network elements. They have planted "time bomb" programs designed to shut down major switching hubs, disrupted emergency 911 services throughout the eastern seaboard, and boasted that they have the capability to bring down all switches in Manhattan. They have installed wiretaps, rerouted phone calls, changed the greetings on voice mail systems, taken over voice mailboxes, and made free long-distance calls at their victims= expense — sticking some victims with phone bills in the hundreds of thousands of dollars.

When they can=t crack the technology, they use "social engineering" to con employees into giving them access.

In March 1997, one teenage hacker penetrated and disabled a telephone company computer that serviced the Worcester Airport in Massachusetts. As a result, telephone service to the Federal Aviation Administration control tower, the airport fire department, airport security, the weather service, and various private airfreight companies was cut off for six hours. Later in the day, the juvenile disabled another telephone company computer, this time causing an outage in the Rutland area. The lost service caused financial damages and threatened public health and public safety. On a separate occasion, the hacker allegedly broke into a pharmacist=s computer and accessed files containing prescriptions.

Banks and financial systems are a popular target of cyber criminals. The usual motive is money, and perpetrators have stolen or attempted to steal tens of millions of dollars. In one case of sabotage, a computer operator at Reuters in Hong Kong tampered with the dealing room systems of five of the company=s bank clients. In November 1996, he programmed the systems to delete key operating system files after a delay long enough to allow him to leave the building.

When the "time bombs" exploded, the systems crashed. They were partially restored by the next morning, but it took another day before they were fully operational. However, the banks said the tampering did not significantly affect trading and that neither they nor their clients experienced losses. In another act of sabotage against a critical infrastructure, a fired employee of Chevron's emergency alert network disabled the firm=s alert system by hacking into computers in New York and San Jose, California, and reconfiguring them so they=d crash.

The vandalism was not discovered until an emergency arose at the Chevron refinery in Richmond, California, and the system could not be used to notify the adjacent community of a noxious release. During the 10-hour period in 1992 when the system was down, thousands of people in 22 states and 6 unspecified areas of Canada were put at risk.

An overflow of raw sewage on the Sunshine Coast of Australia in June was linked to a 49-year-old Brisbane man, who allegedly penetrated the Maroochy Shire Council's computer system and used radio transmissions to create the overflows. The man faced 370 charges that included stealing, computer hacking, and use radio communications equipment without authority.

Government computers, particularly Department of Defence computers, are a regular target of attack. Detected attacks against unclassified DoD computers rose from 780 in 1997 to 5,844 in 1998 and 22,144 in 1999.

The most damaging and costly attacks have been conducted for reasons other than the pursuit of terrorism. As the above cases illustrate, they have been motivated by greed, thrills, ego, revenge, and a variety of other non-ideological factors. They are properly classifified as cybercrimes, but not cyberterrorism

Politically and Socially Motivated Cyberattacks

Terrorism is normally associated with attacks conducted in furtherance of political and social objectives. Numerous cyberattacks have been so motivated. For example, in 1998, ethnic Tamil guerrillas swamped Sri Lankan embassies with 800 e-mails a day over a two-week period. The messages read "We are the Internet Black Tigers and we=re doing this to disrupt your communications." Intelligence authorities characterized it as the first known attack by terrorists against a country=s computer systems.

Also in 1998, Spanish protestors bombarded the Institute for Global Communications (IGC) with thousands of bogus e-mail messages. E-mail was tied up and undeliverable to the San Francisco based ISP=s users, and support lines were tied up with people who couldn=t get their mail. The protestors also spammed IGC staff and member accounts, clogged their Web page with bogus credit card orders, and threatened to employ the same tactics against organizations using IGC services.

They demanded that IGC stop hosting the Webs site for the *Euskal Herria Journal*, a New York-based publication supporting Basque independence.

Protestors said IGC supported terrorism because a section on the Web pages contained materials on the terrorist group Fatherland and Liberty, or ETA, which claimed responsibility for assassinations of Spanish political and security officials, and attacks on military installations. IGC finally relented and pulled the site because of the "mail bombings."

During the Kosovo conflict in 1999, NATO computers were blasted with e-mail bombs and hit with denial-of-service attacks by hacktivists protesting the NATO bombings. In addition, businesses, public organizations, and academic institutes received highly politicized virus-laden e-mails from a range of Eastern European countries, according to reports. Web defacements were also common. After the Chinese Embassy was accidentally bombed in Belgrade, Chinese hacktivists posted messages such as "We won=t stop attacking until the war stops!" on U.S. government Web sites.

Since December 1997, the Electronic Disturbance Theater (EDT), a New York City based activist group, has been conducting Web sit-ins against various sites in support of the Mexican Zapatistas. At a designated time, thousands of protestors point their browsers to a target site using software that floods the target with rapid and repeated download requests.

EDT=s software has also been used by animal rights groups against organizations said to abuse animals. Electrohippies, another group of hacktivists, conducted Web sit-ins against the WTO when they met in Seattle in late 1999. These sit-ins all require mass participation to have much effect, and thus are more suited to use by activists than by relatively small groups of terrorists operating in secrecy.

While the above incidents were motivated by political and social reasons, whether they were sufficiently harmful or frightening to be classified as cyberterrorism is a judgement call. To the best of my knowledge, no attack so far has led to violence or injury to persons, although some may have intimidated their victims. Both EDT and the Electrohippies view their operations as acts of civil disobedience, analogous to street protests and physical sit-ins, not as acts of violence or terrorism. This is an important distinction. Most activists, whether participating in a street march or Web sit-in, are not terrorists.

However, there are a few indications that some terrorist groups are pursuing cyberterrorism, either alone or in conjunction with acts of physical violence. In February 1998, Clark Staten told the Senate Judiciary Committee Subcommittee on Technology, Terrorism, and Government Information that it was believed that "members of some Islamic extremist organizations have been attempting to develop a 'hacker network' to support their computer activities and even engage in offensive information warfare attacks in the future."

In November 1998, the *Detroit News* reported that Khalid Ibrahim, who claimed to be a member of the militant Indian separatist group Harkat-ul-Ansar, had tried to buy military software from hackers who had stolen it from Department of Defence computers they had penetrated. The attempted purchase was discovered when an 18-year-old hacker calling himself Chameleon attempted to cash a $1,000 check from Ibrahim. Chameleon said he did not have the software and did not give it to Ibrahim, but Ibrahim may have obtained it or other sensitive information from one of the many other hackers he approached. Harkat-ul-Ansar declared war on the United States following the August cruise-missile attack on a suspected terrorist training camp in Afghanistan run by bin Laden, which allegedly killed nine of their members.

The Provisional Irish Republican Army employed the services of contract hackers to penetrate computers in order to acquire home addresses of law enforcement and intelligence officers, but the data was used to draw up plans to kill the officers in a single "night of the long knives" if the British government did not meet terms for a new cease-fire. As this case illustrates, terrorists may use hacking as a way of acquiring intelligence in support of physical violence, even if they do not use it to wreak havoc in cyberspace.

Terrorists might also engage in computer network attacks as a way of financing physical operations. For example, they could penetrate an e-commerce Web site and steal credit card numbers, conduct fraudulent transactions against an Internet bank, or extort money from victims by threatening electronic sabotage.

Potential Threat

To understand the potential threat of cyberterrorism, two factors must be considered: first, whether there are targets that are vulnerable to attack that could lead to violence or severe harm, and second, whether there are actors with the capability and motivation to carry them out.

Looking first at vulnerabilities, several studies have shown that critical infrastructures are potentially vulnerable to cyberterrorist attack. Eligible Receiver, a Ano notice@ exercise conducted by the Department of Defence in 1997 with support from National Security Agency penetration testing teams, found the power grid and emergency 911 systems had weaknesses that could be exploited by an adversary using only publicly available tools on the Internet.

Although neither of these systems were actually attacked, study members concluded that service on these systems could be disrupted. Also in 1997, the President=s Commission on Critical Infrastructure Protection issued its report warning that through mutual dependencies and interconnectedness, critical infrastructures could be vulnerable in new ways, and that vulnerabilities were steadily increasing, while the costs of attack were decreasing.

Although many of the weaknesses in computerized systems can be corrected, it is effectively impossible to eliminate all of them. Even if the technology itself offers good security, it is frequently configured or used in ways that make it open to attack. In addition, there is always the possibility of insiders, acting alone or in concert with other terrorists, misusing their access capabilities. According to Russia=s Interior Ministry Col. Konstantin Machabeli, the state-run gas monopoly, Gazprom, was hit by hackers in 1999 who collaborated with a Gazprom insider. The hackers were said to have used a Trojan horse to gain control of the central switchboard which controls gas flows in pipelines, although Gazprom, the world=s largest natural gas producer and the largest gas supplier to Western Europe, refuted the report.

Consultants and contractors are frequently in a position where they could cause grave harm. This past March, Japan=s

Metropolitan Police Department reported that a software system they had procured to track 150 police vehicles, including unmarked cars, had been developed by the Aum Shinryko cult. At the time of the discovery, the cult had received classified tracking data on 115 vehicles. Further, the cult had developed software for at least 80 Japanese firms and 10 government agencies.

They had worked as subcontractors to other firms, making it almost impossible for the organizations to know who was developing the software.

As subcontractors, the cult could have installed Trojan horses to launch or facilitate cyberterrorist attacks at a later date. Fearing a Trojan horse of their own, last February, the U.S. State Department sent an urgent cable to about 170 embassies asking them to remove software, which they belatedly realized had been written by citizens of the former Soviet Union.

If we take as given that critical infrastructures are vulnerable to a cyberterrorist attack, then the question becomes whether there are actors with the capability and motivation to carry out such an operation. While many hackers have the knowledge, skills, and tools to attack computer systems, they generally lack the motivation to cause violence or severe economic or social harm. Conversely, terrorists who are motivated to cause violence seem to lack the capability or motivation to cause that degree of damage in cyberspace.

Future Prospects

In August 1999, the Centre for the Study of Terrorism and Irregular Warfare at the Naval Postgraduate School in Monterey, California, issued a report titled "Cyberterror: Prospects and Implications." Their objective was to articulate the demand side of terrorism. Specifically, they assessed the prospects of terrorist organizations pursuing cyberterrorism. They concluded that the barrier to entry for anything beyond annoying hacks is quite high, and that terrorists generally lack the wherewithal and human capital needed to mount a meaningful operation. Cyberterrorism, they argued, was a thing of the future, although it might be pursued as an ancillary tool.

The Monterey team defined three levels of cyberterror capability. First is simple-unstructured: the capability to conduct basic hacks against individual systems using tools created by someone else. The organization possesses little target analysis, command and control, or learning capability.

Second is advanced-structured: the capability to conduct more sophisticated attacks against multiple systems or networks and possibly, to modify or create basic hacking tools. The organization possesses an elementary target analysis, command and control, and learning capability.

Third is complex-coordinated: the capability for a coordinated attacks capable of causing mass-disruption against integrated, heterogeneous defenses (including cryptography). The organization has the ability to create sophisticated hacking tools. They possess a highly capable target analysis, command and control, and organization learning capability.

The Monterey team estimated that it would take a group starting from scratch 2-4 years to reach the advanced-structured level and 6-10 years to reach the complex-coordinated level, although some groups might get there in just a few years or turn to outsourcing or sponsorship to extend their capability.

The study examined five terrorist group types: religious, New Age, ethno-nationalist separatist, revolutionary, and far-right extremists. They determined that only the religious groups are likely to seek the most damaging capability level, as it is consistent with their indiscriminate application of violence. New Age or single issue terrorists, such as the Animal Liberation Front, pose the most immediate threat, however, such groups are likely to accept disruption as a substitute for destruction. Both the revolutionary and ethno-nationalist separatists are likely to seek an advanced-structured capability.

The far-right extremists are likely to settle for a simple-unstructured capability, as cyberterror offers neither the intimacy nor cathartic effects that are central to the psychology of far-right terror. The study also determined that hacker groups are psychologically and organizationally ill-suited to cyberterrorism, and that it would be against their interests to cause mass disruption of the information infrastructure. Thus, at this time, cyberterrorism does not seem to pose an imminent threat.

This could change. For a terrorist, it would have some advantages over physical methods. It could be conducted remotely and anonymously, and it would not require the handling of explosives or a suicide mission. It would likely garner extensive media coverage, as journalists and the public alike are fascinated by practically any kind of computer attack. Indeed cyberterrorism could be immensely appealing precisely because of the tremendous attention given to it by the government and media. Cyberterrorism also has its drawbacks. Systems are complex, so it may be harder to control an attack and achieve a desired level of damage than using physical weapons. Unless people are injured, there is also less drama and emotional appeal. Further, terrorists may be disinclined to try new methods unless they see their old ones as inadequate, particularly when the new methods require considerable knowledge and skill to use effectively.

Terrorists generally stick with tired and true methods. Novelty and sophistication of attack may be much less important than assurance that a mission will be operationally successful. Indeed, the risk of operational failure could be a deterrent to terrorists. For now, the truck bomb poses a much greater threat than the logic bomb.

The next generation of terrorists will grow up in a digital world, with ever more powerful and easy-to-use hacking tools at their disposal. They might see greater potential for cyberterrorism than the terrorists of today, and their level of knowledge and skill relating to hacking will be greater.

Hackers and insiders might be recruited by terrorists or become self-recruiting cyberterrorists, the Timothy McVeigh=s of cyberspace. Some might be moved to action by cyber policy issues, making cyberspace an attractive venue for carrying out an attack. Cyberterrorism could also become more attractive as the real and virtual worlds become more closely coupled, with a greater number of physical devices attached to the Internet. Some of these may be remotely controlled. Terrorists, for example, might target robots used in telesurgery. Unless these systems are carefully secured, conducting an operation that physically harms someone may be easy as penetrating a Web site is today.

Although the violent pursuit of political goals using exclusively electronic methods is likely to be at least a few years into the future, the more general threat of cybercrime is very much a part of the digital landscape today. In addition to cyberattacks against digital data and systems, many people are being terrorized on the Internet today with threats of physical violence. On-line stalking, death threats, and hate messages are abundant. These crimes are serious and must be addressed. In so doing, we will be in a better position to prevent and respond to cyberterrorism if and when the threat becomes more serious.

4

Information Warfare: Issues and Perspectives

INFORMATION WARFARE

What are the implications of these trends for the MTR concept and the future of professional military establishments? Following van Creveld, one might conclude that, since modern high-tech armies are ill-suited to waging unconventional wars, they will either wither away or be transformed into paramilitary security forces. If, on the other hand, one accepts the premise that technology-based information superiority confers the ability to dominate any opponent, a military with this advantage should be able to prevail in unconventional wars. What is needed, however, is a conceptual framework that identifies strategies and requirements for achieving such dominance across the full spectrum of conflict.

DOD has begun to move in this direction by expanding its doctrine of Command and Control Warfare into the broader concept of Information Warfare (IW). According to a provisional DOD definition, IW consists of "actions taken to achieve information superiority in support of national military strategy by affecting adversary information and information systems while leveraging and protecting our own information and information systems now (Note 35)." This formulation is intended to encompass military and non-military actions as well as defensive and offensive aspects. It also covers all levels of war from the tactical to strategic, and applies to troth peacetime and wartime conditions. According to writers like Donald Ryan, IW is based on the assumption that information technologies have developed to the point where they can now be employed as a weapon in their own right rather than as a "handmaiden" of armed combat now (Note 36). It thus becomes possible to envision wars being "won" or "lost" without, a shot being fired.

In contrast to Command and Control Warfare, which aims at victory on the battlefield, IW seeks to avoid the need to resort to lethal force by putting "enemies in positions where their information resources are useless or, worse, unreliable." In this respect, IW aspires to realizing Sun Tzu's famous dictum that "to subdue the enemy without fighting is the acme of skill."

Employed offensively, IW emphasizes the manipulation of electronic information systems to influence an adversary's perceptions and behavior. This might, for example, involve disabling military and civilian telecommunication systems through computer viruses or electromagnetic pulse devices. Infiltration is, however, the "maneuver of choice" since an enemy, unaware that his information sources have been compromised, will continue to trust them, creating opportunities for deception now (Note 37). Offensive IW also emphasizes the use of direct broadcast satellites, the commercial media, and "visual stimulus and illusion" technologies such as holography to conduct propaganda and subversion.

Defensively, IW requires an ability to detect and thwart attempts to tamper with one's own sources of information. In the military sphere, this entails assuring the integrity of command and control, communications, and intelligence systems. Critical elements of the civilian infrastructure such as power grids, financial networks, and telecommunications systems must also be protected. In addition, IW posits an ability to counter enemy propaganda and disinformation. According to the Tofflers, this can best be accomplished in an Information Age context by "precision-targeting" audience segments, disguising propaganda as news and entertainment, and employing computer-generated special effects now (Note 38).

IW theorists like John Arguilla set great store by the techniques of systems analysis to identify enemy and friendly centers of gravity now (Note 39). This approach, which is modeled on the air campaign plan against Iraq, visualizes a state or society as a set of systems and subsystems linked by numerous "nodes." Given sufficient knowledge of such systems, one can isolate the 'critical nodes ' which when destroyed or disabled will cause a systemic collapse. In most cases, the political leadership will be the critical node of the entire state structure, but if it cannot he reached with hard or "soft kill" weapons, belief systems, economic infrastructures, and military forces may have to be attacked. Applied in an IW context, the systems approach presupposes not only comprehensive knowledge about an adversary, but an ability to continually update that knowledge so that one is in a position to react more swiftly to a changing situation. Such "situational awareness" depends, in turn, on the use of artificial intelligence and other advanced data processing technologies to "fuse" large quantities of human and technical intelligence into an accurate, real-time picture of events. While most IW theorists acknowledge that anything resembling omniscience is unattainable, they do claim that these technologies confer a potentially decisive advantage over opponents lacking comparable capabilities now (Note 40).

The United States faces both opportunities and challenges in waging Information Warfare. On the one hand, it enjoys a wide lead over potential competitors in adapting information technologies to military purposes, and its private sector is at the cutting edge of the global Information Revolution. At the same time, however, the American information infrastructure, on which U.S. defense communications depend, is highly vulnerable to infiltration and sabotage. A recent Joint Security Commission Report describes this vulnerability as "the major security challenge of this decade and possibly the next century" and warns that there is "insufficient awareness of the grave risks we face in this area now (Note 41)."

"Hardening" the U.S. national information infrastructure, however, will not be easy. From a purely technical standpoint, it would be a "lengthy and extremely costly" undertaking which might not ensure protection for all types of sensitive date. Moreover, neither DOD nor any other Federal agency currently has the legal authority to enforce information security standards in the private sector, and the imposition of such standards probably would be controversial, especially in the absence of a clear external threat to national security. Despite public concern over privacy and computer crime, reaping the benefits of the "information superhighway" is widely believed to require openness and accessibility now (Note 42).

It will also not be easy for the U.S. to wage Information Warfare at the political level. It is unclear, for example, whether DOD or some other Federal entity would have primary responsibility. Since IW involves issues which affect numerous government agencies and cut across the public and private sectors, a case could be made for the establishment of a separate agency, or coordinating body. However, such organizational problems pale in significance compared to the controversy likely to be generated by the official adoption of a strategy which sanctions, or appears to sanction, systematic "perception management" activities aimed at the American people in the name of national security.

Whatever the means employed, it is questionable whether American public opinion can be induced to support risky foreign policy ventures absent a clear threat to U.S. interests. As Richard Haas points out, building consensus around such ventures is extremely difficult in a political environment characterized by a focus on domestic priorities, an assertive Congress, and heightened media scrutiny now (Note 43).

The unraveling of U.S. policy in Somalia after the October 1993 firefight with Aidid's followers illustrates the problems that can arise in this kind environment, especially when the executive branch neglects to build a reservoir of public support by explaining the costs and risks of its policies.

Information Warfare also poses potential foreign policy and international legal complications. Eliot Cohen, for example, worries that "a military fighting the shadowy battles of "information warfare" may find itself engaging the country in foreign policy tangles of a particularly messy kind now (Note 44)." IW operations undertaken in peacetime by the United States for purposes of deterrence or compellence, such as electronically sabotaging the power grid of a rogue state, might well be considered "terrorism," exposing the U.S. to international criticism and possible retaliation in kind. Operations of this type could also stiffen the resolve of the leaders and populace of a hostile state rather than coerce them.

The possibility should be considered that Information Warfare may be more effective against some kinds of adversaries than others. In general, the "critical nodes" of nation-states are easier to identify than those of nonstate entities, especially ones organized as networks and camouflaged within civilian populations. Given "precision intelligence," the vulnerabilities of any group can, in theory, be targeted, and the Information Revolution is enhancing the prospects of acquiring such intelligence through improved surveillance and data processing techniques. As is demonstrated by the growth of computer crime, however, the Information Revolution is also enlarging opportunities for concealment.

According to Robert Steele, the U.S. intelligence community as presently constituted is "virtually worthless" in assuring information dominance over terrorists, criminals, guerrillas and other non-state actors who are able to operate beyond the reach of its technical collection capabilities now (Note 45).

To, deal with the threats posed by such groups, Steele argues that radically new approaches to intelligence gathering and analysis are needed, including greater reliance on human as opposed to technical collection methods: closer cooperation among military, law enforcement and private-sector organizations; and a concerted effort to tap "open source" data available from the media, academia and business.

The inconclusive U.S. "war" against foreign drug traffickers suggests, however, that better intelligence by itself may not be enough to "defeat" some non-state actors. Drug trafficking is rooted in intractable political, social and economic conditions -- including endemic poverty and corruption in producer countries and the demand for illicit drugs in the United States -which can be addressed only at the margins through interdiction.

Thus, while improved intelligence and surveillance methods may enable military and law enforcement authorities to break up some trafficker organizations and raise the cost of doing business for others, trafficking itself is unlikely to be stamped out by such methods now (Note 46).

It might be objected that "raising the cost of doing business" is a viable objective in many conflict situations, and Information Warfare offers the U.S. a means of achieving it at a lower human and material cost than reliance on military force alone.

It is not difficult. for example, to envision U.S. forces successfully using IW techniques in "peace operations" to calm civil disturbances or induce the participants to settle their differences by nonviolence means. Even when armed conflicts cannot be averted or resolved, moreover, these techniques might be helpful in weakening the aggressive capabilities of a target group by sowing distrust among its members or undermining its base of popular support.

By the same token, however, the United States itself presents an inviting target for Information Warfare since its "centers of gravity" are highly visible and difficult to defend. As noted above, these include the vulnerability of the civilian information infrastructure to electronic attack and the tenuous nature of domestic support for foreign military interventions. The sensitivity of American public opinion to military casualties, collateral damage, and the taking of hostages, is another obvious pressure point which foreign adversaries -- aided by media coverage of such events -- have sometimes manipulated to coerce U.S. policymakers and will no doubt continue to try to exploit.

In sum, the United States faces significant constraints and handicaps in waging Information Warfare despite its undoubted military and technological process. Most of those who advocate the adoption of an IW strategy by the U.S. deal with this subject within a military frame of reference, ignoring or glossing over its broader political, legal, foreign policy, ethical and cultural implications.

Critical questions therefore tend not to be addressed. Perhaps the most fundamental of these is whether the American people are willing, in the absence of a clearly defined external threat, to accept the increased government intervention and regulation that would be required to implement such a strategy.

If waging Information Warfare is problematic for United States, it also poses difficulties for other states, including totalitarian regimes. Such regimes are less inhibited by legal, political and moral constraints than democratic governments. But even a garrison state like North Korea cannot completely protect its infrastructure against electronic manipulation and disruption. Moreover, the tight bureaucratic controls needed to sustain totalitarian system exact a heavy price in economic efficiency, national competitiveness and, ultimately, living standards. The 1989-1991 collapse of most communist states indicates that discontents bred by these systems contains the seeds of their own demise.

As John Patrick suggests, Information Warfare may be best suited to non-state entities like guerrilla movements, drug cartels, and terrorist networks now (Note 47). Such groups have several advantages over formal military organizations, including a decentralized organization and an ability to blend in with their surroundings.

They are also adept at manipulating ideas and information to defeat opponents politically. Furthermore, the Information Revolution is enhancing their capabilities by making them more competitive in terms of firepower, increasing their ability to conduct "pyschological operations" through the media, and enabling them to inflict "electronic Pearl Harbors" on vulnerable nation-states.

INFORMATION BASED WARFARE -THE NEW BATTLEFIELDS

Exiled to France, the Ayatollah Khomeni sought to maintain contact with the faithful. A cleric who espoused the return of his country to an Islamic theocracy-something: that many argued would move Iran back into the 16th century-the Ayatollah turned to 20th century tools to begin his crusade. Through the medium of cassettes, he began to record his message. After being mass-produced m 20th century studios, his 16th century message was smuggled back to Iran. Those tapes both planted the seed and inspired the flowering of a movement that brought Khomeni back to power m 1979.

For at least a decade, the American military had tinkered with devices for sabotaging enemy electrical systems. Some of the results were serendipitous. In the early 1980's, during a Navy exercise code-named Hey [Rube, long strands of rope chaff-glass filaments in which metal shards were embedded-had been dropped over the Pacific Ocean as part of a standard tactic to befuddle an opponent's radar. An unexpectedly skiff wind carried some of the chaff ninety miles to the coastline, where it got draped across power lines, shorting out transformers and causing power failures in parts of San Diego. The Navy quietly settled the damages- while carefully noting the effects of its unintended attack.

Information warfare has as many meanings as it has proponents, detractors and observers. Airpower theorists see it on the wings of Desert Storm; tank commanders see it in the American army's Force XXI; simulator designers see it in their virtual realities...and strategic-war planners see it as a way to lay waste to whole societies. Information warfare studies are proliferating within the American armed forces almost as quickly as the networks that carry them from desktop to desktop. The confusing planoply stems from the fact that the information revolution, whether it is in uniform or mufti, relies upon the fastest technology to do the oldest things. Thus it is always a peculiar mixture of the familiar and the shockingly new. In that war is all about strategies, command and morale, it has always been about information. All war is information war, and so every aspect of fighting wars in the information age can be called "information warfare" by someone. If information driven warfare means something new, it is the use of information as a substitute for traditional ways of fighting, rather than an adjunct to them. There are three ways that this might be achieved by:

- the high technology equivalent of brute force;
- subversion; and,
- a new form of deterrence. (Note 22)

For the purpose of this chapter, we focus on the second element-subversion. It is our belief that because of the unique relationship between Americans and computers, IBW launched subversive acts-a prelude to, or the actual execution of "quiet wars"-may be accomplished.

The evolution and ultimate "blurring" of military and civilian sectors came about in large part because of the growth in hardware and software. It was not so long ago, in the early 1960's, that the Pentagon provided the market for sophisticated electronics. Today, it makes up less than 1% of that market. In many ways, the military is following the revolution, not leading it. In 1962 Paul Baran of RAND developed a concept that permitted the linking of computers from distant locations. It was designed to preserve the integrity of the military command and control network in case of a nuclear attack. In 1969, the Defense Advanced Research Projects Agency (DARPA) funded the first test of the concept, and the first node was installed at RAND. The test consisted of scientists from remote locations passing findings and research notes back and forth. However, a year later it was being used like a mail box for the users and it proceeded to grow rapidly in use. In 1983, the military part and the nonmilitary part grew apart and finally split, the nonmilitary section grew up into what is now called the Internet.

For the first time in our nation's history, technology is no longer the sole domain of the military. The speed of the growth and application of technology is clearly a concern for defense planners. While the US used some of the world's most advanced weaponry and technology in the Gulf War (much of which proved inaccurate) it also used a great deal of older technology, some of which dated back to the 1960's. As B.R. Inman and Daniel F. Burton Jr. note in their article "Technology and US. National Security, "the 8088 microprocessor used in the Patriot missile was developed by the Intel Corporation fifteen years ago." (Note 23) This technology is not competitive today.

Opening and Closing Pandora's Box

In the center of Strike the battleship's commander, Captain David S. Bill, Ferched in his high backed padded chair. Although he occasionally glanced at the screens above, the captain s attention was largely fixed on the men clustered around four computers lining the far bulkhead. Something had gone awry with the ship's Tomahawk missile system. . For reasons no one could fathom, the Tomahawk computers seemed confused, refusing to transfer the necessary commands from the engagement-planning console to the launch console. The resulting impasse_"casualty" in Navy jargon_meant the missiles could not be fired. ..On Wisconsin, where the scheduled launch was now just moments away, the men in Strike were running out of solutions. ..As the request for additional time flashed up the chain of command, an excited voice from one of the nearby ships crackled through Strike: "Alpha, alpha." This is the Paul F Foster. Happy trails." Happy trails: the code phrase for missiles away. Operation Desert Storm had begun without Wisconsin.

As the most technologically vulnerable nation, the US defense planners must recognize several concepts about the technical end of the IBW battlefield:

It must be assumed that everyone has access to technology, therefore the US is the most vulnerable to attack;

As the US's ability to wage IBW increases, so to do the IBW capabilities, and response capabilities, of other nation-states and non-state actors;

While at first glance it would appear that IBW is most effective against adversaries with like technological capabilities and infrastructure-the top end of the IBW target spectrum-it must be remembered that technology comes in two forms-high and appropriate-and it is the latter that will always defeat the former. Thus, the benefits of IBW in arena's of conflict as found in the Gray Areas are a target rich environment must be pursued alongside the force on force approach.

The technical realm of information based warfare can be split into two major areas: Netwar and Cyberwar. Netwar is the information related conflict between nations, societies, governments, or non-state actors with the targets being information systems and communications, and it consists of destruction of communications, acquisition of information, release of misinformation, and destruction or deletion of data. Cyberwar consists of militaries conducting their operations according to information based theories and principles. These terms can be broken down even further. Netwar can be broken into three main categories: Personal, Corporate, and Global.

We are constantly warned about the personal level of Netwar, we have passwords to computer accounts, never give our social security number over the telephone, and generally try to be careful about our own information. But protecting yourself from someone who genuinely wants to conduct information war against you is nearly impossible. Corporations are subject to a barrage of information security problems to an even greater extent. The stealing of company secrets is a new form of economic war that is plaguing many companies. It is also possible for one company to release false findings that indicate that a competitor has a poor or dangerous product. IBW spawned misinformation-a fertile area for denial and deception techniques-are very difficult to combat and correct. Finally, on the global level, Netwar can be waged against industries, economies, nations, or non-state groups. It ranges from intelligence and information leads, to the terrifying possibilities of terrorist groups breaking into such communications as an air traffic control system at a major US airport. The impact at the global level can be much more wide spread and all threatening than that of the personal or corporate levels of netwar.

On both sides of the war, Netwar and Cyberwar, the key to good protection and offense is good software to run the systems, encode the data, and peck holes in other's data. The vital link for the information and the technology is software, which relies heavily upon implanted logic. The newest and brightest theories and concepts of logic center around what is called 'fuzzy logic'. The name fuzzy logic makes one think of a system that is inexact, but that is not the case, instead it has an infinite exactness. Fuzzy logic expands our normal computer principle of 0 or 1, true or false, and in the place of this is infinite degrees between 0 and 1. Fuzzy logic is used every day in the development of everything from smart washers to train systems in Japan. With a smart washer, you merely press a start button and the machine figures the cycle, how much detergent, and the water use; the logic train systems are smooth as silk, quick, and always on time. The theory started with a few paradoxes one of which is The Paradox of Theseus' ship: When Theseus returned from slaying the Minotaur, says Plutarch, the Athenians preserved his ship, and as planks rotted, replaced them with new ones. When the first plank was replaced, everyone agreed it was still the same ship. Adding a second plank made no difference either. At some point, the Athenians may have replaced every plank in the ship. Was it a different ship? At what point did it become one?

At different points in time the ship was certain degrees the original ship, for instance when half the planks were replaced, it was .5 the original ship. This same principle of degrees can be applied to many concepts around us, and what you end up with is a very exact and reliable process for computers. When you tie this concept into ideas such as artificial intelligence, you may obtain a computer that has the capacity to learn because it can start to work with more than 0 and 1.

Because of the importance of the technical tools of IBW-and their fragility-we list below the possible contents of an IBW techno "kit-bag": Computer Viruses - A piece of code, or code fragment, designed to begin replicating itself when a host program begins to run. It's objective is to erase data, software programs, or memory in order to interrupt the action of the computer it infests. These can be loaded unwittingly by a user off the Internet or some other disk.

Worms - Instead of being just a code fragment, a worm is an entire program in and of itself. The code begins to replicate as soon as it touches a computer system, not dependent on the start of execution of any other program. Its aim is to eat up computer resources and/or delete data to result in a crippling effect on the host computer. Trojan Horses - As the name would suggest, a Trojan horse is a program, or code fragment inside a program, that performs a function unbeknownst to the user. It usually performs a simple task on the outside, while unleashing a virus or a worm on the inside. It can also perform information retrieval while performing a task, leaving no trace.

Logic Bombs - Similar to a Trojan horse, a logic bomb is used to release a virus, worm, or complete some other secret task. These are usually planted by a programmer or system developer. This could be useful in US military strategy, instead of open bombs, the US could plant logic bombs to retrieve specific data from foreign users. This is plausible because many of the main software development in the world occurs in the US. Trap Doors - The use of this is similar to a logic bomb. It is a secret way back into a system left by a programmer or designer. Unlike a logic bomb that executes, a trap door is merely an unknown security flaw. Chipping - This is the term for doing any of the above to the hardware of a system instead of to the software. One can build in circuitry to a chip that performs specific functions.

Machines and Microbes - Although one thinks of Star Trek and other science fiction when the subject of nanny machines comes up, it is actually a feasible plan. machines and microbes are tiny machines, like a small insect, that "eat" electronic circuits, oil, plastics, etc. If unleashed on a computer center, the result would be total shut down. Electronic Jamming, HERF guns, and EM bombs- These are all forms of electronic signal jamming. One can jam communications, stopping computer information flow; shoot radio signals at an electronic target to shut it down with a High Energy Radio Frequency (HERF) gun; or send out a high powered electromagnetic pulse, an EMP bomb.

Hitch-hiking- This is a group of people, a subsection of hackers, that merely sit on the net and wait. They wait for any information and interesting code to go by and then hitch a ride with it, they follow and delete it, or they simply copy and steal it. Thinking in terms of closing Pandora's Box, the following techniques will have to be considered as an IBW operational security plan is built:

Firewalls - A limited gateway to the Interment from a company or group. Only passwords and certain configurations can get in, and everything is checked for viruses, etc. Only privileged personnel, or personnel with certain system configurations can get out. If implemented correctly they can be useful.

Encryption - This growing area of interest consists on coding data so that others can not place bombs in or around it or read the data. This is growing more difficult as hackers and other groups become more efficient at breaking the codes. This is one of the areas that fuzzy logic could come into serious play. (Note 24) If, at first glance, the foregoing appears to be merely a "laundry list," a reading of the following paragraph will surely prove sobering to the IBW planner:

The Defense Information Security Agency (DISA) conducts vulnerability studies of military and government computer systems. Their figures are truly alarming: 88% of defense computer systems are easily penetrated. Of the successful penetrations, 96% are not detected. Even worse, 95% of the detected penetrations are not reported or responded to. Even when an intrusion is detected, it is usually impossible to determine who did it. DISA studies indicate that there were possibly 300,000 intrusions into government computer systems in 1994 alone. (Note 25)

THE DOMAIN OF INFORMATION AND INFORMATION WARFARE

The read-ahead package for the workshop included a paper that stressed the size and complexity of the information warfare domain. As illustrated in the paper, three relatively independent dimensions are required to capture and describe the information warfare arena: the degree of conflict/cooperation, substantive focus (political, military, social, economic, etc.), and the nature of the actors involved (individuals, private organizations, nation states, international organizations, the general public, media, etc.).

The workshop participants generally accepted the broad nature of the information warfare domain and the central role of information systems and processes in the world today. However, they inferred several very important implications from this broad characterization of the relevant domain.

- First, the term "information warfare" is used to mean many things, but is often focused on the military domain or the cyber-war domain dominated by computers. This narrow definition is inconsistent with the broad policy questions relevant to competition and conflict using information media.
- Because information warfare is really a broad and diverse arena, analysis of it must be focused on selected elements,

which must be clearly defined in each application. Overall, the field is so broad that virtually no meaningful generalizations can be drawn about it.

- Isolation, except in rare instances, of military, national, public, and private information systems is all but impossible today. Even very important military traffic is likely to be carried on national infrastructure systems. Public and private sectors are heavily interdependent, and this linkage will continue to grow.
- A whole raft of information systems make potential targets -- banking systems, control systems for railway operations, air control systems, control systems for pipelines, media systems, and others. Only a fraction of these are primarily military or under the direct protection of the Department of Defense (DoD).
- As has been stressed by ADM Owens as Vice Chairman of the Joint Chiefs of Staff, the civilian sector is no longer a sanctuary that can be protected by interposing military forces between adversaries and their targets. Traditional military forces can be flanked at the speed of light by information age attacks on the general population or key economic systems.
- More profoundly, there is no consensus on the appropriate boundary between the military and Department of Defense roles and missions, those of the law enforcement and intelligence systems, and those of the commercial sector.

Workshop participants were aware of a variety of policy initiatives to create interagency working groups and coordinating mechanisms as well as public-private dialogues and mechanisms for both exchanging information and developing plans for dealing with information age threats that cut across communities. Considerable progress has been made in generating better awareness of the threat and some effort has been made toward cooperation.

However, the general consensus was that these helpful activities were only now developing momentum and were far from successful completion.

INFORMATION WARFARE AND DETERRENCE

At the abstract level, the interface between these two concepts is dependent on setting the context clearly. First, deterrence is always from an actor toward a target. The very nature of the actor and target, as well as the degree of asymmetry between them, is important.

Moreover, the nature of the relationship between the parties is important to the analysis. Hence, specification of the context (type of relationship, nature of the actors, substantive domain) is essential before any conclusion is possible about the potential or actual effectiveness of deterrence.

The most important insight arising from looking at the two concepts, however, is the fact that they are only relevant to one another in highly selective contexts. The analogy that emerged was that of a steamroller and a wrench.

Both are tools and, depending on the situation, appropriate wrenches may be useful for, or even crucial to, the operation of the steamroller. However, most of the things the steamroller does are irrelevant to the wrench and most of the things the wrench can be used for do not involve a steamroller. In many cases, therefore, the workshop found itself venturing away from a pure consideration of the two concepts and into meaningful discussions in areas related to one or more of the central topics.

CONCLUSIONS

One is thus led back to the issue posed at the outset of this essay -whether the advent of the Information Age marks the beginning of the end of the monopoly of war by nation-states and their professional military establishments. This issue is largely ignored in discussions of the Military Technical Revolution, which assume that information technologies are merely the latest in a series of innovations which have revolutionized the character of armed conflict among nation-states.

The possibility raised by van Creveld that larger changes may be underway in the nature of war itself with which nation-state armies are ill-prepared to cope is thrust into the background or even dismissed as "elegant irrelevance now (Note 48)." Information Warfare theorists, on the other hand, do address the broader societal impact of the Information Revolution and the challenges this poses for conventional militaries. As suggested above, however, they tend to frame these challenges in narrowly technological and military terms, with the result that they often fail to take into account the political, cultural and legal dimensions of the subject. As long as Information Warfare continues to be viewed chiefly as a problem of military modernization, rather than as part of a larger global transformation affecting every facet of society, it will be difficult to transcend the limitations of this approach and to formulate more persuasive recommendations for coping with it.

A precondition for addressing the challenge of Information Warfare is recognizing that there is a problem. This requires moving beyond the horizons of the MTR concept in which dealing with today's low-intensity conflicts is seen as a "small but irksome" task "compared to potentially more critical but totally unknown tasks that may face the nation two decades from now (Note 49)." A second requirement is acknowledgment that the ability of the U.S. government and military to "solve" the problem may be limited. Technology is unlikely to provide all the answers and the American political environment is not conducive to peacetime mobilization for "total war" against still largely hypothetical threats.

5

Information Warfare and Information Strategy

Information warfare is often thought of as being defined by a particular target setudecision makers, information, information processes, and information systems. The "battlespace" associated with IW has been a constantly expanding one, moving far beyond traditional military situations. In some quarters, IW has even been associated with the leveraging of information technologies to achieve greater effectiveness and efficiency.

This has stretched the meaning of IW to the breaking point and has sowed more confusion than enlightenment. For this reason, this treatment of the subject uses the term "information strategies" to refer to the recognition and utilization of information and information technologies as an instrument of national power that can be independent of, or complementary to, military presence and operations.

The scope, or battlespace, of information warfare and strategy (IWS) can be defined by the players and three dimensionsùthe nature of their interactions, the level of their interactions, and the arena of their interactions. Nation states or combinations of nation states are not the only players. Non-state actors (including political, ethnic, and religious groups; organized crime; international and transnational organizations; and even individuals empowered by information technology) are able to engage in information attacks and to develop information strategies to achieve their desired ends.

The term "war" has been used so loosely in recent times (e.g., War on Poverty, War on Drugs, War on Crime) that is should be no surprise that IW has evolved over the past several years to become a "catch-all" term that encompasses many disparate activities, some of which have long been associated with competition, conflict, and warfare, and others that are of more recent origin.

These include activities that range from propaganda campaigns (including Media War), to attacks (both physical and non-physical) against commanders, their information sources, and the means of communicating with their forces. Under this rather large umbrella that has become known as IW, one can find activities long associated with military concepts and operations, including deception, command and control warfare (C2W), and psychological operations (Psyops). Technological advances have added new forms such as electronic warfare (EW) and "hacker warfare."

The term "defensive information warfare" (IW-D) is used here to refer to all actions taken to defend against information attacks, that is, attacks on decision makers, the information and information-based processes they rely on, and their means of communicating their decisions. Strictly speaking, since these attacks can be launched during peace time at nonmilitary targets by nonmilitary groups, both foreign and domestic, the term IW-D should be IWS-D. However, IW-D is currently in wide use.

This overview of IW-D does not attempt to deal with the problems of defending against all of the different kinds of information attacks, but rather focuses its attention on the subset of IW that involves attacks against our information infrastructure, including what has become known as "hacker warfare" and in its more serious form, "digital warfare."

ANALOGIES AND REALITIES

Defending against information attacks has a number of characteristics in common with societal efforts to combat disease, drugs, and crime. Noting these similarities helps to put this problem into perspective, provides some potential useful lessons learned, and serves as a benchmark.

Before reviewing the specific similarities between combating IWS and these long-standing problems, it should be noted that, while eradicating information attacks may not be a realistic expectation, significant progress can be made in defending against all forms of information attacks, enough so that the risks can be kept at acceptable levels. Defending, as it is used here, includes preventing attacks, blunting attacks, and controlling the damage caused by attacks.

The problem of IW-D is similar to the problems encountered in the "wars" on disease, drugs, and crime in a number of dimensions. First, the solution to any of these problems requires the efforts of a number of organizations, both public and private. Second, it is unlikely, given the competition for resources, that any of these efforts will be fully funded. Therefore, we can expect that there will never be what those who have IW-D responsibilities think are a sufficient level of funding for IW-D programs. Third, these are not static problems. Drug cartels and criminals certainly learn from their mistakes.

Even viruses "learn." Thus, defense forces will be continuously locked in a battle to keep up with attackers. Fourth, public awareness and concern will reach peaks, often accompanied by frenzied efforts to solve the problem. These relatively short periods of interest will be followed by longer periods when the urgency to solve the problem will give way to apathy. Maintaining funding and progress during these periods of waning public interest will be one of the key challenges of leadership in this area. Fifth, organizations and individuals will learn to make adjustments in their behavior to deal with IW attacks and their often unintended consequences.

These adjustments will be made so that those organizations and individuals can accommodate some level of painùa dynamic equilibrium of sortsùas the cost of doing business in the Information Age. Finally, solutions will, of necessity, involve compromises. This is due to the natural tensions that exist among the various stakeholders. Tensions between the law enforcement and the protection of civil liberties are classic examples that have already arisen in the information domain.

CURRENT SITUATION

Attacks on information systems are already a fact of life in the Information Age. Although a small portion of these attacks result in significant loss or damage, the vast majority of them result in little or no damageù the crime equivalents of trespassing, public nuisance, minor vandalism, and petty theft. It has been estimated that more than 90 percent of these attacks are perpetrated using available tools and techniques (based upon incidents reported to CERT), that only 1 attack in 20 is noticed by the victim, and that only 1 in 20 gets reported (these last two statistics were a result of a Defense Information Systems Agency (DISA) study and similar rates have been reported by others). However, it appears that reporting rates may be on the increase.

Of more concern is the presence of a technically feasible "strategic" threat. That is, the means exist to cause significant damage and disruption to U.S. public and private information assets, processes, and systems, and to compromise the integrity of vital information. Analysts also have no difficulty identifying groups with the motivations and opportunities to launch such attacks. Given our present vulnerabilities as a nation, a well-planned, coordinated IW attack could have strategic consequences. Such an attack, or the threat of such an attack, could thwart our foreign policy objectives, degrade military performance, result in significant economic loss, and perhaps even undermine the confidence of our citizens in the Government's ability to protect its citizens and interests.

While no "smoking keyboard" has been found to validate such a threat, the very existence of the means to carry out such an attack, when coupled with the myriad of motives and opportunities that exist, results in our present state of vulnerability. These circumstances have created a situation that calls for prudent defensive actions to be taken in the public interest. We need to be proactive rather than be forced to react after an Information Age "Pearl Harbor." Moreover, a successful strategic attack would point the way and encourage others to plan similar attacks. Hence, we need to go on the offensive with a vigorous defense.

DIGITAL WAR

Each age has seen war transformed by modern technologies and concepts. The Information Age promises to be no different. Some have called the Gulf War the first "Information War" - others have called it the last "Industrial Age" war. The power of information was clearly demonstrated in the context of traditional conflict. Information was leveraged to significantly improve the effectiveness of all aspects of warfare from logistics to command, control, communications, and computers, intelligence, surveillance, and reconnaissance (C4ISR).

The effectiveness of the U.S. and its allies in the Gulf War has surely deterred potential adversaries from taking on our forces in the rather symmetrical manner that Iraq attempted and has stimulated thinking about other strategies for countering conventional forces. Digital war, enabled by advances in technology and its widespread adoption as well as the globalization of economics and commerce, is surely a strategy that potential adversaries are thinking about to achieve some of the objectives that have previously been sought by means of traditional warfare.

Digital war, a subset of what we call information war, involves non-physical attacks on information, information processes, and information infrastructure that compromise, alter, damage, disrupt, or destroy information and/or delay, confuse, deceive, and disrupt information processing and decision making.

Digital war intrinsically possesses in ultimate form some of the same characteristics that traditional military planners are striving for, including low-cost precision, standoff, and stealth. Digital war threatens the ability of a nation state's military to interpose itself between its population and "enemies of the state," thereby causing a loss of sanctuary. The importance of sanctuary can be inferred by our willingness to spend significant resources on air, sea, and missile defenses to provide our citizens with a workable sanctuary with respect to territorial intrusions.

Another characteristic of information attacks stems from the loss of sanctuary. Attacks of this sort, particularly when they consist of more than an isolated incident, create a perception of vulnerability, loss of control, and loss of confidence in the ability of the state to provide protection. Thus, the impact can far exceed the actual damage that has occurred. This non-linear relationship between actual damage and societal damage makes the problem of digital war a particularly challenging one because it creates a mismatch between rational defense responses and their effectiveness.

How does one respond to a serious set of information attacks? Responding with traditional military forces may be politically unacceptable or in fact, may be ineffectual. Currently there is no consensus, even among those in the defense establishment who think about these issues, regarding how to deal with such an attack.

Given the potential effectiveness of digital war, particularly as an instrument of power for niche competitors and non-state actors, we need, as a society, to take this Information Age form of war very seriously. If we do not, and if we rely solely on traditional weapons and concepts of war, we may be building our own 21st Century Maginot line that can be flanked with the speed of light.

INADVERTENT ROBUSTNESS

There are some who have suggested that we are not as vulnerable to information attacks as has been claimed because the collection of our legacy systems provides a certain amount of inherent robustness and resiliency. They point to the overlaps and duplications in these systems and argue that it would be very hard for anyone to completely disrupt a given set of services. They point to the lack of interoperability among legacy systems and the firewalls that are thereby created and argue that it would be impossible for attackers to get very far by penetrating the weakest systems and using them as launching pads for attacks on other systems. They argue that our current legacy systems and their interrelationships are difficult (even for us) to understand, so it must follow that potential adversaries will also be confused.

Clearly there is some truth in each of these arguments. But this unruly collection of legacy systems also carries with it significant disadvantages. As far as security considerations are concerned, five points need to be made. First, this issue is not whether or not an attack could totally destroy or disrupt a particular system or type of service, but whether or not there could be sufficient damage to trigger the perception of a failure and result in panic behavior that could in turn create a significant national problem. Second, the redundancies in the systems are only partial and unplanned. Hence, they are neither complete nor reliable. Third, our legacy systems, many having been designed and built with little or no attention to security, are difficult to protect and secure. Fourth, as the need for interconnectivity and interoperability increases, more and more systems are being lashed together with "work-arounds." These patches, in many cases, compromise security. Lastly, the lack of security that these systems provide is dampening the demand for services that could make operations more effective and efficient in many areas. Our current collection of legacy systems has other disadvantages as well. For example, the lack of interoperability wastes resources and impairs operations. Thus, it should be clear that the disadvantages of our current collection of legacy systems are not a blessing in disguise but rather the source of problems that need to be addressed so that we can take full advantage of the opportunities that information technologies can provide.

RESPONSIBILITIES FOR POTENTIALLY STRATEGIC THREATS

The division of responsibilities for this region of the threat topology is not as clear-cut or as familiar as for the other two regions. In this zone of collaboration, public and private sector organizations need to find ways and create mechanisms that foster a shared perception of the nature of the threat, particularly those aspects of a situation that increase the likelihood of strategic consequences. In addition, ways should be found to enhance our defenses and improve our ability to mitigate the effects of attacks in this region to prevent them from having strategic consequences.

In this region, the Government needs to take the lead in helping to develop the necessary understanding of the threat, while the private sector needs to support Government efforts by providing incident data. The Government also needs to take the lead in developing coordinating mechanisms designed to both support improved understanding and the coordination of defenses.

The two biggest challenges associated with this pivotal threat region are first, the recognition of when an attack of strategic significance has begun and in characterizing the nature and scope of the attack and second, in the effecting of a transition from a "peace time" to a "war time" footing. The success of the processes and mechanisms developed to coordinate this transition will be critical to the success of any IW-D strategy.

The private sector needs to take the lead in this region by turning improvements in understanding into more effective defenses. This includes not only enhanced detection tools and techniques but also an improved ability to contain an attack, thereby limiting its spread, damage, and consequences. The Government needs to assist the private sector in these efforts by providing resources and technical support. Resources might take the form of tax incentives, or as was recommended in the case of some private sector systems that were deemed to be strategic, direct payments.

IW-D CHALLENGES

For anyone who thrives on challenges, defending against information warfare is a great line of work. There are five key challenges we face. The first challenge involves the development of a better understanding of the nature and characteristics of the threat among society and its institutions. Success requires that everyone be on board. Therefore, it is important that we continue to work to increase awareness of this problem and to develop a better understanding of both the nature of the threat and our vulnerabilities.

The second challenge is to develop a strategy for deterring digital information attacks. The first line of defense is deterrence. Not enough effort is being devoted to developing and gaming possible strategies. In February 1996, ACTIS sponsored a workshop on this subject. This workshop was a highly successful endeavor, giving those who attended a better idea where the latest thinking is on this subject, stimulating more thinking about the subject, and bringing some key issues into sharper focus. (The proceedings of this workshop, "IW and Deterrence," have been published and are available from ACTIS.)

The third and fourth challenges involve developing means of providing warning for attacks and ways of successfully defending against attacks that do occur. Improving our ability to see an attack coming, or providing indications and warning (I&W) of attacks in a timely fashion, is perhaps the most single difficult challenge we face. Developing an I&W capability involves not only the traditional strategic and tactical warning capabilities, but also the ability to know that an attack has begun and to ascertain the likely scope of such an attack. Given that currently, in many cases, an attack in progress is not even recognized, this will be a tall order. This is not only a technical challenge, but it is, as mentioned earlier, an organizational challenge. This is because of the information necessary to provide warning of an imminent action or an attack in its early stages would most likely need to come primarily from private sector organizations whose "peace time" reporting structures may not either require reporting of all relevant incident data or require it in near real time. Thus an attack of strategic significance may be well underway before we realize it and are able to move to a "war time" footing, which would bring with it the increased reporting requirements and coordination necessary to assess the situation and respond accordingly.

As a result of my participation in a series of "day after" games developed by RAND for ASD(C3I), I have concluded that we will not be able to respond to such attacks in a timely and effective manner unless there is 1) more awareness and understanding of the nature of strategic IW capabilities and our own vulnerabilities among not only key officials in public and private organizations but also among Congress, the Media and the Public; 2) more understanding of the offense arsenal at our disposal, particularly the direct, indirect, and collateral damage they might cause; 3) a pre-agreed systematic system of alerts similar to the DEFCON system, each level of which carries with it known, understood, and practiced processes and actions; and 4) a "battle damage" assessment process suitable for IW.

The construction of a DEFCON-type system for IW-D will require the investment of a considerable amount of intellectual capital as well as a considerable amount of coordination among a wide variety of Government departments and agencies, the Congress, industrial associations, and private organizations. Given the nature of the problem, time will be of the essence should problems with our information infrastructure begin to appear. Well thought-out options that address both the need for increased collection and analyses and the need to take measures to prevent or control damage are essential to countering this threat. Given the trifurcated threat topology and the very different nature of each of the three threat regions, implementing the proposed "defense-in-depth" strategy will be a considerable undertaking.

The fifth challenge is to develop appropriate and effective responses to such attacks. Responses to attacks include identification, interdiction, apprehension, and punishment (possibly including retaliation).

IWS AWARENESS AND UNDERSTANDING

We have much to learn and many to educate. When many of the individuals who need to become more aware of the threat and its potential consequences are exposed to the subject only by reading novels or going to the movies, we cannot really expect to develop the degree of understanding required. When the only exposure to the subject is through fiction, it is no wonder that the threat may be dismissed as fictional. There are still many individuals in key positions in both the public and private sector who need to have a better appreciation for this problem and to be more motivated to address the issues. On the other hand, admittedly we do not possess a great abundance of factual information. While we have clear indications that some potentially serious attacks, even crippling attacks, are technically feasible, as has been pointed out, there is no "smoking keyboard" to show. Yet it should be pointed out that the time it took to create a working atomic bomb from the time its theoretical feasibility was recognized surprised many, even the most knowledgeable scientists. Our ignorance about the nature of potential attacks is mirrored by a lack of knowledge about the effectiveness of current and developing defensive techniques and strategies.

When our systems are not being adequately monitored and incidents are not being adequately recorded and investigated, it is hard to see how we can develop the vastly improved understanding of both the threat and the effectiveness of defenses we require. Increased collection and analysis is clearly needed to provide the empirical foundation required to a) increase awareness, b) increase our understanding, c) support planning, and d) develop effective defenses. Given our tendencies to value privacy, both in terms of individuals and corporations, and the limitations we have imposed upon the collection of domestic intelligence, it is unlikely that sufficient information will be collected and analyzed by the Government to quickly determine the nature and extent of an ongoing IW attack in its early stages. Therefore, it is extremely important that when it appears that such an attack may be imminent or in progress, that "peace time" data collection and analysis arrangements be quickly shifted to a "war time" footing. In designing a DEFCON-like process, it will be important to define "trigger" events that will automatically cause information to flow to a situation assessment organization. This is because of the time criticality of providing up-to-date information to the decision makers who will be considering appropriate DEFCON-like decisions involving potentially costly actions to safeguard the NII and prevent further damage to our information infrastructure and the key public safety and economic functions that it supports.

CHANGING THE ENDS, WAYS, AND MEANS MODEL OF STRATEGY

The ends, ways, and means paradigm posits that strategy equals ends plus ways plus means. Ends are expressed as national objectives drawn from national values and interests. Ways are courses of action to achieve ends. Means are the resources (manpower, materiel, money, forces, logistics, etc.) required to support each course of action. Unless ends, ways, and means are compatible and in balance, the strategy will be at risk. And the greater the imbalance, the greater the risk. The information age changes all three elements of the strategy equation.

Ends. In the information age, national objectives (ends), other than the protection of the national information infrastructure, are not easily identifiable. Clearly, the emergence of global economic networks delink national corporations from national markets and turn them multinational. For example, profits from the sale of a new Boeing 777 aircraft find their way into countries worldwide. Boeing is a broker in the global economic network, buying materials and components worldwide, basing its acquisitions on price, availability, quality and any other number of factors. In effect, Boeing attempts to optimize its entire operation globally. As it does so, it pays little attention to national allegiance. In such an environment, governmental influence over Boeing's purchases becomes problematic. Then the implications of a power struggle between government and industry are very real. (Note 24)

Economic security and prosperity in the information age are functions of a kind of equality between nations and firms. The more firms act internationally, as in the Boeing example, the less they can be held to national accountability. Walter Wriston asserts that "Capital will go where it is wanted and stay where it is well treated." (Note 25) Multinational firms play one nation-state against the other as they seek the greatest profit. (Note 26) Now trade agreements among sovereign nations are really inadequate when they don't include the concerns of global business organizations. (Note 27) The North American Free Trade Agreement and the European Union are recent attempts of nations to achieve competitive equality with the growing multinational economic networks. Yet, in a global information age economy, it will be futile for sovereign states to attempt to cut off and control even part of the world market. (Note 28) The organizing principles for the analysis of power have changed. Multinational firms anticipate events and react quickly in global markets. But governments, whose policies are geographically bound, react more slowly. (Note 29) Power in the information age depends more on the ability to influence access and interconnection than on the capacity to enforce borders. It follows that the ends of our national security strategy will depend less on confrontation with opponents and more on cooperation and trust among competitors. (Note 30) Moreover, total agreement on objectives within a globally linked network is virtually impossible.

If national economic objectives can't be achieved due to the emergent global and networked nature of markets, why not ignore global markets completely? Well, ignoring the networked global markets is risky business, if not impossible, for either a nation-state or a business concern. Each year since 1965, the U.S. commercial sector has invested more of its dollars in research and development than has the Department of Defense (DoD). (Note 31) If our military services are to preserve their technological superiority over potential foes, they must have access to these commercial products. Similarly, individual businesses can afford neither the enormous costs nor bear the high risks of remaining on the leading edge of all information age technologies. Yet they can't afford to miss a breakthrough that could create new product lines. When businesses share intellectual capital (knowledge) through participation in global markets, they avoid isolation from new technologies. (Note 32)

Obviously, the ends of our strategy equation have become unclear, since it may be difficult to achieve all desired national objectives in the globally networked information age. At best, a sovereign nation might effectively pursue its interests only as it paradoxically subordinates those interests to the common interests of all networked partners. (Note 33)

Ways. It is not difficult to show how the ways of security strategy change with the information age. For example, information age weapons are equalizers. They help small nations against large nations and favor the weak over the strong. Examples include Stinger missiles used by the Mujahedin against the Russians and computer viruses designed to invade individual weapon systems or an entire defense computer network. (Note 34) However, the real problem lies in the fact that today's breakthrough technologies in electronics, computer systems, software, and telecommunications come from the commercial marketplace and are available to anyone in the world. Furthermore, foes may use these technologies to their advantage without even resorting to military applications.

In broadest terms, information warfare is not new. It encompasses any hostile activity directed against our knowledge and belief systems. (Note 35) Cyberwar, the newest subset of information warfare, needs no battlefield -- it is fought in cyberspace. Cyberspace includes information itself, the communication nets that move it, and the computers that make it useful. (Note 36) Cyberspace can be influenced and at times dominated by anyone possessing inexpensive computers linked into existing global communication nets.

The enemy may exploit global business organizations that produce cyber technology and determine the patterns of change. (Note 37) He may attempt to propagate waves of data big enough to crash the network by overloading network switches. (Note 38) Cyberwar operations can blind us electronically and may change the definition of what is a hostile attack and what determines defeat. (Note 39)

Under the microscope of world opinion formed by means of pervasive communication satellites, open warfare is no longer an option for sovereign nations to pursue their national interests. (Note 40) Cable News Network coverage can rapidly trigger a negative international response, as we have seen during the recent wars in Somalia and Bosnia. However, the information age offers a more subtle approach -- waging a quiet war in cyberspace where digital fingerprints are hard, if not impossible, to trace. (Note 41) When information warfare enters and uses public cyberspace, collateral damage may be significant. Banking, finance, telecommunications, trade, travel, energy, and cultural systems are vulnerable. (Note 42) Misinformation and disinformation campaigns are easily mounted and hard to defend against. Moreover, an adequate defense depends upon gathering, analyzing, and distributing intelligence to a flexible, networked interagency team. (Note 43)

So, the information age introduces at least three new concepts in the ways of strategy. First, information age weapons are equalizers and can negate the military principle of mass. Second, cyberwar needs no battlefield and therefore no specially trained military organization -- even civilians may participate. Finally, the initial offensive strike in a quiet cyberwar would be hard to detect and to defend against. It is also impossible to limit the cyberwar battlespace to purely military networks.

Another way of assessing the changes in the ways of strategy is to compare World War I and II warfare to information age warfare. Whereas the world wars used attrition (WW I) and maneuver (WW II), information age war emphasizes control. Whereas the world wars attempted to exhaust (WW I) and annihilate (WW II), cyberwar seeks to paralyze. And whereas the tools of the world wars were firepower weapons (WW I) and mechanization (WW II) produced in mass, the tools of information war are limited numbers of inexpensive computers linked via global communication systems. (Note 44)

Means. Knowledge as a resource is not included in the current resource paradigm of manpower, materiel, money, forces, and logistics. (Note 45) Knowledge, the "ammunition" of information war, is inexhaustible. Once produced (at a cost), knowledge can be used repeatedly -- it will not disappear. In fact, it only increases! Digital knowledge can be copied and never missed. It can be given away but still kept. Digital knowledge can be distributed instantly. It is non-linear; it defies the theory of economy of scale. (Note 46) Knowledge is the key element of wealth in the information age. Compared with industrial age manufacturing, information-based industries can produce more with fewer resources, less energy, and less labor. Production runs of one are possible and even economical with intellectual capital (knowledge) encoded in software and used by smart machines. (Note 47) The result is an explosion of personalized products and services. (Note 48) Moreover, knowledge to inform people, coded as digital bits, can be turned into audio, video, or even graphics -- it is "mediumless." (Note 49) Manpower, materiel, and forces, on the other hand, possess none of these characteristics. Knowledge as a resource is often cheaper than materiel. It uses limited manpower or forces and may require little or no logistics. Thus the information age opens the doors to the resource poor. Knowledge diffuses and redistributes power to the weaker actors. It redraws boundaries and time and space horizons. It enables organizations to open up. (Note 50) When it comes to balancing means with ends and ways, knowledge as a resource offers an economical solution.

In sum, it is difficult to apply the ends, ways, and means paradigm of strategy to information age security. Unlike traditional means, knowledge is relatively cheap and easy to balance with ends and ways. Unlike conventional ways, cyberwar defies the military principle of mass. And its primary objectives are control and paralysis. Unlike the clearly articulated ends of Cold War security strategies, national objectives in a globally networked information age are more difficult to define and thus to achieve. Clearly, we need a new framework for formulating information age knowledge strategies.

INFORMATION WAR DEFINED

Information Warfare (IW) was formally launched in December 1992 with the dissemination of DOD Directive 3600.1. (Note 1) From the outset, widespread discussion and understanding of IW were hampered by its Top Secret classification. (Note 2) In September 1995 the Assistant Secretary of Defense for Command, Control, Communications and Intelligence (ASD(C3I)) published the formal DOD unclassified definition of IW:

Actions taken to achieve information superiority by affecting adversary information, information-based processes, and information systems, while defending one' s own information, information-based processes, and information systems.

This description clearly underscores both the defensive, as well as offensive aspects of IW. In the summer of 1994, the Defense Science Board(Note 3) (DSB), drawing heavily from expertise within DOD, published the most comprehensive and authoritative discussion of IW to date. The report highlighted the distinction between information in warfare and information warfare. Information in warfare pertains to "getting [information] it where it is needed in a timely and reliable manner. (Note 4) " It encompasses the collection, processing, and dissemination of information and is synonymous with the "C4I for the Warrior" vision released by the Joint Staff in 1992.

C4I for the Warrior addresses the concept of a global Command, Control, Communications, Computer, and Intelligence system directly linking military units around the globe in an interoperable, fully integrated fashion spanning the range of military operations from peace to war. (Note 5) Information in warfare capitalizes on the national information infrastructure (NII). Characterized as an "information highway,6 the NII is the growing worldwide information infrastructure which transcends industry, media, and the military and includes government and non-government entities. Most activities now rely on the information infrastructure including the banking' transportation, manufacturing, and electrical power industries. The Defense Information Infrastructure (DII) is an integral part of the NII with over 95 percent of DOD' s worldwide telecommunications needs satisfied by commercial telecommunications carriers. (Note 7) Military activities relying on the DII include transportation, logistics, financial, manpower, and personnel and training.

While C4I for the Warrior focuses on harnessing ever-increasing computer storage and exchange capabilities, IW targets these information systems. The distinction between C4I for the Warrior and IW is extremely important. IW employs offensive techniques such as deception, electronic jammers, munitions and advanced technologies to deceive, deny, exploit, damage, or destroy adversary information systems, while at the same time protecting friendly information systems from disruption, exploitation and damage by an adversary. (Note 8) The target of IW may range from influencing national level decisionmakers to corrupting the automated control of transportation systems. (Note 9) defensive IW protects friendly information systems from disruption, exploitation and damage by an adversary. (Note 10) or example, the Army's ongoing digitization of the battlefield is an application of information in warfare at the operational and tactical levels. Defensive IW, on the other hand, focuses on identifying and protecting vulnerabilities which arise from this increased reliance on technology.

The emergence of Command and Control Warfare (C2W) has been fundamental in understanding IW. (Note 12) In article in

Signal magazine LTGen James Clapper, then Director Defense Intelligence Agency (DIA), wrote "the closest description of information warfare might be found in the definition of command and control warfare." (Note 12) IW and C2W, however, are not interchangeable terms. C2W is a subset of IW. The Chairman of the Joint Chiefs of Staff (CJCS) Memorandum of Policy (MOP) 3O, states "C2W is the military strategy which implements IW on the battlefield." (Note 13) C2W is designed as an essential part of an overall theater campaign plan.

It is implemented during "joint military operations when U.S. military forces unilaterally or as part of an allied/coalition force are opposed or threatened by an organized military or paramilitary force." (Note 14) C2W focuses on an adversary's military command and control when military force is applied. On the other hand, the use of the word "warfare" in the term IW does not limit IW to a military conflict, declared or otherwise. is IW targets the entire information infrastructure of an adversary - political, economic, and military throughout the continuum of operations from peace to war.

ORGANIZATIONAL IMPERATIVE

IW, as this definitional discussion highlights, is a complex issue. Organizations are essential in actually implementing this new concept and achieving a viable IW architecture. IW will only become institutionalized if activities actually take responsibility for planning and executing IW. Today IW offices have been stood up throughout DOD focusing on offensive and defensive IW capabilities, but for the most part the budgets and staffs of these elements are very limited. They represent an important start in what will likely be a long and slow process.

IWExecutive Board: The Deputy Secretary of Defense chairs an IW Executive Board established in May 1995 which comprises senior officials within the department including the Vice Chairman Joint Chief of Staff (VCJCS) (Note 16). Supporting the IW Executive Board is an IW Council chaired by the Assistant Secretary of Defense for Command, Control, Communications and Intelligence (ASD(C3I)).

The Executive Board is chartered to address IW roles and responsibilities and serve as the DOD focal point for IW discussion at the national level. The Board is a welcome addition as it demonstrates an awareness by senior DOD officials of the need to coordinate IW, not only within the department, but in the interagency arena. However, senior officials are too busy to spend a great deal of time on any one issue, particularly one that has not reached crisis proportions. This is the point Robert McNamara makes in his book In Retrospect when discussing the evolution of U.S. policy in Vietnam during the Kennedy and Johnson administrations and the same is true today. (Note 17) You need to have the pull from the top, but it is important that lower levels are fully energized.

ASD C31: The ASD(C3I), as the senior IW advisor to the Secretary of Defense, has organized a small IW Directorate comprising less than ten personnel to help him execute his responsibilities. It was the forerunner to this office which drafted the original IW directive in 1992. The IW Directorate conducts centralized planning, coordination, and oversight for IW and conducts program reviews of selected Service and defense agency IW efforts. In May 1995 the IW Directorate sponsored an IW wargame for senior government officials designed to raise the profile of the threat to the U.S. information infrastructure. (Note 18)

The IW Directorate has also focused on initiating a DOD "Red Team" effort. This was one of the IW recommendations from the 1994 Defense Science Board report to "jump start Defensive IW." (Note 19) Under this concept personnel knowledgeable in adversaries' offensive IW form a team to "attack" the DOD information infrastructure. Given the magnitude of the vulnerabilities, the objective would be to have this capability distributed throughout DOD and carried out at various levels and locations. This concept dovetails with the Computer Emergency Response Team (CERT) which reacts to real world intrusions into computer systems. The Defense Information Systems Agency (DISA) has stood up small offices which accomplish both these tasks, but a more comprehensive program is necessary. In the twelve months prior to July 1994 DISA detected roughly 3,600 attacks on military networks, but officials estimate they detected only two percent of all the attacks, raising the estimated number to 182,000. (Note 20)

The "Red Team" program is designed to increase awareness throughout DOD of the vulnerabilities of automated systems and improve the overall security posture. A comprehensive "Red Team" effort can significantly reduce vulnerabilities in the near term as many existing problems are attributed to inadequate training of operators and system administrators. As the head of a CERT team stated, "the problem...is a lack of understanding and awareness and a lack of training and technical competence on the part of the user community." (Note 21) The "Red Team" is a laudable objective, but ASD(C3I) presently only coordinates and does not direct action. The Joint Staff has designated the Joint Command and Control Warfare Center (JC2WC) at San Antonio, Texas as executive agent to support the OSD IW Red Team effort. However, implementation of the "Red Team" concept is evolving slowly given budget constraints and manpower reductions in the Services and defense agencies.

USD(P): In 1995 the Under Secretary of Defense (Policy) (USD(P)) created an Infrastructure Policy Directorate. This office focuses on emergency preparedness and shaping the role of DOD in the protection of infrastructures, including coordination between DOD and nonDOD government, and civilian/corporate owned infrastructures. (Note 22) These are important responsibilities which clearly fall under the heading of defensive IW. As this office matures, it will be incumbent upon the IW Council and Executive Board to insure IW activities within ASD(C3I) and USD(P) are delineated and deconflicted, if necessary.

Joint Staff: In the Joint arena, IW organizations have also emerged. On the Joint Staff, proponency for IW is now shared between the Directorate for Operations, J3, and the J6, Directorate for Command, Control, Communications, Computers, and Intelligence (C4I) under a Memorandum of Understanding signed in October 1994. While conceptually this may have merits with each directorate bringing a unique dimension of IW, in reality as

Lt Gen Clapper, former Director, DIA, has recommended, the Operations Officer should be the overall staff coordinator as he is for all other operations issues. (Note 23)

The current arrangement on the Joint Staff presents some unique challenges as no one is actually in charge. The J3 and J6 principals are too busy to dedicate the constant attention this area requires and day-to-day responsibility for IW on the Joint Staff is delegated. A need exists for direct flag officer sponsorship to orchestrate joint IW policy and doctrine development, conduct operational planning, and establish requirements. A dedicated flag officer sponsor would greatly facilitate coordination with Services, OSD, the Intelligence Community and as IW matures, the interagency and civilian sectors. It would also send a strong message that IW is an important joint warfighting issue requiring immediate highlevel attention. Within the Joint Staff J3, responsibility for offensive IW now resides within the Information Warfare /Special Technical Operations Division (IW/STOD). This division is responsible for coordinating compartmented planning between the Services, Combatant Commands, and DOD agencies. Bob Woodward writes in The Commanders, the Special Technical Operations Center (STOC) is "a command and communications center for operations involving the sensitive "black" programs known only to those cleared to the special-access compartments." (Note 24) The IW/STOD also has responsibility for coordinating all facets of C2W for the Joint Staff including policy, doctrine, and operational issues. It is this office which authored MOP 30, led the preparation of Joint Pub 3-13 and will draft IW doctrine. This arrangement underscores the important linkage between C2W and IW. As the military proceeds to operationalize IW, the IW/STOD represents the linchpin for ensuring the integration of all dimensions of joint IW.

It has been suggested that, just as we continue to use a Single Integrated Operational Plan (SIOP) for strategic nuclear warfare, DOD might consider the use of an "IW SIOP" which addresses offensive and defensive deconfliction and intelligence equity issues. (Note 25) If this were implemented, the task would be assigned to the IW/STOD to coordinate the task. Today the IW/STOD focuses principally on support to the Combatant Commands, but as IW matures with both its non- lethal and deterrence potentials, greater interagency participation and coordination will undoubtedly occur.

JC2WC: The activation of the Joint Command and Control Warfare Center (JC2WC) at San Antonio, Texas in October 1994 provided a valuable resource for the Commanders of the Combatant Commands (CINCs). (Note 26 As a field-operating agency of the Joint Chiefs of Staff and headed by a flag officer, (Note 27) the JC2WC is fully engaged in the warfighting application of IW. With 163 assigned personnel, the JC2WC dispatches tailored teams to augment CINC and Joint Task Force staffs and provide C2W expertise in all joint exercises and contingency operations. Personnel from the JC2WC have participated in U.S. efforts in Bosnia and contingency operations in both Kuwait and Haiti. Given the high turnover of personnel on CINC staffs, the JC2WC is very much in demand for its C2W expertise. (Note 28) The JC2WC is in the unique position of being able to cross fertilize and share C2W lessons learned between the Combatant Commands. Accordingly, the organization has played a major role in developing joint C2W doctrine and will contribute significantly to the preparation of a follow-on C2W Joint Tactics, Techniques, and Procedures (JTTP) publication. At the present time, the JC2WC is fully engaged accomplishing its assigned tasks with respect to C2W. It is only now beginning to analyze its newly assigned responsibilities as executive agent in support of the OSD IW Red Team effort. As IW evolves and DOD' s role in the larger IW arena is clarified, a natural progression will be for this organization to serve as the nucleus for a Joint IW center.

Joint COMSEC Monitoring Activity. The JCMA is another field operating agency of the Joint Chiefs of Staff having IW applications. It was created in 1993 by a Memorandum of Agreement between the Service Operations Deputies and Directors of the Joint Staff and NSA. The JCMA is charged with conducting "COMSEC monitoring (collection, analysis, and reporting) of DOD telecommunications and automated information systems (AIS) and monitoring of related noncommunications signals." (Note 29) Its purpose is to identify vulnerabilities exploitable by potential adversaries and recommend countermeasures and corrective actions. The JCMA focuses on unencrypted DOD systems and "does not perform traditional telephone monitoring," as this function remains a Service responsibility. (Note 30) The Joint Staff Director for Operations has been assigned primary responsibility for JCMA affairs. This facilitates coordination between the JC2WC and the JCMA. The JCMA supports both real-world operations, as well as joint exercises and DOD systems monitoring. The JCMA, more so than the JC2WC, already has the expertise to perform the Red Team mission. Rather than further diluting the already stretched resources and expertise of the JC2WC, it would make better sense to designate the JCMA as executive agent to support the OSD Red Team IW initiative.

Joint Spectrum Center. The DOD Joint Spectrum Center (JSC) was activated in September 1994 under the direction of the Joint Staff J6. The JSC assumed all the mission and responsibilities previously performed by the Electromagnetic Compatibility Center, as well as additional functions. The JSC deploys teams in support of the CINCs and serves as the DOD focal point for supporting spectrum supremacy aspects of IW. Notably the JSC assists warfighters in developing and managing the Joint Restricted Frequency List (JRFL) and assisting in the resolution of operational interference and jamming incidents. While informal coordination occurs on IW related issues between the Joint Spectrum Center, the Joint COMSEC Monitoring Activity, and the Joint C2W Center, each organization interfaces separately with the CINC staffs. No formal mechanism is yet in place to ensure the warfighters obtain a coordinated IW support package.

Combatant Commands: The focus of warfighters at the Combatant Commands remains planning and executing C2W. All of the geographic CINCs now have C2W staff officers assigned in their Operations Directorates, but organizing the diverse elements which comprise C2W is a challenge for CINC staffs. U.S. Central Command (CENTCOM) has actually physically consolidated the staff officers responsible for orchestrating electronic warfare, operational security, military deception and psychological operations into a single branch. This organization can serve as the nucleus as new IW capabilities emerge and are apportioned to the CINCs. Defensive IW poses a more significant challenge. While the CINCs can take incremental measures to unilaterally reduce vulnerabilities of their information systems, given their ultimate dependence on the national information infrastructure, defensive IW must be undertaken as part of a larger DOD sponsored initiative.

Services: Each of the Services have created or are participating in Information Warfare Centers or Activities. The Air Force leads the Services and in September 1995, the Chief of Staff and Secretary of the Air Force published the 17 page, Cornerstones of Information Warfare which describes how "Air Force doctrine should evolve to accommodate information warfare." (Note 31) The Air Force was also the first to establish their Information Warfare Center (AFIWC) at San Antonio, Texas in October 1993. This was accomplished by consolidating the Air Force cryptologic support center and the electronic warfare center. The AFIWC serves as the Air Force command and control warfare executive agent with approximately 1000 military and civilian personnel assigned. The Center is subordinate to the Air Intelligence Agency closely aligning it with the Intelligence Community. The Center applies the teaming concept integrating the intelligence component with operators, engineers, communications and computer specialists, both offensive and defensive. (Note 32) The AFIWC also has an ongoing "Red Team" and CERT effort designed to improve network security in the Air Force. The Center is collocated with the JC2WC and both organizations work closely together. Personnel from the AFIWC regularly team with the JC2WC on major deployments.

On 1 October 1995, the Air Force created its first Information Warfare Squadron at Shaw Air Force Base, South Carolina. The squadron's primary purpose will be to protect Air Force computers and communications, as well as assisting in "infiltrating an enemy's computer and communications systems." (Note 33) The squadron will support the 9th Air Force commander who is assigned the Central Command area of operations. Eventually, the Air Force will set up more squadrons to assist air commanders responsible for other geographic areas. While the IW Squadron at Shaw AFB presently only has two officers assigned, there will be as many as 40 by August 1996, when the squadron is slated to be operational. Eventually, the squadron might grow to 85 people. (Note 34) The Air Force recognizes it is pushing the envelope, but as General Joseph Ralston, chief of Air Combat Command, stated:

You can sit around for another 10 years and debate about what some of the problems might be [with setting up an information warfare squadron]...but you will never know until you actually get into them and try to make it work operationally. (Note 35)

The Navy established the Navy Information Warfare Activity (NIWA) in August 1994 to serve as their focal point for IW activities. (Note 36) Directly subordinate to the Naval Security Group, the NIWA is located at Fort Meade, Maryland and is closely linked to the National Security Agency.

Given the rapid pace of advancing technology the Navy has given the NIWA special authority to generate requirements and procure systems. Traditionally there has been a sharp separation in the Navy between organizations responsible for setting requirements and those charged with overseeing their acquisition. However, with new generations of computers and information systems unveiled on average about every 18 months, the Navy has adopted a more streamlined approach. As John Davis, technology adviser to the Navy's Space and Electronic Warfare Directorate, indicated, "If we fall more than one cycle behind. we could find industry putting information warfare systems into potentially hostile nations at the same time that US force receive the same equipment." (Note 37)

The Navy also has established the Fleet Information Warfare Center (FIWC) at Little Creek, Virginia from existing Fleet Deception/C2W Group assets. (Note 38) The FIWC serves as the link between the NIWA and the Atlantic and Pacific Fleets. With personnel deployed on carrier battle groups throughout the world, the FIWC fulfills a similar mission for the Navy that the JC2WC does for the joint warfighter. The IW organizational structure created by the Navy enables the FIWC to focus on near term operational requirements, while the NIWA assumes a more long-term perspective keeping abreast of IW advances and developing and acquiring systems. Rather than create a separate IW organization, the Marines intend to assign liaison officers to the respective Service IW centers to benefit from their efforts. The Navy and Marines have also teamed up to develop policy guidance for Navy and Marine IW/C2W operations. In February 1995, the Marine Corps Commandant and Chief of Naval Operations approved a plan which states, "Navy and Marine Corps must have a fully integrated IW/C2W capability...team must organize, train, and equip its forward deployed forces to conduct IW/C2W."

The Army is the latest Service to establish an IW activity. Officially activated in May 1995, the Land Information Warfare Center (LIWA) is subordinate to the Army Intelligence and Security Command (INSCOM) but is under the operational control of the Headquarters Department of the Army, Deputy Chief of Staff for Operations (DCSOPS). As with the Air Force and Navy, the Army has closely aligned its IW effort with the Intelligence Community. The LIWA is a totally new organization in contrast to the Air Force and Navy efforts which reorganized existing activities. It is also the smallest of the three Service IW activities with a projected end strength of 50-75 personnel. The primary focus of the LIWA is to provide operational support at the Army Corps and higher levels. The Army is also coordinating closely with the Marines to assign personnel to the LIWA. Given its small size, the LIWA draws upon existing capabilities in the Army including psychological operations, electronic warfare, and operational security. The Army is in the process of institutionalizing a "Red Team" effort from existing INSCOM assets, and there is close coordination and collaboration with NSA on mutual IW efforts.

The Services' efforts during a period of serious budget constraints underscore a recognition of the importance of IW. Except for the general responsibilities delineated in the original DOD IW directive, Services have received no additional policy guidance on how to implement IW. In reviewing Service responses to IW, they have established organizations which best suit their near term needs. Manpower and funding for Service IW initiatives have been reallocated internally with the Air Force taking the most aggressive approach.

Over time Service organizations can be expected to evolve as IW matures. Today much of their focus is on implementing C2W, the military application of IW. Services have also implemented "Red Teams" to train personnel and improve security awareness of the vulnerabilities associated with information systems. Additionally, while the linkages of Service IW organizations with the Intelligence Community is valuable, it is important IW does not become an intelligence activity. IW needs to be controlled and fully managed by the warfighters as an integral part of an overall strategy. In that regard, the recent activation of the IW Squadron by the Air Force, separate and distinct from the AFIWC, is a positive step.

Intelligence Community: Within the Intelligence Community there exists an acute appreciation of the enormous impact IW has on their efforts. Each organization, DIA, CIA and NSA has established an office to orchestrate IW related activities and satisfy the needs of their consumers. NSA, in addition to it its intelligence mission, has a unique responsibility for developing "standards, techniques, systems, and equipment" for classified information. (Note 40) NSA has demonstrated success at protecting classified systems, but has achieved less success in the increasingly vulnerable area of unclassified computer networks where it plays a supporting role.

Under the 1987 Computer Security Act, the National Institute for Standards and Technology (NIST) was assigned responsibility for developing government wide standards and guidelines for "unclassified, sensitive information." (Note 41) The law also directed NIST to draw upon technical computer security guidelines developed by NSA. (Note 42) To clarify the relationship between NIST and NSA, a Memorandum of Agreement (MOW) was formalized in 1989 establishing mechanisms for implementing the Computer Security Act of 1987. The MOU has been controversial because of concerns in Congress and elsewhere that it cedes NSA much more authority than was intended under the act. (Note 43) The act envisioned NIST requesting NSA expertise as needed, but instead the MOU has involved NSA in all NIST activities related to information security.

Protecting unclassified, sensitive information is essential in developing an effective IW architecture. Given the growing threat to our information system, NSA officials are lobbying for increased efforts to protect unclassified networks. (Note 44) While NSA certainly has tremendous expertise and is the national authority on cryptographic protection, there are reservations about having it assume a greater role. Some perceive a conflict of interest between NSA's information protection role and its principal intelligence mission. Additionally, leadership in cryptography does not imply leadership in other areas of defensive IW. DOD has assigned the responsibility of protecting its own information infrastructure to the Defense Information Systems Agency. (Note 45) As national defensive IW policy is formulated, the security of unclassified, sensitive information must be addressed.

Non DOD Organizations: Although defensive IW has not been officially embraced outside of DOD, several standing organizations focus on this issue. The National Communication System (NCS) was established in 1963 to coordinate the planning of national security and emergency preparedness communications for the federal government under all circumstances, including crisis or emergency, attack, recovery, and reconstitution. The NCS receives policy direction directly from the National Security Council (NSC) but is managed through the Department of Defense. (Note 45) The NCS's National Coordinating Center for Telecommunications is staffed full time by both government and telecommunications industry representatives whose mission is to respond to both military and civil emergencies: ea., Desert Storm, Hurricane Andrew and, more recently, the bombing of the Federal building in Oklahoma city. (Note 47)

The National Security Telecommunications Advisory Council (NSTAC) was established during the Reagan Administration to advise the President on national security and emergency preparedness issues. This senior body is composed of presidents and CEOs of major telecommunications and defense information systems companies. NSTAC works closely with NCS.

The Federal Communications Commission (FCC) also plays a strong role in reliability and privacy issues regarding the public switched telephone network. The Network Reliability Council (NRC) was created in 1992 by the FCC to investigate the reliability of the public switched network following a series of service outages in 1991. The efforts culminated in a one-thousand page document, "Network Reliability." The FCC expanded the membership of the NRC in July 1994 and gave it a new charter. Today the NRC is composed of CEOs from telephone companies, equipment suppliers, state agencies, and federal, corporate, and consumer users.

Each of these organizations, as well as NIST, are involved in aspects of defensive IW. What is lacking, however, is an overarching framework linking these disparate efforts into a coordinated effort. Within the government someone needs to be in charge. The NCS may serve as a blueprint for this effort. Not only does it have in place representatives and links to all major government agencies, including the Intelligence Community, but it is a model for governmentindustry cooperation. To be successful, defensive IW must have the support of private industry. Not only must awareness of vulnerabilities be increased, but coordinated steps taken to reduce the risk. That is the exactly the success which NCS has achieved in the telecommunications sector. As national policy is developed for IW, strong consideration should be given to creating an organization like the NCS to serve as the focal point for this effort and having it possibly work directly for the Vice President. DOD should play a role in the organization but as an active participant, not the leader.

AN AZIMUTH FOR THE FUTURE

There has been a proliferation of IW activities within the Services, OSD, joint activities and defense agencies, but up to this point it has been very decentralized. Revised policy and formal doctrine will go a long way in improving everyone' s understanding of IW and their responsibilities. Within the Office of the Secretary of Defense (OSD), one central office needs to remain as the focal point for IW. It is important that the offensive and defensive dimensions of IW are fully coordinated and it made clear to everyone in the department and in the interagency arena who has the lead in OSD. This can be helped through strong leadership by the IW Executive Board.

Similarly on the Joint Staff, a single office needs to be designated as the locus for IW related issues. The central clearing house should be the, J3, Director for Operations. While both the J6 and J2 play key roles in the areas of defensive IW and intelligence support respectively, to be successful, IW must be integrated into operations and that is the purview of the J3. Given the complexity and sensitivity of the issues involved with IW, a flag officer within the J3 should be assigned full time to oversee the development of policy, doctrine, operational planning and the IW component of the Joint Warfighting Capability Assessment. IW has enormous potential for the joint warfighter. A flag officer focusing on this issue will ensure the joint perspective and associated equities are skillfully articulated as this concept is hotly debated within DOD and the interagency process.

At the joint level, strong consideration should be given to more effectively leveraging the capabilities of the Joint Command and Control Warfare Center, Joint COMSEC Monitoring Activity and the Joint Spectrum Center. Each of these organizations is a field operating agency of the Joint Staff and brings a unique dimension to IW. However, aside from informal coordination, no formal mechanism or oversight exists to ensure they provide optimum IW support to the CINCs. For example, while the JC2WC was recently designated responsibility for the joint "Red Team" mission, the Joint COMSEC Monitoring Activity already contains the nucleus for an effective joint "Red Team" capability, with responsibility for monitoring DOD automated information systems and related noncommunications signals. At the same time, close coordination is essential between the Joint Spectrum Center and the JC2WC regarding the Joint Restricted Frequency List and its impact on the planning and conduct of electronic warfare.

The Joint Staff needs to capitalize on the full potential of each of these organizations and ensure there is unity of effort in planning and executing IW. Serious consideration should be given to creating an umbrella Joint Information Warfare Activity with the JC2WC, JCMA, JSC and any other related activities, as subordinate elements.

The flag officer position now assigned to the Joint C2W Center should be reallocated to provide senior leadership at the Joint IW Center. Working directly for the Director for Operations on the Joint Staff, he can ensure the Combatant Commands leverage the full potential of IW. While each of the Services has undertaken a different organizational response to IW, these activities are critical in laying the foundation. They serve as the nucleus upon which the Services can build their respective IW architectures. These organizations will almost certainly evolve over time, but the initial framework is in place. Training the force, particularly operators and system administrators on the defensive aspects of IW, must be tackled in the near term and enable the military to function more effectively in this new environment.

While it may be premature to specify a structure at the interagency level, the National Communication System model cannot be overlooked. Staffed with full time government and telecommunications industry representatives, the NCS serves as a microcosm of the effort that is needed to truly implement a comprehensive national defensive IW campaign. Just as within DOD, there needs to be a focal point to function as the national information assurance coordinator within the government as a whole. Chronic vulnerabilities in the NII must be addressed and coordinated actions undertaken, not only in the telecommunications and automation industries, but across the spectrum of activities involving finance, transportation, power generation and most certainly the military.

6

Use of Nuclear Weapons in War

The Cold War dominated the world in the decades following World War II. On one side was the "West", dominated by the capitalist United States of America and acting mainly through the North Atlantic Treaty Organization (NATO), while on the other side was the "East", dominated by the communist United Soviet Socialists Republic (Soviet Union or USSR). The two sides were opposed ideologically, both in government styles and financial systems, and geographically. Nearly all events that occurred in the world during this time, such as the Vietnam War and the war in Afghanistan, became an exercise of will between the two super powers, the US and the USSR. The threat of a total nuclear war that will end life on Earth hung over the world during this era, even though neither side wanted to use their large nuclear arsenals.

The Soviet Union, after losing nearly 20 million people during World War II, was determined that it would never again be invaded and built the world's largest military at the time. While it did rely on numbers over technology, they still built some of the most advanced war machines in the world, and many were as good, if not better, than those of the more technologically advanced western countries. Realizing that they could never realistically match the Soviet Union in military size for any great period of time, NATO decided to use nuclear weapons as a deterrent for war. Most NATO countries built and maintained a large stockpile of nuclear arms, which were significantly cheaper to maintain then a large standing army. This caused the Soviet Union to respond by building its own large stockpile of nuclear weapons, but their numbers of lower than NATO's.

During the 1980's, the Soviet Union suffered a demoralizing setback when their military failed to defeat rebel factions in Afghanistan and increased military spending was tearing the country's economy to shreds. NATO and the United States did not realize the extent of collapse in the Soviet Union until in 1989 they allowed the reunification of Germany, which had been split into two countries following World War II, one side controlled by NATO, the other by the Soviet Union. Soon after, the entire Soviet Union collapsed leaving many former republics independent for the first time ever and a much weaker Russian Republic.

The now democratic Russia was suffering from economic collapse and many western countries were too used to viewing the Russians as enemies to offer any help. This forced the Russians, and many of the independent Republics to sell many of their weapons to third world countries, such as China, the Middle East, and many countries in Africa. Some of the weapons sold were even rumored to be nuclear warheads, which would garner a huge price on the black market.

In contrast, this was an impressive time for the western countries: they had easily won a war in the Middle East against Iraq and advances in space technology allowed the concept of a space station become a reality. Since Russia had one of the world's largest space agencies and the world's only existing space station, they were reluctantly included in the US dominated international space agency. As computers became widespread, information became more accessible to those that opposed the world's current notion of peace. With the Cold War over, and with many countries looking forward to a time of real pace, many powerful countries forgot that most of the world had been dominated by only a few countries and that with the collapse of colonialism, imperialism, and the end of the Cold War many of these countries were truly free for the first time ever. These countries, particularly China, India, Iran, and several countries in Africa, did not appreciate that the world had decided that there would be no more wars, no more taking from other countries what you wanted, which is exactly what the current Super Powers had done to achieve their power.

Tensions would rise continuously throughout the early half of the 1990's, as many countries fought the "world powers" both in the United Nations General Assembly, and in world markets to achieve what they believed was their fair share. Support ebbed and waned for international cooperation throughout the world and many countries felt cheated by the United States, as the US would treat them as partners with one hand and as enemies with the other.

New alliances were formed throughout the world, such as a growing bond between Islamic countries in the Middle East, between former enemies in Africa, and between China and India, but the United States viewed these alliances as strategic threats that it could not counter with traditional methods. A new world order was being built around the United States claiming the world had moved past imperialism and other countries finally moving into positions where they could execute their own imperialist goals. The International Space Station, named Freedom Station, was the focal point for the anger that had grown among the countries of the world.

HISTORY OF NUCLEAR WEAPONS

The history of nuclear weapons chronicles the development of nuclear weapons. Nuclear weapons are devices that possess enormous destructive potential derived from nuclear fission or nuclear fusion reactions. Starting with the scientific breakthroughs of the 1930s which made their development possible, and continuing through the nuclear arms race and nuclear testing of the Cold War, the issues of proliferation and possible use for terrorism still remain in the early 21st century. The first fission weapons, also known as "atomic bombs," were developed jointly by the United States, Britain and Canada during World War II in what was called the Manhattan Project to counter the assumed Nazi German atomic bomb project. In August 1945 two were dropped on Japan ending the Pacific War. An international team was dispatched to help work on the project. The Soviet Union started development shortly thereafter with their own atomic bomb project, and not long after that both countries developed even more powerful fusion weapons called "hydrogen bombs."

During the Cold War, the Soviet Union and United States each acquired nuclear weapons arsenals numbering in the thousands, placing many of them onto rockets which could hit targets anywhere in the world. Currently there are at least nine countries with functional nuclear weapons. A considerable amount of international negotiating has focused on the threat of nuclear warfare and the proliferation of nuclear weapons to new nations or groups. There have been (at least) four major false alarms, the most recent in 1995, that resulted in the activation of either the US's or Russia's nuclear attack early warning protocols.

Physics and Politics in the 1930s

In the first decades of the twentieth century, physics was revolutionized with developments in the understanding of the nature of atoms. In 1898, French physicist Pierre Curie and his Polish wife Maria Sklodowska-Curie had discovered that present in pitchblende, an ore of uranium, was a substance which emitted large amounts of radioactivity, which they named radium. This raised the hopes of both scientists and lay people that the elements around us could contain tremendous amounts of unseen energy, waiting to be tapped. Experiments by Ernest Rutherford in 1911 indicated that the vast majority of an atom's mass was contained in a very small nucleus at its core, made up of protons, surrounded by a web of whirring electrons. In 1932, James Chadwick discovered that the nucleus contained another fundamental particle, the neutron, and in the same year John Cockcroft and Ernest Walton "split the atom" for the first time, the first occasion on which an atomic nucleus of one element had been successfully changed to a different nucleus by artificial means.

In 1934 the idea of chain reaction via neutron was proposed by Leó Szilárd, who patented the idea of the atomic bomb. The patent was transferred in secret to Britain's Royal Navy in 1936. In a very real sense, Szilárd was the father of the atomic bomb academically. In 1934, French physicists Irène and Frédéric Joliot-

Curie discovered that artificial radioactivity could be induced in stable elements by bombarding them with alpha particles, and in the same year Italian physicist Enrico Fermi reported similar results when bombarding uranium with neutrons. In December 1938, the German chemists Otto Hahn and Fritz Strassmann sent a manuscript to *Naturwissenschaften* reporting they had detected the element barium after bombarding uranium with neutrons; simultaneously, they communicated these results to Lise Meitner. Meitner, and her nephew Otto Robert Frisch, correctly interpreted these results as being nuclear fission. Frisch confirmed this experimentally on 13 January 1939. Even before it was published, Meitner's and Frisch's interpretation of the work of Hahn and Strassmann crossed the Atlantic Ocean with Niels Bohr, who was to lecture at Princeton University. Isidor Isaac Rabi and Willis Lamb, two Columbia University physicists working at Princeton, heard the news and carried it back to Columbia. Rabi said he told Fermi; Fermi gave credit to Lamb. Bohr soon thereafter went from Princeton to Columbia to see Fermi. Not finding Fermi in his office, Bohr went down to the cyclotron area and found Herbert Anderson. Bohr grabbed him by the shoulder and said: "Young man, let me explain to you about something new and exciting in physics."

It was clear to a number of scientists at Columbia that they should try to detect the energy released in the nuclear fission of uranium from neutron bombardment. On 25 January 1939, an experimental team at Columbia University conducted the first nuclear fission experiment in the United States, which was done in the basement of Pupin Hall; the members of the team were Herbert L. Anderson, Eugene T. Booth, John R. Dunning, Enrico Fermi, G. Norris Glasoe, and Francis G. Slack. As the Nazi army marched into first Czechoslovakia in 1938, and then Poland in 1939, beginning World War II, many of Europe's top physicists had already begun to flee from the imminent conflict. Scientists on both sides of the conflict were well aware of the possibility of utilizing nuclear fission as a weapon, but at the time no one was quite sure how it could be done. In the early years of the Second World War, physicists abruptly stopped publishing on the topic of fission, an act of self-censorship to keep the opposing side from gaining any advantages.

From Los Alamos to Hiroshima

By the beginning of World War II, there was concern among scientists in the Allied nations that Nazi Germany might have its own project to develop fission-based weapons. Organized research first began in Britain as part of the "Tube Alloys" project, and in the United States a small amount of funding was given for research into uranium weapons starting in 1939 with the Uranium Committee under Lyman James Briggs. At the urging of British scientists, though, who had made crucial calculations indicating that a fission weapon could be completed within only a few years, by 1941 the project had been wrested into better bureaucratic hands, and in 1942 came under the auspices of a Military Policy Committee led by General Leslie Groves as the Manhattan Project.

Scientifically led by the American physicist Robert Oppenheimer, the project brought together the top scientific minds of the day (many exiles from Europe) with the production power of American industry for the goal of producing fission-based explosive devices before Germany could. Britain and the U.S. agreed to pool their resources and information for the project, but the other Allied power—the Soviet Union under Joseph Stalin—was not informed. A massive industrial and scientific undertaking, the Manhattan Project involved many of the world's great physicists in the scientific and development aspects. The United States made an unprecedented investment into wartime research for the project, which was spread across more than 30 sites in the U.S. and Canada. Scientific knowledge was centralized at a secret laboratory known as Los Alamos, previously a small ranch school near Santa Fe, New Mexico.

Uranium appears in nature primarily in two isotopes: uranium-238 and uranium-235. When the nucleus of uranium-235 absorbs a neutron, it undergoes nuclear fission, splitting into two "fission products" and releasing energy and 2.5 neutrons on average. Uranium-238, on the other hand, absorbs neutrons but does not split, effectively putting a stop to any ongoing fission reaction. It was discovered that an atomic bomb based on uranium would need to be made of almost completely pure uranium-235 (at least 80% pure), or else the presence of uranium-238 would quickly curtail the nuclear chain reaction. The team of scientists working on the Manhattan Project immediately realized that one of the largest problems they would have to solve was how to remove uranium-235 from natural uranium, which was composed of 99.3% uranium-238. Two methods were developed during the wartime project, both of which took advantage of the fact that uranium-238 has a slightly greater atomic mass than uranium-235: electromagnetic separation and gaseous diffusion—methods which separated isotopes based on their differing weights. Another secret site was erected at rural Oak Ridge, Tennessee, for the large-scale production and purification of the rare isotope. It was a massive investment: at the time, one of the Oak Ridge facilities (K-25) was the largest factory under one roof. The Oak Ridge site employed tens of thousands of employees at its peak, most of whom had no idea what they were working on.

Though uranium-238 cannot be used for the initial stage of an atomic bomb, when U-238 absorbs a neutron, it transforms first into an unstable element, uranium-239, and then decays into neptunium-239, and finally the relatively stable plutonium-239, an element which does not exist in nature. Plutonium is also fissile and can be used to create a fission reaction, and after Enrico Fermi achieved the world's first sustained and controlled nuclear chain reaction in the creation of the first "atomic pile"—a primitive nuclear reactor—in a basement at the University of Chicago, massive reactors were secretly created at what is now known as Hanford Site in the state of Washington, using the Columbia River as cooling water, to transform uranium-238 into plutonium for a bomb.

For a fission weapon to operate, there must be a critical mass—the amount needed for a self-sustaining nuclear chain reaction—of fissile material bombarded with neutrons at any one time. The simplest form of nuclear weapon is a gun-type fission weapon, where a sub-critical mass of fissile material (such as uranium-235) would be shot at another sub-critical mass of fissile material. The result would be a super-critical mass which, when bombarded with neutrons, would undergo fission at a rapid rate and create the desired explosion. The weapons envisaged in 1942 were the two gun-type weapons, Little Boy (uranium) and Thin Man (plutonium), and the Fat Man plutonium implosion bomb. In early 1943 Oppenheimer determined that two projects should proceed forwards: the "Thin Man" project (plutonium gun) and the "Fat Man" project (plutonium implosion). The plutonium gun was to receive the bulk of the research effort, as it was the project with the most uncertainty involved. It was assumed that the uranium gun-type bomb could then be adapted from it.

But in April 1944 it was found by Emilio Segrè that plutonium produced by the Hanford reactors had too high a level of background neutron radiation, and underwent spontaneous fission to a very small extent, due to the presence of impurities of the Pu-240 isotope. If such plutonium were used in a "gun assembly," the chain reaction would start in the split seconds before the critical mass was assembled, blowing the weapon apart before it would have any great effect (this is known as a fizzle). So development of Fat Man, the implosion bomb, was given high priority. Chemical explosives were used to implode a sub-critical sphere of plutonium, thus increasing its density and making it into a critical mass. The difficulties with implosion were in the problem of making the chemical explosives deliver a perfectly uniform shock wave upon the plutonium sphere— if it were even slightly asymmetric, the weapon would fizzle (which would be expensive, messy, and not a very effective military device). This problem was circumvented by the use of hydrodynamic "lenses"—explosive materials of differing densities—which would focus the blast waves inside the imploding sphere, akin to the way in which an optical lens focuses light rays.

After D-Day, General Groves had ordered a team of scientists—Project Alsos—to follow eastward-moving victorious Allied troops into Europe in order to assess the status of the German nuclear program (and to prevent the westward-moving Russians from gaining any materials or scientific manpower). It was concluded that while Nazi Germany had also had an atomic bomb program, headed by Werner Heisenberg, the government had not made a significant investment in the project, and had been nowhere near success. Historians claim to have found a rough schematic showing a Nazi nuclear bomb. Research was conducted in the German nuclear energy project. In March 1945, a Nazi scientific team was directed by the physicist Kurt Diebner to develop a primitive nuclear device in Ohrdruf, Thuringia.

By the unconditional surrender of Germany on May 8, 1945, the Manhattan Project was still months away from a working weapon. That April, after the death of American President Franklin D. Roosevelt, former Vice-President Harry S. Truman was told about the secret wartime project for the first time. Because of the difficulties in making a working plutonium bomb, it was decided that there should be a test of the weapon, and Truman wanted to know for sure if it would work before his meeting with Joseph Stalin at an upcoming conference on the future of postwar Europe. On July 16, 1945, in the desert north of Alamogordo, New Mexico, the first nuclear test took place, code-named "Trinity," using a device nicknamed "the Gadget." The test, a plutonium implosion type device, released the equivalent of 19 kilotons of TNT, far mightier than any weapon ever used before. The news of the test's success was rushed to Truman, who used it as leverage at the upcoming Potsdam Conference, held near Berlin.

After hearing arguments from scientists and military officers over the possible uses of the weapons against Japan (though some recommended using them as "demonstrations" in unpopulated areas, most recommended using them against "built up" targets, a euphemistic term for populated cities), Truman ordered the use of the weapons on Japanese cities, hoping it would send a strong message which would end in the capitulation of the Japanese leadership and avoid a lengthy invasion of the island. There were suggestions to drop the atomic bomb on Tokyo, the capital of Japan, but concerns about Tokyo's cultural heritage changed the plan. On May 10–11, 1945 The Target Committee at Los Alamos, led by J. Robert Oppenheimer, recommended Kyoto, Hiroshima, Yokohama, and the arsenal at Kokura as possible targets. On August 6, 1945, a uranium-based weapon, "Little Boy", was let loose on the Japanese city of Hiroshima. Three days later, a plutonium-based weapon, "Fat Man", was dropped onto the city of Nagasaki. The atomic bombs killed at least one hundred thousand Japanese outright, most of them civilians, with the heat, radiation, and blast effects. Many tens of thousands would die later of radiation sickness and related cancers. Truman promised a "rain of ruin" if Japan did not surrender immediately, threatening to eliminate Japanese cities, one by one; Japan surrendered on August 15. Truman's threat was in fact a bluff, since the US had but one remaining uranium-gun type bomb completed.

Soviet Atomic Bomb Project

The Soviet Union was not invited to share in the new weapons developed by the United States and the other Allies. During the war, information had been pouring in from a number of volunteer spies involved with the Manhattan Project (known in Soviet cables under the code-name of *Enormoz*), and the Soviet nuclear physicist Igor Kurchatov was carefully watching the Allied weapons development. It came as no surprise to Stalin when Truman had informed him at the Potsdam conference that he had a "powerful new weapon." Truman was shocked at Stalin's lack of interest. The Soviet spies in the U.S. project were all volunteers and none were Russians. One of the most valuable, Klaus Fuchs, was a German émigré theoretical physicist who had been a part in the early British nuclear efforts and had been part of the UK mission to Los Alamos during the war. Fuchs had been intimately involved in the development of the implosion weapon, and passed on detailed cross-sections of the "Trinity" device to his Soviet contacts. Other Los Alamos spies—none of whom knew each other—included Theodore Hall and David Greenglass. The information was kept but not acted upon, as Russia was still too busy fighting the war in Europe to devote resources to this new project.

In the years immediately after World War II, the issue of who should control atomic weapons became a major international point of contention. Many of the Los Alamos scientists who had built the bomb began to call for "international control of atomic energy," often calling for either control by transnational organizations or the purposeful distribution of weapons information to all superpowers, but due to a deep distrust of the intentions of the Soviet Union, both in postwar Europe and in general, the policy-makers of the United States worked to attempt to secure an American nuclear monopoly. A half-hearted plan for international control was proposed at the newly formed United Nations by Bernard Baruch ("The Baruch Plan"), but it was clear both to American commentators—and to the Soviets—that it was an attempt primarily to stymie Russian nuclear efforts. The Soviets vetoed the plan, effectively ending any immediate postwar negotiations on atomic energy, and made overtures towards banning the use of atomic weapons in general.

All the while, the Soviets had put their full industrial and manpower might into the development of their own atomic weapons. The initial problem for the Soviets was primarily one of resources—they had not scouted out uranium resources in the Soviet Union and the U.S. had made deals to monopolise the largest known (and high purity) reserves in the Belgian Congo. The USSR used penal labour to mine the old deposits in Czechoslovakia—now an area under their control—and searched for other domestic deposits (which were eventually found). Two days after the bombing of Nagasaki, the U.S. government released an official technical history of the Manhattan Project, authored by Princeton physicist Henry DeWolf Smyth, known colloquially as the Smyth Report. The sanitized summary of the wartime effort focused primarily on the production facilities and scale of investment, written in part to justify the wartime expenditure to the American public.

The Soviet program, under the suspicious watch of former NKVD chief Lavrenty Beria (a participant and victor in Stalin's Great Purge of the 1930s), would use the Report as a blueprint, seeking to duplicate as much as possible the American effort. The "secret cities" used for the Soviet equivalents of Hanford and Oak Ridge literally vanished from the maps for decades to come. At the Soviet equivalent of Los Alamos, Arzamas-16, physicist Yuli Khariton led the scientific effort to develop the weapon. Beria distrusted his scientists, however, and he distrusted the carefully collected espionage information. As such, Beria assigned multiple teams of scientists to the same task without informing each team of the other's existence. If they arrived at different conclusions, Beria would bring them together for the first time and have them debate with their newfound counterparts. Beria used the espionage information as a way to double-check the progress of his scientists, and in his effort for duplication of the American project even rejected more efficient bomb designs in favour of ones which more closely mimicked the tried-and-true "Fat Man" bomb used by the U.S. against Nagasaki.

Working under a stubborn and scientifically ignorant administrator, the Soviet scientists struggled on. On August 29, 1949, the effort brought its results, when the USSR tested its first fission bomb, dubbed "Joe-1" by the U.S., years ahead of American predictions. The news of the first Soviet bomb was announced to the world first by the United States, which had detected the nuclear fallout it generated from its test site in Kazakhstan. The loss of the American monopoly on nuclear weapons marked the first tit-for-tat of the nuclear arms race. The response in the U.S. was one of apprehension, fear, and scapegoating, which would lead eventually into the Red-baiting tactics of McCarthyism. Yet recent information from unclassified Venona intercepts and the opening of the KGB archives after the fall of the Soviet Union show that the USSR had useful spies that helped their program, although none were identified by the McCarthy. Before this, though, President Truman would announce his decision to begin a crash program to develop a far more powerful weapon than those which were used against Japan: the hydrogen bomb.

The First Thermonuclear Weapons

The notion of using a fission weapon to ignite a process of nuclear fusion can be dated back to 1942. At the first major theoretical conference on the development of an atomic bomb hosted by J. Robert Oppenheimer at the University of California, Berkeley, participant Edward Teller directed the majority of the discussion towards Enrico Fermi's idea of a "Super" bomb which would utilize the same reactions which powered the Sun itself.

It was thought at the time that a fission weapon would be quite simple to develop and that perhaps work on a hydrogen bomb would be possible to complete before the end of the Second World War. However, in reality the problem of a "regular" atomic bomb was large enough to preoccupy the scientists for the next few years, much less the more speculative "Super." Only Teller continued working on the project—against the will of project leaders Oppenheimer and Hans Bethe.

After the atomic bombings of Japan, many scientists at Los Alamos rebelled against the notion of creating a weapon thousands of times more powerful than the first atomic bombs. For the scientists the question was in part technical—the weapon design was still quite uncertain and unworkable—and in part moral: such a weapon, they argued, could only be used against large civilian populations, and could thus only be used as a weapon of genocide. Many scientists, such as Bethe, urged that the United States should not develop such weapons and set an example towards the Soviet Union. Promoters of the weapon, including Teller, Ernest Lawrence, and Luis Alvarez, argued that such a development was inevitable, and to deny such protection to the people of the United States—especially when the Soviet Union was likely to create such a weapon themselves—was itself an immoral and unwise act.

Oppenheimer, who was now head of the General Advisory Committee of the successor to the Manhattan Project, the Atomic Energy Commission, presided over a recommendation against the development of the weapon. The reasons were in part because the success of the technology seemed limited at the time (and not worth the investment of resources to confirm whether this was so), and because Oppenheimer believed that the atomic forces of the United States would be more effective if they consisted of many large fission weapons (of which multiple bombs could be dropped on the same targets) rather than the large and unwieldy predictions of massive super bombs, for which there were a relatively limited amounts of targets of the size to warrant such a development.

Furthermore, were such weapons developed by both the U.S. and the USSR, they would be more effectively used against the U.S. than by it, as the U.S. had far more regions of dense industrial

and civilian activity which would serve as ideal targets for the large weapons than the Soviet Union did.

In the end, President Truman made the final decision, looking for a proper response to the first Soviet atomic bomb test in 1949. On January 31, 1950, Truman announced a crash program to develop the hydrogen (fusion) bomb. At this point, however, the exact mechanism was still not known: the "classical" hydrogen bomb, whereby the *heat* of the fission bomb would be used to ignite the fusion material, seemed highly unworkable. However, an insight by Los Alamos mathematician Stanislaw Ulam showed that the fission bomb and the fusion fuel could be in separate parts of the bomb, and that *radiation* of the fission bomb could first work in a way to *compress* the fusion material before igniting it.

Teller pushed the notion further, and used the results of the boosted-fission "George" test (a boosted-fission device using a small amount of fusion fuel to boost the yield of a fission bomb) to confirm the fusion of heavy hydrogen elements before preparing for their first true multi-stage, Teller-Ulam hydrogen bomb test. Many scientists initially against the weapon, such as Oppenheimer and Bethe, changed their previous opinions, seeing the development as being unstoppable. The first fusion bomb was tested by the United States in *Operation Ivy* on November 1, 1952, on Elugelab Island in the Enewetak (or Eniwetok) Atoll of the Marshall Islands, code-named "Mike". "Mike" used liquid deuterium as its fusion fuel and a large fission weapon as its trigger. The device was a prototype design and not a deliverable weapon: standing over 20 ft (6 m) high and weighing at least 140,000 lb (64 t) (its refrigeration equipment added an additional 24,000 lb as well), it could not have been dropped from even the largest planes.

Its explosion yielded 10.4 megatons of energy—over 450 times the power of the bomb dropped onto Nagasaki— and obliterated Elugelab, leaving an underwater crater 6240 ft (1.9 km) wide and 164 ft (50 m) deep where the island had once been. Truman had initially tried to create a media blackout about the test—hoping it would not become an issue in the upcoming presidential election—but on January 7, 1953, Truman announced the

development of the hydrogen bomb to the world as hints and speculations of it were already beginning to emerge in the press. Not to be outdone, the Soviet Union exploded its first thermonuclear device, designed by the physicist Andrei Sakharov, on August 12, 1953, labeled "Joe-4" by the West. This created concern within the U.S. government and military, because, unlike "Mike," the Soviet device was a deliverable weapon, which the U.S. did not yet have. This first device though was arguably not a "true" hydrogen bomb, and could only reach explosive yields in the hundreds of kilotons (never reaching the megaton range of a "staged" weapon). Still, it was a powerful propaganda tool for the Soviet Union, and the technical differences were fairly oblique to the American public and politicians.

Following the "Mike" blast by less than a year, "Joe-4" seemed to validate claims that the bombs were inevitable and vindicate those who had supported the development of the fusion program. Coming during the height of McCarthyism, the effect was most pronounced by the security hearings in early 1954 which revoked former Los Alamos director Robert Oppenheimer of his security clearance, on the grounds that he was unreliable, had not supported the American hydrogen bomb program, and had made long-standing, left-wing ties in the 1930s. Edward Teller participated in the hearing as the only major scientist to testify against Oppenheimer, a role which resulted in his virtual expulsion from the physics community. On February 28, 1954, the U.S. detonated its first deliverable thermonuclear weapon (which used isotopes of lithium as its fusion fuel), known as the "Shrimp" device of the "Castle Bravo" test, at Bikini Atoll, Marshall Islands. The device yielded 15 megatons of energy, over twice its expected yield, and became the worst radiological disaster in U.S. history. The combination of the unexpectedly large blast and poor weather conditions caused a cloud of radioactive nuclear fallout to contaminate over 7,000 square miles, including Marshall Island natives and the crew of a Japanese fishing boat, as a snow-like mist. The contaminated islands were evacuated (and are still uninhabitable), but the natives received enough of a radioactive dose that they suffered far elevated levels of cancer and birth defects in the years to come.

The crew of the Japanese fishing boat, *Lucky Dragon 5*, returned to port suffering from radiation sickness and skin burns. Their cargo, many tons of contaminated fish, managed to enter into the market before the cause of their illness was determined. When a crew member died from the sickness and the full results of the contamination were made public by the U.S., Japanese concerns were reignited about the hazards of radiation and resulted in a boycott on eating fish (a main staple of the island country) for some weeks. The hydrogen bomb age had a profound effect on the thoughts of nuclear war in the popular and military mind. With only fission bombs, nuclear war could be considered something which could easily be "limited." Dropped by planes and only able to destroy the most built up areas of major cities, it was possible to consider fission bombs simply a technological extension of previous wartime bombing (such as the extensive firebombing which took place against Japan and Germany during World War II), and claims that such weapons could lead to worldwide death or harm were easily brushed aside as grave exaggeration.

Even the decades before the development of fission weapons there had been speculation about the possibility for human beings to end all life on the planet by either accident or purposeful maliciousness, but technology had never allowed for such a capacity. The far greater power of hydrogen bombs made this seem ever closer. The "Castle Bravo" incident itself raised a number of questions about the survivability of a nuclear war. Government scientists in both the U.S. and the USSR had insisted that fusion weapons, unlike fission weapons, were "cleaner" as fusion reactions did not result in the dangerously radioactive by-products as did fission reactions. While technically true, this hid a more gruesome point: the last stage of a multi-staged hydrogen bomb often used the neutrons produced by the fusion reactions to induce fissioning in a jacket of natural uranium, and provided around half of the yield of the device itself.

This fission stage made fusion weapons considerably more "dirty" than they were made out to be, a fact made evident by the towering cloud of deadly fallout which followed the "Bravo" test.

When the Soviet Union tested its first megaton device in 1955, the possibility of a limited nuclear war seemed even more remote in the public and political mind: even if a city or country was not the direct target of a nuclear attack, the clouds of fallout and harmful fission products would disperse along with normal weather patterns and embed themselves in the soil and water of non-targeted areas of the planet as well. Speculation began to look towards what would happen as the fallout and dust created by a full-scale nuclear exchange would affect the world as a whole, rather than just the cities and countries which had been directly involved. In this way, the fate of the world was now tied to the fate of the bomb-wielding superpowers.

Deterrence and Brinkmanship

Throughout the 1950s and the early 1960s a number of trends were enacted between the U.S. and the USSR as they both endeavored in a tit-for-tat approach to disallow the other power from acquiring nuclear supremacy. This took form in a number of ways, both technologically and politically, and had massive political and cultural effects during the Cold War. The first atomic bombs dropped on Hiroshima and Nagasaki were large, custom-made devices, requiring highly trained personnel for their arming and deployment. They could be dropped only from the largest bomber planes—at the time the B-29 Superfortress—and each plane could only hold a single bomb in its hold.

The first hydrogen bombs were similarly massive and complicated. This ratio of one plane to one bomb was still fairly impressive in comparison with conventional, non-nuclear weapons, but against other nuclear-armed countries it was considered to be a grave danger. In the immediate postwar years, the U.S. expended much effort on making the bombs "G.I.-proof"—capable of being used and deployed by members of the U.S. Army, rather than Nobel Prize–winning scientists, and in the 1950s a program of nuclear testing was undertaken in order to improve the nuclear arsenal. Starting in 1951, the Nevada Test Site (in the Nevada desert) became the primary location for all U.S. nuclear testing (in the USSR, Semipalatinsk Test Site in Kazakhstan served a similar

role). Tests were divided into two primary categories: "weapons related" (verifying that a new weapon worked or looking at exactly how it worked) and "weapons effects" (looking at how weapons behaved under various conditions or how structures behaved when subjected to weapons).

In the beginning, almost all nuclear tests were either "atmospheric" (conducted above ground, in the atmosphere) or "underwater" (such as some of the tests done in the Marshall Islands). Testing was used as a sign of both national and technological strength, but also raised questions about the safety of the tests, which released nuclear fallout into the atmosphere (most dramatically with the Castle Bravo test in 1954, but in more limited amounts with almost all atmospheric nuclear testing). Because testing was seen as a sign of technological development (the ability to design usable weapons without some form of testing was considered dubious), halts on testing were often called for as stand-ins for halts in the nuclear arms race itself, and many prominent scientists and statesmen lobbied for a ban on nuclear testing. In 1958, the U.S., USSR, and the United Kingdom (a new nuclear power) declared a temporary testing moratorium for both political and health reasons, but by 1961 the Soviet Union had broken the moratorium and both the USSR and the U.S. began testing with great frequency.

As a show of political strength, the Soviet Union tested the largest-ever nuclear weapon in October 1961, the massive Tsar Bomba, which was tested in a reduced state with a yield of around 50 megatons—in its full state it was estimated to have been around 100 Mt. The weapon was largely impractical for actual military use, but was hot enough to induce third-degree burns at a distance of 62 mi (100 km) away. In its full, "dirty" design, it would have increased the amount of worldwide fallout since 1945 by 25%. In 1963, all nuclear and many non-nuclear states signed the Limited Test Ban Treaty, pledging to refrain from testing nuclear weapons in the atmosphere, underwater, or in outer space. The treaty permitted underground tests.

Most tests were considerably more modest, and worked for direct technical purposes as well as their potential political

overtones. Weapons improvements took on two primary forms. One was an increase in efficiency and power, and within only a few years fission bombs were being developed which were many times more powerful than the ones created during World War II. The other was a program of miniaturization, reducing the size of the nuclear weapons themselves. Smaller bombs meant that bombers could carry more of them, and thus become even more of a threat against even the most rigorous air defenses, and they could also be used in conjunction with the development in rocketry during the 1950s and 1960s. U.S. rocket efforts had received a large boost in the postwar years, largely from the acquiring of engineers who had worked on the Nazi rocketry program during the war, such as Wernher von Braun, who had been involved in the design and manufacture of the V-2 rockets which were launched across the English Channel. An American program, Project Paperclip, had endeavored to move scientists of this sort into American hands (and kept out of Soviet hands) and put them to work on projects for the U.S.

Weapons Improvement

The first nuclear-tipped rockets, such as the MGR-1 Honest John, first deployed by the U.S. in 1953, were surface-to-surface missiles with relatively short ranges (around 15 mi/25 km maximum) with yields around twice the size of the first fission weapons. The limited range of these weapons meant that they could only be used in certain types of potential military situations—the U.S. rocket weapons could not, for example, threaten the city of Moscow with the threat of an immediate strike, and could only be used as "tactical" weapons (that is, for small-scale military situations). For "strategic" weapons—weapons which would serve to threaten an entire country—for the time being, only long-range bombers capable of penetrating deep into enemy territory would work. In the U.S. this resulted in the creation of the Strategic Air Command in 1946, a system of bombers headed by General Curtis LeMay (who had previously presided over the firebombing of Japan during WWII), which kept a number of nuclear-armed planes in the sky at all times, ready to receive orders to attack Moscow whenever commanded.

These technological possibilities enabled nuclear strategy to develop a logic considerably different than previous military thinking had allowed. Because the threat of nuclear warfare was so awful, it was first thought that it might make any war of the future impossible.

President Dwight D. Eisenhower's doctrine of "massive retaliation" in the early years of the Cold War was a message to the USSR, saying that if the Red Army attempted to invade the parts of Europe not given to the Eastern bloc during the Potsdam Conference (such as West Germany), nuclear weapons would be used against the Soviet troops and potentially the Soviet leaders. With the development of more rapid-response technologies (such as rockets and long-range bombers), this policy began to shift. If the Soviet Union also had nuclear weapons and a policy of "massive retaliation" was carried out, it was reasoned, then any Soviet forces not killed in the initial attack, or launched while the attack was ongoing, would be able to serve their own form of nuclear "retaliation" against the U.S. Recognizing this to be an undesirable outcome, military officers and game theorists at the RAND think tank developed a nuclear warfare strategy that would eventually become known as Mutually Assured Destruction (MAD).

MAD divided potential nuclear war into two stages: first strike and second strike. A first strike would be the first use of nuclear weapons by one nuclear-equipped nation against another nuclear-equipped nation.

If the attacking nation did not prevent the attacked nation from a nuclear response, then a second strike could be deployed against the attacking nation. In this situation, whether the U.S. first attacked the USSR or the USSR first attacked the U.S., the end result would be that both nations would be damaged perhaps to the point of utter social collapse. According to game theory, because starting a nuclear war would be suicidal, no logical country would willfully enter into a nuclear war. However, if a country were capable of launching a first strike which would utterly destroy the ability of the attacked country to respond in kind, then the balance of power would be disturbed and nuclear war could then be safely undertaken.

MAD played on two seemingly opposed modes of thought: cold logic and emotional fear. The phrase by which MAD was often known, "nuclear deterrence", was translated as "dissuasion" by the French and "terrorization" by the Russians. This apparent paradox of nuclear war was summed up by British Prime Minister Winston Churchill as "the worse things get, the better they are"—the greater the threat of mutual destruction, the safer the world would be. This philosophy made a number of technological and political demands on participating nations. For one thing, it said that it should always be assumed that an enemy nation may be trying to acquire "first strike capability," something which must always be avoided. In American politics this translated into demands to avoid "missile gaps" and "bomber gaps" where the Soviet Union could potentially "out shoot" American efforts (most of these supposed "gaps" proved to be political figments, but this hardly mattered at the time). It also encouraged the production of thousands of nuclear weapons by both the U.S. and the USSR, far more than would be needed to simply destroy the major civilian and military infrastructures of the opposing country.

These policies and strategies were satirized in the 1964 Stanley Kubrick film Dr. Strangelove, in which the Soviets, unable to keep up with the US's first strike capability, instead plan for MAD by building a Doomsday Machine, and thus, after a (literally) mad US General orders a nuclear attack on the USSR, the end of the world is brought about. The policy also encouraged the development of the first early warning systems. Conventional war, even at its fastest, was fought over time scales of days and weeks. With long-range bombers, the time from the start of an attack to its conclusion was reduced to mere hours. With rockets, it could be reduced to minutes. It was reasoned that conventional command and control systems could not be expected to adequately respond to a nuclear attack, and so great lengths were taken to develop the first computers which could look for enemy attacks and direct rapid responses. In the U.S., massive funding was poured into the development of SAGE, a system which would track and intercept enemy bomber aircraft using information from remote radar stations, and was the first computer system to feature real-time processing, multiplexing, and display devices—the first

"general" computing machine, and a direct predecessor of modern computers.

Anti-nuclear

Bombers and short-range rockets were not reliable: planes could be shot down, and earlier nuclear missiles could cover only a limited range— for example, the first Soviet rockets' range limited them to targets in Europe. However, by the 1960s, both the United States and the Soviet Union had developed intercontinental ballistic missiles, which could be launched from extremely remote areas far away from their target; and submarine-launched ballistic missiles, which had less range but could be launched from submarines very close to the target without any radar warning. This made any national protection from nuclear missiles increasingly impractical. The military realities made for a precarious diplomatic situation. The international politics of brinkmanship led leaders to exclaim their willingness to participate in a nuclear war rather than concede any advantage to their opponents, feeding public fears that their generation may be the last. Civil defence programs undertaken by both superpowers, exemplified by the construction of fallout shelters and urging civilians about the "survivability" of nuclear war, did little to ease public concerns.

The climax of brinksmanship came in early 1962, when an American U-2 spy plane photographed a series of launch sites for medium-range ballistic missiles being constructed on the island of Cuba, just off the coast of the southern United States, beginning what became known as the Cuban Missile Crisis. The U.S. administration of John F. Kennedy concluded that the Soviet Union, then led by Nikita Khrushchev, was planning to station Russian nuclear missiles on the island, which was under the control of Communist Fidel Castro. On October 22, Kennedy announced the discoveries in a televised address, and declared that a naval quarantine would be put around Cuba to turn back any Soviet nuclear shipments, and warned that the military was prepared "for any eventualities." The missiles would have a range of 2,400 miles (4,000 km), and allow the Soviet Union to easily destroy many major American cities on the Eastern Seaboard if a nuclear war were started. The leaders of the two superpowers stood nose to nose, seemingly poised over the beginnings of a third world war. Khrushchev's ambitions for putting the weapons on the island were motivated in part by the fact that the U.S. had stationed similar weapons in Britain, Italy, and nearby Turkey, and had previously attempted to sponsor an invasion of Cuba the year before in the failed Bay of Pigs Invasion. On October 26, an offer was sent from Khrushchev to Kennedy offering to withdraw all missiles if Kennedy would commit to a policy of no future invasions of Cuba. Khrushchev worded the threat of assured destruction eloquently: "You and I should not now pull on the ends of the rope in which you have tied a knot of war, because the harder you and I pull, the tighter the knot will become. And a time may come when this knot is tied so tight that the person who tied it is no longer capable of untying it, and then the knot will have to be cut. What that would mean I need not explain to you, because you yourself understand perfectly what dreaded forces our two countries possess."

A day later, however, the Russians put forward another offer, this time demanding that the U.S. remove its missiles from Turkey before any missiles would be withdrawn from Cuba. On the same day, a U-2 plane was shot down over Cuba and another was almost intercepted over Russia, and Soviet merchant ships were nearing the quarantine zone. Kennedy responded by accepting the first deal publicly, and sending his brother Robert to the Soviet embassy to accept the second deal in private. On October 28, the Soviet ships stopped at the quarantine line and, after some hesitation, turned back towards the Soviet Union. Khrushchev announced that he had ordered the removal of all missiles in Cuba, and U.S. Secretary of State Dean Rusk was moved to comment, "We went eyeball to eyeball, and the other fellow just blinked."

The Crisis was later seen as the closest the U.S. and the USSR ever came to nuclear war and had been narrowly averted by last-minute compromise by both superpowers. Fears of communication difficulties led to the installment of the first hotline, a direct link between the superpowers which would allow them to more easily discuss future military activities and political maneuverings. It had been made clear that with their missiles, bombers, submarines, and computerized firing systems, the escalation of any situation to Armageddon could be done far more easily than anybody desired. After stepping so close to the brink, both the U.S. and the USSR worked to reduce their nuclear tensions in the years immediately following. The most immediate culmination of this work was the signing of the Partial Test Ban Treaty in 1963, in which the U.S. and USSR agreed to no longer test nuclear weapons in the atmosphere, underwater, or in outer space. Testing underground continued, allowing for further weapons development, but the worldwide fallout risks were purposefully reduced, and the era of using massive nuclear tests as a form of saber-rattling ended.

In December 1979, NATO decided to deploy cruise and Pershing II missiles in Western Europe in response to Soviet deployment of intermediate range mobile missiles, and in the early 1980s, a "dangerous Soviet-US nuclear confrontation" arose. In New York on June 12, 1982, one million people gathered to protest nuclear weapons, and to support the second UN Special Session on Disarmament. As the nuclear abolitionist movement grew, there were many protests at the Nevada Test Site. For example, on February 6, 1987, nearly 2,000 demonstrators, including six members of Congress, protested against nuclear weapons testing and more than 400 people were arrested. Four of the significant groups organizing this renewal of anti-nuclear activism were Greenpeace, The American Peace Test, The Western Shoshone, and Nevada Desert Experience.

Initial Proliferation

The United Kingdom had been an integral part of the Manhattan Project following the Quebec Agreement in 1943. The passing of the McMahon Act by the United States in 1946 unilaterally broke this partnership and prevented the passage of any further information to the United Kingdom. The British Government under Clement Attlee determined that it would be essential for there to be a British Bomb. Because of the involvement in the Manhattan Project Britain had extensive knowledge in some areas, but not in others.

An improved version of 'Fat Man' was developed, and on 26 February 1952, Prime Minister Winston Churchill announced that the United Kingdom also had an atomic bomb and a successful test took place on the 3rd October 1952. At first these were free-fall bombs and then there was a missile, Blue Steel, and a later-canceled MRBM, Blue Streak. Anglo-American cooperation on Nuclear weapons was restored by the 1958 US-UK Mutual Defence Agreement. As a result of this and the Polaris Sales Agreement, the United Kingdom has bought United States designs for submarine missiles and fitted its own warheads. It retains full independent control over the use of the missiles. It no longer possesses any free-fall bombs. France had been heavily involved in nuclear research before World War II through the work of the Joliot-Curies. This was discontinued after the war because of the instability of the Fourth Republic and the lack of finance available. However, in the 1950s a civil nuclear research program was started, a byproduct of which would be plutonium.

In 1956 a secret Committee for the Military Applications of Atomic Energy was formed and a development program for delivery vehicles started. With the return of Charles de Gaulle to the presidency of France in 1958 the final decisions to build a bomb were taken, and a successful test took place in 1960. Since then France has developed and maintained its own nuclear deterrent. In 1951 China and the Soviet Union signed an agreement whereby China would supply uranium ore in exchange for technical assistance in producing nuclear weapons. In 1953 China had established a research program under the guise of civilian nuclear energy. Throughout the 1950s the Soviet Union provided large amounts of equipment, but as the relations between the two countries worsened, the amount of assistance was reduced, and in 1959 the donation of a bomb for copying purposes was refused. Despite this, rapid progress was made with the test of an atomic bomb on the 16th October 1964 at Lop Nur, a nuclear missile on 25 October 1966, and of a hydrogen bomb on the 14th June 1967.

Nuclear warheads were produced from 1968 and thermonuclear warheads from 1974. It is also thought that Chinese warheads have been successfully miniaturised from 2200 kg to

700 kg through the use of designs obtained by espionage from the United States. The current number of weapons is unknown owing to strict secrecy, but it is thought that up to 2000 warheads may have been produced, though far fewer may be available for use. China is the only nuclear weapons state to have guaranteed the non-first use of nuclear weapons.

NUCLEAR WEAPONS USES IN WAR

An all-out nuclear war between Russia and the United States would be the worst catastrophe in history, a tragedy so huge it is difficult to comprehend. Even so, it would be far from the end of human life on earth. The dangers from nuclear weapons have been distorted and exaggerated, for varied reasons. These exaggerations have become demoralizing myths, believed by millions of Americans.

While working with hundreds of Americans building expedient shelters and life-support equipment, I have found that many people at first see no sense in talking about details of survival skills. Those who hold exaggerated beliefs about the dangers from nuclear weapons must first be convinced that nuclear war would not inevitably be the end of them and everything worthwhile.

Only after they have begun to question the truth of these myths do they become interested, under normal peacetime conditions, in acquiring nuclear war survival skills. Therefore, before giving detailed instructions for making and using survival equipment, we will examine the most harmful of the myths about nuclear war dangers, along with some of the grim facts.

- Myth: Fallout radiation from a nuclear war would poison the air and all parts of the environment. It would kill everyone. (This is the demoralizing message of On the Beach and many similar pseudoscientific books and articles.)
- Facts: When a nuclear weapon explodes near enough to the ground for its fireball to touch the ground, it forms a crater.

Many thousands of tons of earth from the crater of a large explosion are pulverized into trillions of particles. These particles are contaminated by radioactive atoms produced by the nuclear explosion. Thousands of tons of the particles are carried up into a mushroom-shaped cloud, miles above the earth. These radioactive particles then fall out of the mushroom cloud, or out of the dispersing cloud of particles blown by the winds thus becoming fallout.

Each contaminated particle continuously gives off invisible radiation, much like a tiny X-ray machine while in the mushroom cloud, while descending, and after having fallen to earth. The descending radioactive particles are carried by the winds like the sand and dust particles of a miles-thick sandstorm cloud except that they usually are blown at lower speeds and in many areas the particles are so far apart that no cloud is seen. The largest, heaviest fallout particles reach the ground first, in locations close to the explosion. Many smaller particles are carried by the winds for tens to thousands of miles before falling to earth. At any one place where fallout from a single explosion is being deposited on the ground in concentrations high enough to require the use of shelters, deposition will be completed within a few hours.

The smallest fallout particles those tiny enough to be inhaled into a person's lungs are invisible to the naked eye. These tiny particles would fall so slowly from the four-mile or greater heights to which they would be injected by currently deployed Soviet warheads that most would remain airborne for weeks to years before reaching the ground. By that time their extremely wide dispersal and radioactive decay would make them much less dangerous. Only where such tiny particles are promptly brought to earth by rain- outs or snow-outs in scattered "hot spots," and later dried and blown about by the winds, would these invisible particles constitute a long-term and relatively minor post-attack danger.

The air in properly designed fallout shelters, even those without air filters, is free of radioactive particles and safe to breathe except in a few' rare environments as will be explained later. Fortunately for all living things, the danger from fallout radiation lessens with time. The radioactive decay, as this lessening is called, is rapid at first, then gets slower and slower. The dose rate (the amount of radiation received per hour) decreases accordingly. Fallout meters called dosimeters measure the dose received by recording the number of R. Fallout meters called survey meters, or dose-rate meters, measure the dose rate by recording the number of R being received per hour at the time of measurement. Notice that it takes about seven times as long for the dose rate to decay from 1000 roentgens per hour (1000 R/hr) to 10 R/hr (48 hours) as to decay from 1000 R/hr to 100 R/hr (7 hours). (Only in high-fallout areas would the dose rate 1 hour after the explosion be as high as 1000 roentgens per hour.)

If the dose rate 1 hour after an explosion is 1000 R/hr, it would take about 2 weeks for the dose rate to be reduced to 1 R/hr solely as a result of radioactive decay. Weathering effects will reduce the dose rate further,' for example, rain can wash fallout particles from plants and houses to lower positions on or closer to the ground. Surrounding objects would reduce the radiation dose from these low-lying particles.

Within two weeks after an attack the occupants of most shelters could safely stop using them, or could work outside the shelters for an increasing number of hours each day. Exceptions would be in areas of extremely heavy fallout such as might occur downwind from important targets attacked with many weapons, especially missile sites and very large cities. To know when to come out safely, occupants either would need a reliable fallout meter to measure the changing radiation dangers, or must receive information based on measurements made nearby with a reliable instrument.

The radiation dose that will kill a person varies considerably with different people. A dose of 450 R resulting from exposure of the whole body to fallout radiation is often said to be the dose that will kill about half the persons receiving it, although most studies indicate that it would take somewhat less. Almost all persons confined to expedient shelters after a nuclear attack would be under stress and without clean surroundings or antibiotics to fight infections. Many also would lack adequate water and food. Under these unprecedented conditions, perhaps half the persons who received a whole-body dose of 350 R within a few days would die. Fortunately, the human body can repair most radiation damage if the daily radiation doses are not too large. A person who is healthy and has not been exposed in the past two weeks to a total radiation dose of more than 100 R can receive a dose of 6 R each day for at least two months without being incapacitated.

Only a very small fraction of Hiroshima and Nagasaki citizens who survived radiation doses some of which were nearly fatal have suffered serious delayed effects.

The reader should realize that to do essential work after a massive nuclear attack, many survivors must be willing to receive much larger radiation doses than are normally permissible. Otherwise, too many workers would stay inside shelter too much of the time, and work that would be vital to national recovery could not be done. For example, if the great majority of truckers were so fearful of receiving even non-incapacitating radiation doses that they would refuse to transport food, additional millions would die from starvation alone.

- Myth: Fallout radiation penetrates everything; there is no escaping its deadly effects.
- Facts: Some gamma radiation from fallout will penetrate the shielding materials of even an excellent shelter and reach its occupants. However, the radiation dose that the occupants of an excellent shelter would receive while inside this shelter can be reduced to a dose smaller than the average American receives during his lifetime from X rays and other radiation exposures normal in America today. The design features of such a shelter include the use of a sufficient thickness of earth or other heavy shielding material. Gamma rays are like X rays, but more penetrating.

The actual paths of gamma rays passing through shielding materials are much more complicated, due to scattering, etc., than are the straight-line paths. But when averaged out, the effectiveness of a halving-thickness of any material is approximately as shown. The denser a substance, the better it serves for shielding material. Thus, a halving-thickness of concrete is only about 2.4 inches (6.1 cm). If additional halving-thicknesses of packed earth shielding are successively added to the five thicknesses, the protection factor

(PF) is successively increased from 32 to 64, to 128, to 256, to 512, to 1024, and so on.

- Myth: A heavy nuclear attack would set practically everything on fire, causing "firestorms" in cities that would exhaust the oxygen in the air. All shelter occupants would be killed by the intense heat.
- Facts: On aclear day, thermal pulses (heat radiation that travels at the speed of light) from an air burst can set fire to easily ignitable materials (such as window curtains, upholstery, dry newspaper, and dry grass) over about as large an area as is damaged by the blast. It can cause second-degree skin burns to exposed people who are as far as ten miles from a one-megaton (1 MT) explosion. (A 1-MT nuclear explosion is one that produces the same amount of energy as does one million tons of TNT.) If the weather is very clear and dry, the area of fire danger could be considerably larger. On a cloudy or smoggy day, however, particles in the air would absorb and scatter much of the heat radiation, and the area endangered by heat radiation from the fireball would be less than the area of severe blast damage.

"Firestorms" could occur only when the concentration of combustible structures is very high, as in the very dense centers of a few old American cities.

At rural and suburban building densities, most people in earth- covered fallout shelters would not have their lives endangered by fires.

- Myth: In theworst-hit parts of Hiroshima and Nagasaki where all buildings were demolished, everyone was killed by blast, radiation, or fire.
- Facts: InNagasaki, some people survived uninjured who were far inside tunnel shelters built for conventional air raids and located as close as one-third mile from ground zero (the point directly below the explosion). This was true even though these long, large shelters lacked blast doors and were deep inside the zone within which all buildings were destroyed. (People far inside long, large, open shelters

are better protected than are those inside small, open shelters.)

Many earth-covered family shelters were essentially undamaged in areas where blast and fire destroyed all buildings. This shelter was essentially undamaged, although less than 100 yards from ground zero at Nagasaki. The calculated maximum overpressure (pressure above the normal air pressure) was about 65 pounds per square inch (65 psi). Persons inside so small a shelter without a blast doorwould have been killed by blast pressure at this distance from the explosion. However, in a recent blast test,5 an earth-covered, expedient Small-Pole Shelter equipped with blast doors was undamaged at 53 psi. The pressure rise inside was slight not even enough to have damaged occupants' eardrums. If poles are available, field tests have indicated that many families can build such shelters in a few days.

The great life-saving potential of blast-protective shelters has been proven in war and confirmed by blast tests and calculations. For example, the area in which the air bursting of a 1-megaton weapon would wreck a 50-psi shelter with blast doors in about 2.7 square miles. Within this roughly circular area, practically all them occupants of wrecked shelters would be killed by blast, carbon monoxide from fires, or radiation. The same blast effects would kill most people who were using basements affording 5 psi protection, over an area of about 58 square miles.

- Myth: Because some modern H-bombs are over 1000 times as powerful as the A-bomb that destroyed most of Hiroshima, these H-bombs are 1000 times as deadly and destructive.
- Facts: A nuclear weapon 1000 times as powerful as the one that blasted Hiroshima, if exploded under comparable conditions, produces equally serious blast damage to wood-frame houses over an area up to about 130 times as large, not 1000 times as large.

For example, air bursting a 20-kiloton weapon at the optimum height to destroy most buildings will destroy or severely damage houses out to about 1.42 miles from ground zero.6 The circular area of at least severe blast damage will be about 6.33 square miles.

(The explosion of a 20 kiloton weapon releases the same amount of energy as 20 thousand tons of TNT.) One thousand 20-kiloton weapons thus air burst, well separated to avoid overlap of their blast areas, would destroy or severely damage houses over areas totaling approximately 6,330 square miles. In contrast, similar air bursting of one 20- megaton weapon (equivalent in explosive power to 20 million tons of TNT) would destroy or severely damage the great majority of houses out to a distance of 16 miles from ground zero.6 The area of destruction would be about 800 square miles - not 6,330 square miles.

Today few if any of Russia's huge intercontinental ballistic missiles (ICBMs) are armed with a 20-megaton warhead. Now a huge Russian ICBM, the SS-18, typically carries 10 warheads, each having a yield of 500 kilotons, each programmed to hit a separate target. See Jane's Weapon Systems, 1987-88.

- Myth: A Russian nuclear attack on the United States would completely destroy all American cities.
- Facts: As long as Soviet leaders are rational they will continue to give first priority to knocking out our weapons and other military assets that can damage Russia and kill Russians. To explode enough nuclear weapons of any size to completely destroy American cities would be an irrational waste of warheads. The Soviets can make much better use of most of the warheads that would be required to completely destroy American cities; the majority of those warheads probably already are targeted to knock out our retaliatory missiles by being surface burst or near-surface burst on their hardened silos, located far from most cities and densely populated areas.

Unfortunately, many militarily significant targets - including naval vessels in port and port facilities, bombers and fighters on the ground, air base and airport facilities that can be used by bombers, Army installations, and key defense factories - are in or close to American cities. In the event of an all-out Soviet attack, most of these "'soft" targets would be destroyed by air bursts. Air bursting a given weapon subjects about twice as large an area to blast effects severe enough to destroy "soft" targets as does surface bursting the same weapon. Fortunately for Americans living outside blast and fire areas, air bursts produce only very tiny particles.

Most of these extremely small radioactive particles remain airborne for so long that their radioactive decay and wide dispersal before reaching the ground make them much less life- endangering than the promptly deposited larger fallout particles from surface and near-surface bursts. However, if you are a survival minded American you should prepare to survive heavy fallout wherever you are. Unpredictable winds may bring fallout from unexpected directions. Or your area may be in a "hot spot" of life-endangering fallout caused by a rain-out or snow-out of both small and tiny particles from distant explosions. Or the enemy may use surface or near-surface bursts in your part of the country to crater long runways or otherwise disrupt U.S. retaliatory actions by producing heavy local fallout.

Today few if any of Russia's largest intercontinental ballistic missiles (ICBMs) are armed with a 20-megaton warhead. A huge Russian ICBM, the SS-18, typically carries 10 warheads each having a yield of 500 kilotons, each programmed to hit a separate target. See "Jane's Weapon Systems. 1987-1988." However, in March 1990 CIA Director William Webster told the U.S. Senate Armed Services Committee that ".... The USSR's strategic modernization program continues unabated," and that the SS-18 Mod 5 can carry 14 to 20 nuclear warheads. The warheads are generally assumed to be smaller than those of the older SS-18s.

- Myth: So much food and water will be poisoned by fallout that people will starve and die even in fallout areas where there is enough food and water.
- Facts: If the falloutparticles do not become mixed with the parts of food that are eaten, no harm is done. Food and water in dust-tight containers are not contaminated by fallout radiation. Peeling fruits and vegetables removes essentially all fallout, as does removing the uppermost several inches of stored grain onto which fallout particles have fallen. Water from many sources -- such as deep wells and covered reservoirs, tanks, and containers -- would not be contaminated. Even water containing dissolved

radioactive elements and compounds can be made safe for drinking by simply filtering it through earth, as described later in this book.

- Myth: Most of the unborn children and grandchildren of people who have been exposed to radiation from nuclear explosions will be genetically damaged will be malformed, delayed victims of nuclear war.
- Facts: The authoritative study by the National Academy of Sciences, A Thirty Year Study of the Survivors qf Hiroshima and Nagasaki, was published in 1977. It concludes that the incidence of abnormalities is no higher among children later conceived by parents who were exposed to radiation during the attacks on Hiroshima and Nagasaki than is the incidence of abnormalities among Japanese children born to un-exposed parents.

This is not to say that there would be no genetic damage, nor that some fetuses subjected to large radiation doses would not be damaged. But the overwhelming evidence does show that the exaggerated fears of radiation damage to future generations are not supported by scientific findings.

- Myth: Overkill would result if all the U.S. and U.S.S.R, nuclear weapons were used meaning not only that the two superpowers have more than enough weapons to kill all of each other's people, but also that they have enough weapons to exterminate the human race.
- Facts: Statements that the U.S. and the Soviet Union have the power to kill the world's population several times over are based on misleading calculations. One such calculation is to multiply the deaths produced per kiloton exploded over Hiroshima or Nagasaki by an estimate of the number of kilotons in either side's arsenal. (A kiloton explosion is one that produces the same amount of energy as does 1000 tons of TNT.) The unstated assumption is that somehow the world's population could be gathered into circular crowds, each a few miles in diameter with a population density equal to downtown Hiroshima or Nagasaki, and then a small (Hiroshima-sized) weapon would be exploded

over the center of each crowd. Other misleading calculations are based on exaggerations of the dangers from long-lasting radiation and other harmful effects of a nuclear war.

- Myth: Blindness and a disastrous increase of cancers would be the fate of survivors of a nuclear war, because the nuclear explosions would destroy so much of the protective ozone in the stratosphere that far too much ultraviolet light would reach the earth's surface. Even birds and insects would be blinded. People could not work outdoors in daytime for years without dark glasses, and would have to wear protective clothing to prevent incapacitating sunburn. Plants would be badly injured and food production greatly reduced.
- Facts: Large nuclear explosions do inject huge amounts of nitrogen oxides (gasses that destroy ozone) into the stratosphere. However, the percent of the stratospheric ozone destroyed by a given amount of nitrogen oxides has been greatly overestimated in almost all theoretical calculations and models. For example, the Soviet and U.S. atmospheric nuclear test explosions of large weapons in 1952-1962 were calculated by Foley and Ruderman to result in a reduction of more than 10 percent in total ozone. (See M. H. Foley and M. A. Ruderman, 'Stratospheric NO from Past Nuclear Explosions", Journal of Geophysics, Res. 78, 4441-4450.) Yet observations that they cited showed no reductions in ozone. Nor did ultraviolet increase. Other theoreticians calculated sizable reductions in total ozone, but interpreted the observational data to indicate either no reduction, or much smaller reductions than their calculated ones.

A realistic simplified estimate of the increased ultraviolet light dangers to American survivors of a large nuclear war equates these hazards to moving from San Francisco to sea level at the equator, where the sea level incidence of skin cancers (seldom fatal) is highest- about 10 times higher than the incidence at San Francisco. Many additional thousands of American survivors might get skin cancer, but little or no increase in skin cancers might result if in the post-attack world deliberate sun tanning and going around hatless went out of fashion.

Furthermore, almost all of today's warheads are smaller than those exploded in the large- weapons tests mentioned above; most would inject much smaller amounts of ozone-destroying gasses, or no gasses, into the stratosphere, where ozone deficiencies may persist for years.

And nuclear weapons smaller than 500 kilotons result in increases (due to smog reactions) in upper tropospheric ozone. In a nuclear war, these increases would partially compensate for the upper-level tropospheric decreases-as explained by Julius S. Chang and Donald J. Wuebbles of Lawrence Livermore National Laboratory.

- Myth: Unsurvivable "nuclear winter" surely will follow a nuclear war. The world will be frozen if only 100 megatons (less than one percent of all nuclear weapons) are used to ignite cities. World-enveloping smoke from fires and the dust from surface bursts will prevent almost all sunlight and solar heat from reaching the earth's surface. Universal darkness for weeks! Sub-zero temperatures, even in summertime! Frozen crops, even in the jungles of South America! Worldwide famine! Whole species of animals and plants exterminated! The survival of mankind in doubt!
- Facts: Unsurvivable "nuclear winter" is a discredited theory that, since its conception in 1982, has been used to frighten additional millions into believing that trying to survive a nuclear war is a waste of effort and resources, and that only by ridding the world of almost all nuclear weapons do we have a chance of surviving.

Non-propagandizing scientists recently havecalculated that the climatic and other environmental effects of even an all-out nuclear war would be much less severe than the catastrophic effects repeatedly publicized by popular astronomer Carl Sagan and his fellow activist scientists, and by all the involved Soviet scientists.

Conclusions reached from these recent, realistic calculations are summarized in an article, "Nuclear Winter Reappraised", featured in the 1986 summer issue of Foreign Affairs, the prestigious quarterly of the Council on Foreign Relations.

The authors, Starley L. Thompson and Stephen H. Schneider, are atmospheric scientists with the National Center for Atmospheric Research. They showed " that on scientific grounds the global apocalyptic conclusions of the initial nuclear winter hypothesis can now be relegated to a vanishing low level of probability."

Their models indicate that in July (when the greatest temperature reductions would result) the average temperature in the United States would be reduced for a few days from about 70 degrees Fahrenheit to approximately 50 degrees. (In contrast, under the same conditions Carl Sagan, his associates, and the Russian scientists predicted a resulting average temperature of about 10 degrees below zero Fahrenheit, lasting for many weeks!)

Persons who want to learn more about possible post-attack climatic effects also should read the Fall 1986 issue of Foreign Affairs. This issue contains a long letter from Thompson and Schneider which further demolishes the theory of catastrophic "nuclear winter." Continuing studies indicate there will be even smaller reductions in temperature than those calculated by Thompson and Schneider.

Soviet propagandists promptly exploited belief in unsurvivable "nuclear winter" to increase fear of nuclear weapons and war, and to demoralize their enemies. Because raging city firestorms are needed to inject huge amounts of smoke into the stratosphere and thus, according to one discredited theory, prevent almost all solar heat from reaching the ground, the Soviets changed their descriptions of how a modern city will burn if blasted by a nuclear explosion. Russian scientists and civil defense officials realistically described - before the invention of "nuclear winter" - the burning of a city hit by a nuclear weapon.

Buildings in the blasted area for miles around ground zero will be reduced to scattered rubble - mostly of concrete, steel, and other nonflammable materials - that will not burn in blazing fires.

Thus in the Oak Ridge National Laboratory translation (ORNL-TR-2793) of Civil Defense.

Second Edition (500,000 copies), Moscow, 1970, by Egorov, Shlyakhov, and Alabin, we read: "Fires do not occur in zones of complete destruction . . . that are characterized by an overpressure exceeding 0.5 kg/cm2 [- 7 psi]., because rubble is scattered and covers the burning structures. As a result the rubble only smolders, and fires as such do not occur."

Firestorms destroyed the centers of Hamburg, Dresden, and Tokyo. The old-fashioned buildings of those cities contained large amounts of flammable materials, were ignited by many thousands of small incendiaries, and burned quickly as standing structures well supplied with air. No firestorm has ever injected smoke into the stratosphere, or caused appreciable cooling below its smoke cloud.

The theory that smoke from burning cities and forests and dust from nuclear explosions would cause worldwide freezing temperatures was conceived in 1982 by the German atmospheric chemist and environmentalist Paul Crutzen, and continues to be promoted by a worldwide propaganda campaign.

This well funded campaign began in 1983 with televised scientific-political meetings in Cambridge and Washington featuring American and Russian scientists. A barrage of newspaper and magazine articles followed, including a scaremongering article by Carl Sagan in the October 30, 1983 issue of Parade, the Sunday tabloid read by millions.

The most influential article was featured in the December 23,1983 issue of Science (the weekly magazine of the American Association for the Advancement of Science): "Nuclear winter, global consequences of multiple nuclear explosions," by five scientists, R. P. Turco, O. B. Toon, T. P. Ackerman, J. B. Pollack, and C. Sagan. Significantly, these activists listed their names to spell TTAPS, pronounced "taps," the bugle call proclaiming "lights out" or the end of a military funeral.

Until 1985, non-propagandizing scientists did not begin to effectively refute the numerous errors, unrealistic assumptions, and computer modeling weakness' of the TTAPS and related "nuclear winter" hypotheses.

A principal reason is that government organizations, private corporations, and most scientists generally avoid getting involved in political controversies, or making statements likely to enable antinuclear activists to accuse them of minimizing nuclear war dangers, thus undermining hopes for peace. Stephen Schneider has been called a fascist by some disarmament supporters for having written "Nuclear Winter Reappraised," according to the Rocky Mountain News of July 6, 1986. Three days later, this paper, that until recently featured accounts of unsurvivable "nuclear winter," criticized Carl Sagan and defended Thompson and Schneider in its lead editorial, "In Study of Nuclear Winter, Let Scientists Be Scientists." In a free country, truth will out - although sometimes too late to effectively counter fast-hitting propaganda.

Effective refutation of "nuclear winter" also was delayed by the prestige of politicians and of politically motivated scientists and scientific organizations endorsing the TTAPS forecast of worldwide doom. Furthermore, the weakness' in the TTAPS hypothesis could not be effectively explored until adequate Government funding was made available to cover costs of lengthy, expensive studies, including improved computer modeling of interrelated, poorly understood meteorological phenomena.

Serious climatic effects from a Soviet-U.S. nuclear war cannot be completely ruled out. However, possible deaths from uncertain climatic effects are a small danger compared to the incalculable millions in many countries likely to die from starvation caused by disastrous shortages of essentials of modern agriculture sure to result from a Soviet-American nuclear war, and by the cessation of most international food shipments.

7

Aerial Warfare

Aerial warfare is the use of military aircraft and other flying machines in warfare, including military airlift of cargo to further the national interests as was demonstrated in the Berlin Airlift. Developing from unpowered observation hot air balloons in the 18th century and even older kite, aerial warfare has become a high-technology affair that has led to many advances in technology and techniques such as propulsion, radar, and use of composites and engineered materials such as carbon fibers.

Kite Warfare

The earliest documented aerial warfare took place in ancient China, when a manned Kite was set off to spy for military intelligence and communication. Ancient Chinese soldiers also mounted massive aerial fire arrow attacks from war kites, where they would send a volley of flaming arrows from the war kite onto the ground target, carrying out the world's first-ever air attacks.

Balloon Warfare— Balloon warfare in Ancient China

In or around the 2nd or 3rd century, a prototype Hot air balloon, the Kongming lantern was invented in China serving as military communication.

Balloon Warfare in Europe

Some minor warfare use was made of balloons in the infancy of aeronautics. The first instance was by the French Aerostatic Corps at the Battle of Fleurus in 1794, who used a tethered balloon,

L'entreprenant, to gain a vantage point. Balloons had disadvantages. They could not fly in bad weather, fog, or high winds. They were at the mercy of the winds and were also very large targets.

AMERICAN CIVIL WAR–UNION ARMY BALLOON CORPS

The American Civil War was the first war to witness significant use of aeronautics in support of battle.. Thaddeus Lowe made noteworthy contributions to the Union war effort using a fleet of balloons he created In June 1861 Professor Thaddeus S. C. Lowe left his work in the private sector as a scientist/balloonist and offered his services as an aeronaut to President Lincoln, who took some interest in the idea of an air war. Lowe's demonstration of flying his balloon *Enterprise* over Washington, DC, and transmitting a telegraph message to the ground was enough to have him introduced to the commanders of the Topographical Engineers; initially it was thought balloons could be used for preparing better maps.

Lowe's first action was at the First Battle of Bull Run in July 1861 with General Irvin McDowell and the Grand Army of the Potomac. *Enterprise* did a free flight observation of the Confederate positions.

In another demonstration, Lowe was called to Fort Corcoran by artillery General W. F. Smith. Lowe ascended to a given altitude in order to spot rebel encampments at Falls Church, Virginia. With flag signals he directed artillery fire onto the sleeping encampment. As the General put it, *"The signals from the balloon have enabled my gunners to hit with a fine degree of accuracy an unseen and dispersed target area."*

By October, Lowe had orders in hand to build four balloons with portable hydrogen gas generators for use in aerial reconnaissance. Working with several other prominent American balloonists he formed the Union Army Balloon Corps who never received commissions, working as civilian contractors, This was of great concern should the aeronauts be shot down over enemy lines, as civilian spying is summarily punishable by death. Therefore Lowe insisted on the strict use of tethered (as opposed to free) flight. By attaining altitudes from 1,000 feet (300 m) to as much as 3-1/2 miles, an expansive view of the battle field and beyond could be had.

Lowe built seven balloons: *Eagle,* his first; *Constitution,* one of the smaller balloons; its sister, *Washington; Intrepid,* a larger balloon and his favorite; a sister, *Union; Excelsior;* and *United States,* which never came out of storage. As the Confederates retreated toward Richmond, the War turned into the Peninsular Campaign. Due to the heavy forests on the peninsula, the balloons were unable to follow on land. Lowe was introduced to *George Washington Parke Custis,* a coal barge converted to operate balloons. The balloons and their gas generators were loaded aboard and taken down the Potomac, where reconnaissance of the peninsula could continue. *Custis* was taken up the Pawmunkey River, where Lowe was reunited with McClellan's army.

Lowe's most dramatic action came in the Battle of Fair Oaks, where he was able to view the advancing of Lee's army onto the isolated detachment of General Heintzelman. Working from two balloon camps, one at Mechanicsville and one at Gaine's Farm, Lowe galloped six miles (10 km) twice daily to keep up with the reconnaissance reports. McClellan was sure the rebels were feigning an attack, but Lowe could see differently. Heintzelman was left stranded on the other side of the Chickahominy River with the bridges having been taken out overnight by the swollen waters. Lowe sent a dispatch of utmost urgency to have the bridge repaired immediately and reserves sent to Heintzelman's aid. He then sent dispatch from Mechanicsville to Gaine's Farm calling for the immediate inflation of the large balloon *Enterprise,* which would aid him in overlooking the imminent battle.

When Lowe arrived at Gaine's Farm, *Intrepid* will still far from being inflated. In a quick work of inventive ingenuity, Lowe had the bottom of a camp kettle cut out and joined the valve ends of the *Intrepid* and the partially inflated *Constitution* hooked together, thereby transferring the gas from the latter into the former. Within 15 minutes he was in the air to oversee the battle.

Lowe fell prey to malaria during Fair Oaks and was out of commission for more than a month. On his return he found the

Balloon Corps had been stripped of horses and wagons and left out of service for Antietam. Lowe was called back into service at Sharpsburg and later responded to Gen. Burnside's army at Vicksburg. The ensuing defeat of the Union Army in what was referred to as the "Mud March" led to Gen. Joseph Hooker relieving Burnside. By this time, the Balloon Corps had been assigned to the Engineers Corps, and a newly promoted Captain Comstock cut Lowe's pay dramatically. Lowe tendered his resignation and was released from military duty in May 1863. The Balloon Corps continued to operate with Lowe's handlers, but Union generals' continuing ignoring and mistrust of ballooning resulted in balloon-intelligence not being utilized. By August, the Union Army Balloon Corps was disbanded.

Silk Dress Balloons

Due to the effectiveness of the Union Army Balloon Corps, the Confederates felt compelled to incorporate balloons as well. As coke gas was not always available in Richmond, the first balloons were made of the Montgolfier rigid style, cotton stretched over wood framing and filled with hot smoke from fires made of oil-soaked pinecones. They were piloted by Captain John R. Bryant for use at Yorktown. Though Bryant's performance was not all that bad, his handlers were poorly experienced and his balloon was left in the air spinning like a top. Another incident had one of the handlers becoming entangled in the ascending tether rope which had to be chopped loose, leaving the Captain free-flying over his own Confederate positions whose troops threatened to shoot him down.

Attempts at making gas-filled silk balloons were hampered by the South's inability to obtain any imports at all. They did fashion a balloon from dress silk (purportedly silk for making dresses, not from silk dresses themselves). The inflated spheres appeared as multi-colored orbs over Richmond and were piloted by Captain Landon Cheeves. Before the first balloon could be used it was captured during transportation on the James River by the crew of the Monitor. A second balloon did see action until summer 1863, when it was blown from its mooring and taken by Union forces only to be divided up as souvenirs for members of the Federal

Congress. As the Union Army reduced its use of balloons, so did the Confederates—much to their relief.

Zeppelins, Airships and Blimps

As powered aircraft with wings dominated military aviation during World War I, rigid dirigibles and zeppelins were used by the Germans to attack cities. After World War I, the United States Navy researched the use of airships, including their use as a base for fighter aircraft, but efforts were cancelled after losses in storms. In World War II, barrage balloons were used as obstacles against aircraft, and blimps were used as observation and radar platforms.

Before World War I

The armies of many countries evaluated the use of aircraft for observation purposes. Naval aviation was pursued as well; several tests were made in which floatplanes were launched by catapult from ships at sea, and recovered later by crane.

The U.S. Navy had been interested in naval aviation since the turn of the 20th century. In August 1910 Jacob Earl Fickel did the first experimenting with Glenn Curtiss shooting a gun from an airplane. In 1910–1911, the Navy conducted experiments which proved the practicality of carrier-based aviation. On November 14, 1910, near Hampton Roads, Virginia, civilian pilot Eugene Ely took off from a wooden platform installed on the scout cruiser *USS Birmingham* (CL-2). He landed safely on shore a few minutes later. Ely proved several months later that it was also possible to land on a ship. On January 18, 1911, he landed on a platform attached to the American cruiser *USS Pennsylvania* (ACR-4) in San Francisco harbor.

The first use of airplanes in an actual war occurred in the 1911 Italo-Turkish War with the Italian Army Air Corps bombing a Turkish camp at Ain Zara, Libya, and in the 1912 First Balkan War with the Bulgarian Air Force bombing Turkish positions at Adrianople. Airplanes were also used by the U.S. against Pancho Villa. Air reconnaissance was carried out in both wars too. The air-dropped bomb was extensively used during the First Balkan War (including in the first ever night bombing on 7 November 1912), and subsequently shared with the Imperial German Air Service during World War I.

World War I

Initially during that war both sides made use of tethered balloons and airplanes for observation purposes, both for information gathering and directing of artillery fire. A desire to prevent enemy observation led to airplane pilots attacking other airplanes and balloons, initially with small arms carried in the cockpit, but due to the technology of the time pilots couldn't have forward facing machine guns. Although the addition of deflector plates to the back of propellers by French pilot Roland Garros and designer Raymond Saulnier in the Morane-Saulnier monoplane was the first example of an aircraft able to fire through its propeller, it wasn't until the Dutch aircraft designer Anthony Fokker developed the gun synchronizer in 1915 that it became possible to aim the gun and the airplane at the same time, resulting in German *Leutnant* Kurt Wintgens scoring the first known victory for a synchronized gun-equipped fighter aircraft, on July 1, 1915.

The Allies were able to capture a Fokker *Eindecker* with a Fokker-designed *Stangensteuerung* synchronizer mechanism intact and reverse engineer it, leading to the birth of *aerial combat*, more commonly known as the dogfight. Tactics for dogfighting evolved by trial and error. The German ace Oswald Boelcke created eight essential rules of dogfighting, the *Dicta Boelcke*.

Both sides also made use of aircraft for bombing, strafing, sea reconnaissance, antisubmarine warfare, and dropping of propaganda. The German military made use of Zeppelins and, later on, bombers such as the Gotha, to drop bombs on Britain. By the end of the war airplanes had become specialized into bombers, fighters, and observation (reconnaissance) aircraft.

Between the Wars

Between 1918 and 1939 aircraft technology developed very rapidly. In 1918 most aircraft were biplanes with wooden frames, canvas skins, wire rigging and air-cooled engines. Biplanes continued to be the mainstay of air forces around the world and were used extensively in conflicts such as the Spanish Civil War. Most industrial countries also created air forces separate from the army and navy. However, by 1939 military biplanes were in the process of being replaced with metal framed monoplanes, often with stressed skins and liquid cooled engines. Top speeds had tripled; altitudes doubled; ranges and payloads of bombers increased enormously.

Some theorists, especially in Britain, considered that aircraft would become the dominant military arm in the future. They imagined that a future war would be won entirely by the destruction of the enemy's military and industrial capability from the air. The Italian general Giulio Douhet, author of *The Command of the Air*, was a seminal theorist of this school, which has been associated with Stanley Baldwin's statement that "the bomber will always get through"; that is, regardless of air defenses, sufficient raiders will survive to rain destruction on the enemy's cities. This led to what would later be called a strategy of deterrence and a "bomber gap", as nations measured air force power by number of bombers.

Others, such as General Billy Mitchell in the United States, saw the potential of air power to augment the striking power of naval surface fleets. German and British pilots had experimented with aerial bombing of ships and air-dropped torpedoes during World War I with mixed results. The vulnerability of capital ships to aircraft was demonstrated on 21 July 1921 when a squadron of bombers commanded by General Mitchell sank the ex-German battleship SMS *Ostfriesland* with aerial bombs; although the *Ostfriesland* was stationary and defenseless during the exercise, its destruction demonstrated the potency of airplanes against ships.

It was during the Banana Wars, while fighting bandits, freedom fighters and insurgents in places like Haiti, the Dominican Republic and Nicaragua, that United States Marine Corps aviators would begin to experiment with air-ground tactics making the support of their fellow Marines on the ground their primary mission. It was in Haiti that Marines began to develop the tactic of dive bombing and in Nicaraugua where they began to perfect it. While other nations and services had tried variations of this technique, Marine aviators were the first to embrace it and make it part of their tactical doctrine Germany was banned from possessing an air force by the terms of the World War I armistice. The German military continued to train its soldiers as pilots clandestinely until Hitler was ready to openly defy the ban. This was done by forming the *Deutscher Luftsportverband,* a flying enthusiast's club, and training pilots as civilians, and some German pilots were even sent to the Soviet Union for secret training; a trained air force was thus ready as soon as the word was given. This was the beginning of the *Luftwaffe*.

World War II

Military aviation came into its own during the Second World War. The increased performance, range, and payload of contemporary aircraft meant that air power could move beyond the novelty applications of World War I, becoming a central striking force for all the combatant nations. Over the course of the war, several distinct roles emerged for the application of air power.

Strategic Bombing

Strategic bombing of civilian targets from the air was first proposed by the Italian theorist General Giulio Douhet. In his book *The Command of the Air* (1921), Douhet argued future military leaders could avoid falling into bloody World War I–style trench stalemates by using aviation to strike past the enemy's forces directly at their vulnerable civilian populations. Douhet believed such strikes would cause these populations to force their governments to surrender.

Douhet's ideas were paralleled by other military theorists who emerged from World War I, including Sir Hugh Trenchard in Britain. In the interwar period, Britain and the United States became the most enthusiastic supporters of the strategic bombing theory, with each nation building specialized heavy bombers specifically for this task.

Imperial Japanese Air Service

Shôwa strategic bombing was independently conducted during the Second Sino-Japanese war and World War II by the Imperial Japanese Navy Air Service and the Imperial Japanese Army Air

Service. Bombing efforts mostly targeted large Chinese cities such as Shanghai, Wuhan and Chonging. The bombing of Nanjing and Canton, which began on 22 and 23 September 1937, called forth widespread protests culminating in a resolution by the Far Eastern Advisory Committee of the League of Nations.

There were also air raids on Philippines and northern Australia (Bombing of Darwin, 19 February 1942). The Imperial Japanese Navy Air Service used tactical bombing against enemy airfields and military positions, as at Pearl Harbor. The Imperial Japanese Army Air Service also attacked enemy ships and military installations.

Luftwaffe

In the early days of World War II, the Luftwaffe launched devastating air attacks against the besieged cities of Warsaw and Rotterdam. In the case of Warsaw, the bombings had little effect, but in the case of Rotterdam, the psychological effect of the bombings did have the intended effect—a relatively rapid ending of Dutch resistance (Buckley 129).

During the Battle of Britain, the *Luftwaffe,* frustrated in its attempts to gain air superiority in preparation for the planned invasion, turned to bombing of London and other large English cities. However, the *Luftwaffe* found these raids did not have the effect predicted by prewar airpower theorists.

ROYAL AIR FORCE

The British, started in kind-using a strategic bombing campaign in 1940 that was to last for the rest of the war. Early British bombers were all twin-engined designs and were lacking in defensive armament. Therefore, RAF Bomber Command quickly turned to a policy of night bombing, for which the crews were untrained; their inaccuracy meant they were forced to adopt area bombing and were unable to hit specific targets such as factories or power plants until later in the war when pathfinder tactics, radio location plus ground mapping radar (OBOE and H2S) and very low-level bombing such as that used by the Dambusters in Operation Chastise were developed.

Soviet Red Air Force

Although the rapid industrialization the Soviet Union experienced in the 1930s had the *potential* to enable the Voyenno-vozdushnyye sily (VVS) to be effective against the Luftwaffe, Stalin's purges left the organization intellectually and morally weakened. However, when Germany invaded in June 1941 (Operation Barbarossa), the massive size of the VVS, in both planes and people, allowed it to absorb "horrendous" casualties and still maintain capability.

Like Japan was to do in December of that year, Nazi Germany had awoken a sleeping giant which was too large to destroy despite the Wehrmacht's superior experience and the Luftwaffe's superior training. Despite the near collapse of both the Red Army and Red Air Force, Germany's 1941 assault failed to destroy either one, and as the massive resources of the Soviet Union were reorganized toward war, Germany's impending destruction become ever more apparent.

As during the *Battle of Britain*, fundamental flaws in the Luftwaffe were exposed during Germany's war with the Soviet Union. Although strategic bombing requires that the enemy's industrial war capacity be neutralized, some Soviet war factories were moved as much as 1,000 miles (1,600 km) east—far out of reach of the Luftwaffe's bombers. And even factories and VVS facilities that were in reach of the Luftwaffe had to be ignored much of the time because the Luftwaffe's resources were needed for more critical duty in supporting the German army. The Luftwaffe became overstretched, and even victorious battles damaged the overall capability of Germany's air force due to attrition.

By 1943, the Soviets had fully rebounded from the defeats of 1941, and they were able to produce considerably more airplanes than their German rivals; for example, at Kursk, the VVS had twice the number of airplanes that the Luftwaffe had. The VVS's fighter-capability rested on the Yakovlev Yak-9 and Lavochkin La-5, and its primary bombers were the Ilyushin 2 Shturmovik and Petlyakov Pe-2. Utilizing overwhelming numerical superiority, Soviet forces were able to drive the Germans out of Soviet territory and take the war to Germany.

U.S. Army Air Force

When the U.S. Eighth Air Force arrived in England in 1942, the Americans were convinced they could carry out successful daylight raids. The Eighth was equipped with B-17 Flying Fortresses and B-24 Liberators, both high-altitude four-engined designs. The new bombers also featured the strongest defensive armament yet seen-up to 13.50 caliber machine guns, depending on the version, most of them in power-operated turrets. Flying in daylight in large, close formations, U.S. doctrine held tactical formations of heavy bombers would be sufficient to gain air superiority in the absence of escort fighters. The intended raids would hit hard on chokepoints in the German war economy such as oil refineries or ball bearing factories. The U.S.A.A.F. was compelled to change its doctrine since bombers alone, no matter how heavily armed, could not achieve air superiority against single-engined fighters. Loss rates rose from five to twenty *per* cent in a series of missions between August 17 and October 14, 1943, when raids against Regensburg and Schweinfurt, penetrating beyond the range of fighter cover, resulted in the loss of 60 bombers on one mission.

Air Superiority

During the Battle of Britain, many of the best *Luftwaffe* pilots had been forced to bail out over British soil, where they were captured. As the quality of the *Luftwaffe* fighter arm decreased, the Americans introduced the long-range P-38 Lightning and P-51 Mustang escort fighters, carrying drop tanks. Newer, inexperienced German pilots—flying potentially superior aircraft, such as the Focke-Wulf Fw 190, Heinkel He 162, and the Messerschmitt Me 262—gradually became less and less effective at thinning the late-war bomber streams. Adding fighters to the daylight raids gave the bombers much-needed protection and greatly improved the impact of the strategic bombing effort.

Over time, from 1942 to 1944, the Allies' air forces became stronger and stronger while the Luftwaffe became weaker and weaker. During 1944, the Luftwaffe experienced a 78 percent reduction in its strength, and Germany's air force lost control over Germany's skies. As a result *nothing* in Germany could be securely protected—not stationary army units, nor moving army units, nor war factories, nor their workers, nor civilians in cities such as Hamburg and Dresden, nor the nation's capital—Berlin. Germans had to watch as their soldiers and civilians began to be slaughtered in the thousands by aerial bombardment—much as the Germans had done to Poland, Rotterdam, Britain, and the Soviet Union.

Effectiveness

Strategic bombing by non-atomic means did not win the war for the Allies, nor did it succeed in breaking the will to resist of the German (and Japanese) people. But in the words of the German armaments minister Albert Speer, it created "a second front in the air." Speer succeeded in increasing the output of armaments right up to mid-1944 in spite of the bombing. Still, the war against the British and American bombers demanded enormous amounts of resources: antiaircraft guns, day and night fighters, radars, searchlights, manpower, ammunition, and fuel. On the Allied side, strategic bombing diverted material resources, equipment (such as radar) aircraft, and manpower away from the Battle of the Atlantic (where even a couple of squadrons of B-24s could be priceless) and Allied armies. As a result, German army groups in Russia, Italy, and France rarely saw friendly aircraft and constantly ran short of tanks, trucks, and anti-tank weapons. The only option left was to create World War I–style slit trench defenses quite unlike the *blitzkriegs* of 1939–1941.

U.S. Bombing of Japan

The long-range Boeing B-29 was used to bomb Japan. On 15 June 1944, 47 B-29s launched from Chengdu, China, bombed the Imperial Iron and Steel Works at Yawata Japan. This was the first attack on Japanese islands since the Doolittle Raid in April 1942. The entire B-29 effort was gradually shifted to the new bases in the Marianas Islands in the Central Pacific. The first mission against Japan from bases in the Marianas was flown on 24 November 1944, with 111 B-29s sent to attack Tokyo. From that point, increasingly intense raids were launched regularly until the end of the war.

Tactics evolved from high-altitude to lower altitude attacks, largely removing most defensive guns and switching to incendiary bombs. These attacks succeeded in devastating almost all large Japanese cities. The most famous B-29 was the *Enola Gay*, which dropped the atomic bomb 'Little Boy' on Hiroshima on 6 August 1945. *Bockscar*, another B-29, dropped 'Fat Man' on Nagasaki three days later. Although the ethics of nuclear warfare remain controversial, these two actions, along with the Soviet invasion of Manchuria on 9 August 1945, brought about the Japanese surrender, and the official end of World War II.

Tactical Air Support

By contrast with the British strategists, the primary purpose of the *Luftwaffe* was to support the Army. This accounted for the presence of large numbers of dive bombers on strength and the scarcity of long-range heavy bombers. This 'flying artillery' greatly assisted in the successes of the German Army in the Battle of France (1940). Hitler determined air superiority was essential for the invasion of Britain. When this was not achieved in the Battle of Britain, the invasion was canceled, making this the first major battle whose outcome was determined primarily in the air.

The war in Russia forced the Luftwaffe to devote the majority of its resources to providing tactical air support for the beleaguered German army. In that role, the Luftwaffe used the Junkers Ju 87, Henschel Hs 123 and modified fighters—Bf 109 and FW 190. The Red Air Force was also primarily used in the tactical support role, and towards the end of the war was very effective in the support of the Red Army in its advance across Eastern Europe. An aircraft of importance to the Soviets was the *Ilyushin Il-2 Sturmovik*—appropriately called "flying artilery"; the Il-2 was able to make life very difficult for panzer crews, and the Il-2 was an important part of the Soviet victory at Kursk—one of the biggest tank battles in history.

MILITARY TRANSPORT AVIATION AND USE OF AIRBORNE TROOPS

Military transport aviation was invaluable to all sides in maintaining supply and communications of ground troops, and was used on many notable occasions such as resupply of German troops in and around Stalingrad after Operation Uranus, and employment of airborne troops. After the first trials in use of airborne troops by the Red Army displayed in the early 1930s many European nations and Japan also formed the airborne troops, and these saw extensive service on in all Theatres of the Second World War. However their effectiveness as shock troops employed to surprise enemy static troops proved to be of limited success. Most airborne troops served as light infantry by the end of the war despite attempts at massed use in the Western Theatre by US and Britain during the Operation Market Garden.

Naval Aviation

Aircraft and the aircraft carrier first became important in naval battles in World War II. Carrier based aircraft are specialized as dive bombers, torpedo bombers, and fighters, evolving from biplanes such as the Swordfish and fighters such as the F4F Wildcat which were based on biplanes to the F4U Corsair which outperformed many land based types, and the TBF Avenger which had an enclosed gun turret. Surface based aircraft such as the PBY Catalina help find submarines and surface fleets. The aircraft carrier replaces the battleship as the most powerful naval offensive weapons system as battles between fleets are fought entirely out of gun range by aircraft. The Yamato, the most powerful battleship ever built is first turned back by light escort carrier aircraft, and later sunk lacking its own air cover.

In the Doolittle Raid, the US launches normally land-based B-25 Mitchell bombers from carriers in a raid against Tokyo and other Japanese mainland targets. Small escort carriers and light carriers are built in large numbers to escort slow cargo convoys or supplement fast carriers. Aircraft for observation or light raids are also carried by battleships and cruisers, while blimps are used to search for attack submarines.

- Battle of the Atlantic, aircraft carried by low-cost escort carriers are used for antisubmarine patrol, defence, and attack
- Battle of Taranto

- Attack of Pearl Harbor First attack on US territory is carried out entirely by carrier based aircraft, destroying or sinking most US battleships, but not finding any US carriers in port.
- Sinking of *Prince of Wales* and *Repulse*, the first time a battleship underway was sunk solely by aircraft
- Battle of the Coral Sea, the first where neither fleet was in visual contact with the other and all fighting was carried out by aircraft
- Battle of Midway
- Battle of the Bismarck Sea
- Battle of the Philippine Sea
- Battle of Leyte Gulf, with the first appearance of kamikazes, perhaps the largest naval battle in history. Japan's last carriers and pilots are deliberately sacrificed as a decoy, the super battleship *Musashi* is sunk by aircraft. The Japanese Navy ceases to be an effective fighting force.
- Battle off Samar A powerful fleet led by the Japanese battleship Yamato catches the light escort carrier "Taffy" task forces within gun range. Although largely unprepared to attack armored ships, aircraft and screening "tin-can" destroyers caused enough damage, sinking or forcing the scuttling of 3 cruisers and 1 destroyer, to turn the Japanese force back.
- Operation Ten-Go The sinking of a fleet with the Yamato and nine other warships with no air cover demonstrated U.S. air supremacy in the Pacific theatre by this stage in the war and the vulnerability of surface ships without air cover to aerial attack.

Cold War

Military aviation in the post-war years was dominated by the needs of the Cold War. The post-war years saw the almost total conversion of combat aircraft to jet power, which resulted in enormous increases in speeds and altitudes of aircraft. Until the advent of the Intercontinental Ballistic Missile major powers relied on high-altitude bombers to deliver their newly-developed nuclear deterrent; each country strove to develop the technology of bombers and the high-altitude fighters that could intercept them. The concept of air superiority began to play a heavy role in aircraft designs for both the United States and the Soviet Union.

The Americans developed and made extensive use of the high-altitude observation aircraft for intelligence-gathering. The U-2, and later the SR-71 Blackbird were developed in great secrecy. The U-2 at its time was supposed to be invulnerable to defensive measures, due to its extreme altitude. It therefore came as a great shock when the Soviets downed one piloted by Gary Powers with a surface-to-air missile.

Air combat was also transformed through increased use of air-to-air guided missiles with increased sophistication in guidance and increased range. In the 70s and 80s it became clear that speed and altitude was not enough to protect a bomber against air defences. The emphasis shifted therefore to maneuverable attack aircraft that could fly 'under the radar', at altitudes of a few hundred feet.

Korean War

The Korean War was best remembered for jet combat, but was one of the last major wars where propeller-powered fighters such as the P-51 Mustang, F4U Corsair and aircraft carrier-based Hawker Sea Fury and Supermarine Seafire were used. Turbojet fighter aircraft such as F-80s, F-84 Thunderjets and F9F Panthers came to dominate the skies, overwhelming North Korea's propeller-driven Yakovlev Yak-9s and Lavochkin La-9s.

From 1950, North Koreans flew the Soviet-made MiG-15 jet fighters which introduced the near-sonic speeds of swept wings to air combat. Though an open secret during the war, the most formidable pilots today now admit that they were experienced Soviet Air Force pilots, a *casus belli* deliberately overlooked by the UN allied forces who suspected the use of Russians but were reluctant to engage in open war with the Soviet Union and the People's Republic of China.

At first, UN jet fighters, which also included Royal Australian Air Force Gloster Meteors, had some success, but straight winged jets were soon outclassed in daylight by the superior speed of the MiGs. At night, however, radar-equipped Marine Corps F3D Skynight night fighters claimed five MiG kills with no losses of their own, and no B-29s under their escort were lost to enemy fighters.

In December 1950, the U.S. Air Force rushed in their own swept-wing fighter, the F-86 Sabre. The MiG could fly higher, 50,000 vs. 42,000 feet (12,800 m), offering a distinct advantage at the start of combat. In level flight, their maximum speeds were comparable — about 660 mph (1,060 km/h). The MiG could climb better, while the Sabre could turn and dive better with an all-flying tailplane. For weapons, the MiG carried two 23 mm and one 37 mm cannon, compared to the Sabre's six.50 (12.7 mm) caliber machine guns. The American.50 caliber machine guns, while not packing the same punch, carried many more rounds and were aimed with a more accurate radar-ranging gunsight. The U.S. pilots also had the advantage of G-suits, which were used for the first time in this war.

Even after the Air Force introduced the advanced F-86, its pilots often struggled against the jets piloted by Soviet pilots, dubbed "honchos". The UN gradually gained air superiority over most of Korea that lasted until the end of the war — a decisive factor in helping the UN first advance into the north, and then resist the Chinese invasion of South Korea.

After the war, the USAF claimed 792 MiG-15s and 108 additional aircraft shot down by Sabres for the loss of 78 Sabres, a ratio in excess of 10:1, though some other studies show a gap of close to 2:1 against the best Russian pilots. Some post-war research has been able to confirm only 379 victories, although the USAF continues to maintain its official credits and the debate is possibly irreconcilable.

The Soviets claimed about 1,100 air-to-air victories and 335 combat MiG losses at that time. China's official losses were 231 planes shot down in air-to-air combat (mostly MiG-15) and 168 other losses. The number of losses of the North Korean Air Force was not revealed. It is estimated that it lost about 200 aircraft in the first stage of the war, and another 70 aircraft after Chinese intervention. Soviet claims of 650 victories over the Sabres, and China's claims of another 211 F-86s, are considered to be exaggerated by the USAF. According to a recent U.S. publication, the number of F-86s ever present in the Korean peninsula during the war totaled only 674 and the total F-86 losses from all causes were about 230.

The Korean war was the first time the helicopter was used extensively in a conflict. While helicopters such as the YR-4 were used in World War II, their use was rare, and Jeeps like the Willys MB were the main method of removing an injured soldier. In the Korean war helicopters like the H-19 partially took over in the non combat Medevac area.

AIRPOWER AND VALUES

Elaborate security measures like those imposed by Iran and Iraq have clear costs, yet these two ideologically opposed ruling elites each deemed them necessary to the regime's safety. Shifting military priorities from war-fighting effectiveness to internal stability can have debilitating effects.

As these recent examples demonstrate, state value systems may bound modern military capabilities. Rigid command and direction tend to marginalize air forces as instruments of war; each advance in capability that might compensate for inefficient organization makes a repressive state's air force more threatening to the regime it was intended to serve. The values and doctrines required to fully develop and harness the potential of modern airpower clash with those values and mechanisms of state control favoured by unpopular or repressive regimes, as the remainder of this chapter explains.

The security measures imposed on the Iraqi and Iranian air forces by their respective governments attenuated the potential of these forces to a degree that would be viewed as intolerable by the people and the military professionals sworn to protect the people in contemporary Western states. The luxury of concord in public discourse enjoyed by authoritarian regimes comes at an immense price in accurate knowledge and the feedback necessary to tune government operations. Politicized armed forces, compelled to filter and misreport information, lose effectiveness as instruments of the state. The results of manipulation continue in operation, gaining layers of effects. Natural errors may be statistically distributed and self-cancelling in open systems, but imposed biases block such self-regulation. All the armed forces of authoritarian states are clearly affected as military instruments by information distortion, restriction of dialogue, and lack of access to objective sources of feedback. These factors impede air forces disproportionately.

The losses that authoritarian regimes sustain by imposing excessive security measures on their armed forces are proportional to the military possibilities they curtail. Air forces can attack opposing navies, air forces, or armies with great immediacy and effectiveness. They can also attack national war-sustaining means and may destroy or incapacitate specific strategic functions such as internal communications or transportation. The array of airpower's immediate possibilities magnifies the opportunity costs of misapplication and accentuates the importance of air strategy.

In both Iran and Iraq, air strategies appear to have been devised by ruling elites who forbade or dismissed the advice of experienced airmen. It is impossible to say if Iran's religious authorities who oversaw air operations had any understanding of the potential of airpower, but the measures they imposed indicate ignorance of, if not hostility to, the resources at their disposal. Flying then-irreplaceable aircraft without operating IFF equipment subjected Iranian airmen to continuous attack from both Iraqi and Iranian forces.

Operating aircraft supplied with only a minimum of fuel—with no reserve for the vagaries of weather, maneuvering, enemy action, or disorientation—guaranteed needless losses of irreplaceable assets. Likewise, Baghdad's tenuous application of its air force may have stretched out the Iran-Iraq War needlessly. And the awkward locations of Iraq's air bases and Baghdad's restrictions on joint army–air force planning certainly cost soldiers their lives and metered results. Professional airmen in both nations must have understood many of these errors but lacked avenues to communicate even basic professional advice to those in authority.

The understanding required to develop and effectively employ military aviation is technical more than political. However, professional airmen tend to be cosmopolitan, exposed to Western education, and accustomed to thinking rigorously—at least about matters affecting their survival. Iranian airmen were trained in the United States until 1979, while Iraqi airmen traced their traditions to Britain's Royal Air Force and were trained in several European locations in the 1980s. Authoritarian or xenophobic governments may classify airmen as a potentially threatening group. As Richard Hallion observed, "While Saddam Hussein could rely on like-thinking unsophisticates from his home town of Tikrit to run his army, finding equally doctrinaire individuals who could also fly an airplane was a far more difficult task. (Hitler and Goering had the same problem with the Luftwaffe in the Second World War.)" Distorted information can be a death sentence on any sortie. An accurate and thorough preflight briefing arms airmen to minimize risks, affords them the ability to adapt to unforeseen circumstances, and helps them to work together when flying in formation. But to an air force as a body, debriefings are even more important. Debriefings permit organizations to accumulate knowledge, to cease making errors when they are first discerned, to acquire vicarious knowledge that can benefit the whole force, and to hone military capabilities. Debriefings also begin the process of feedback to national decision makers. Regimes that restrict constructive internal communications inadvertently sacrifice external military security.

The airman's appetite for pertinent information is specific but voracious in those particular areas of professional need; the air planner's needs are synoptic. Accurate reporting is important to any military branch; to the airman it is a *personal* priority. Information distribution is a predictable source of tension between the power elites and the airmen of centrist states. Societies ruled by tight control of information cannot tolerate individual access to information, free media, or free speech. This creates a natural tension with the survival values and information requirements of aviators.

All types of forces benefit from societies that permit free speech, free competition, and free markets, but air forces exploit these freedoms in unique ways. Unlike soldiers and sailors, aircrews possess the potential to attack any target within an immense radius each time they fly. This power is concentrated in individuals and small crews. Army forces capable of significant action consist of hundreds or thousands of individuals, none of whom can radically depart from authoritative norms. Similarly, naval vessels are crewed by large numbers, and—while a "Red October" mutiny is theoretically possible—no ship (much less a fleet) is likely to be used to displace a government. Centrally controlled regimes typically compensate for this concentration of power in individual combatants by selecting and advancing airmen based on their political reliability rather than their military competence, but this further reduces the utility of the air forces they acquire. For example, if the primary criterion for entering an air arm is red hair, those with the reddest of hair would be the top candidates, and there would be a cutoff at some degree of redness— regardless of whether hair colour indicates skill or fitness to serve. Even with such selection practices, unpopular or insecure elites cannot afford to trust that their airmen are free of infection from Western ideas.

Western air forces gain advantages stemming from information sharing, the unbiased competition of ideas, scientific objectivity in systems development and testing, and individual initiative. These advantages are likely to remain unchallenged by states that depend for their security on information control and manipulation. The progressive expectation that knowledge accumulates to the benefit of the many is similarly unlikely to benefit repressive regimes. But perhaps the most effective value differential curbing hostile use of airpower is that Western forces are assumed to serve society, not the ruling elite.

THE POLITICAL DIMENSIONS OF AERIAL WARFARE

Any attempt to study the nature of aerial warfare immediately encounters the pervasive and controlling oversight political considerations place on the conduct of aerial war. To discuss aerial warfare without addressing the extent to which political considerations affect the application of airpower in combat is to fail to understand the nature of aerial war. Airmen often lament, with equal measures of pride and shortsightedness, how decisive airpower could be in combat if they were given free rein to prosecute an aerial attack with the full measure of destructive power theoretically at their disposal. However, the utilitarian focus of their enthusiasm entirely misses the point of the larger context against which their actions play out. Simply put, airpower is potentially so destructive and dominant that its effects must be limited. Aerial warfare often becomes a political weapon, rather than a military one, when applied outside the lateral limits of the immediate ground battle. When aerial warfare is used to attack targets of an exclusively military character (like tanks or armored personnel carriers already engaged in combat against friendly ground forces), it obeys and is constrained by the same laws that govern every other purely military instrument of war on the battlefield. However, as aerial warfare is applied further and further from the immediate vicinity of the ground battle, the military effect of its influence decreases, while at the same time, the political effect of its employment becomes potentially more significant.

When opposing forces meet on the battlefield to engage in a violent confrontation for domination and survival, the logic and precedent for action at that moment is martial rather than political.* Kill or be killed. While the decision to employ the military instrument in pursuit of national objectives is a political one, once military forces become engaged in actual combat, the distant political motive for their employment becomes subordinated to the immediate violence, danger, and destruction that make up the character of war. This applies primarily to traditional examples of warfare like Gettysburg, Guadalcanal, or the tank battle at Kursk. Nonetheless, aerial warfare does not fit as neatly into this category of warfare (i.e. traditional warfare directed against strictly military targets) in the same way that it overflows the constricted geography of the traditional battlefield.

Aerial warfare generally ranges far beyond the limits of the immediate ground battle. While airpower is less constrained by the physical dimensions of the battlefield, it is fully and completely constrained by the political dimensions of the objectives underlying the conflict. Airpower advocates have long asserted that airpower's ability to range outside the limits of the traditional battlefield enables it to bring war directly to the heart of the enemy. Many airpower adherents believe that by bombing enemy cities and infrastructure and by disrupting communication with the military forces in the field, airpower provides the capability to extend the limits of the battlefield to bring force to bear on all segments of a society, not just its fielded military forces. In one sense, this assertion is true. The physical capacity of airpower to bring force on the enemy's civil population, infrastructure, and leadership targets is not the question. The questions are (1) do the stakes involved in the conflict warrant this extension of violence outside the traditional arena of the battlefield? and (2) to what extent do attacks on these kinds of targets, outside the traditional battle area, actually affect the outcome of war?

As to the question of whether the stakes involved in the conflict warrant extending violence beyond the limits of the traditional battlefield, the answer, simply put, is that sometimes the situation warrants this kind of attack and sometimes it does not. But, and this is the significant point, the decision to extend the application of violence beyond the zone of the ground battle is a political one. Consequently, Airmen should hardly be surprised if the political constraints applied in such situations fit more tightly than their destructive inclinations might prefer.

Thus, comprehending the effect of politics on the conduct and execution of aerial warfare requires an understanding of the following: The political effects of strategic attack may—and frequently do—outweigh the military effects of the attack.

The decision to extend the application of violence beyond the immediate limit of the traditional battlefield will be a political one. The political constraints placed on the application of airpower in such situations will be more restrictive than those placed on the application of airpower in more traditional warfighting situations.

How Political Effects in Aerial Warfare Outweigh Military Effects

Part of the folklore of the American military experience in the Vietnam War is that President Lyndon Johnson and Secretary of

Defence Robert McNamara selected bombing targets each week at their regular Tuesday luncheons in the west wing of the White House. Airmen often cite this example of political micromanagement of a military operation as axiomatic of the dangers inherent in politicians attempting to perform the work of generals. Yet, there is another lesson in this historical minuet that Airmen overlook. The fact that the president and the secretary of defence took the trouble to select targets in North Vietnam stemmed less from their interest in "playing general" than it did from their recognition of the political ramifications of applying force in the interior of North Vietnam. This is not to imply that we should adopt the example and methods of Johnson and McNamara as model behavior for the application of political oversight to military operations. Rather, Airmen should take this example as emblematic of the political gravity their actions potentially play in the prosecution of war.

For example, how could the actions of a single Airman possibly warrant the time and attention of the president of the United States? Soldiers and sailors rarely receive such unwanted oversight of their actions as they plan for combat. Essentially, three factors differentiate the application of aerial warfare and drive this increased political oversight. They relate to (1) the increase in relative target value, (2) the potential dual use of targets for both civilian and military purposes, and (3) the increased likelihood of civilian casualties from aerial attacks during offbattlefield strikes.

As aerial attacks range further and further from the lateral limits of the ground battlefield, the first political concern that arises relates to the potential variability of target value. On a traditional battlefield, the available targets are primarily, if not exclusively, military. If we destroy a tank, a truck, or an artillery piece on the battlefield, the effect on the enemy is strictly military. The result is that the enemy possesses one less piece of hardware with which to wage war and to threaten friendly forces. The political effect of such an attack is normally minimal, except to the extent to which such losses contribute to the overall outcome of the battle. But if we leave the immediate confines of the traditional battlefield, other targets (of potentially greater value) present themselves: palaces, factories, communication centres, supply depots, bridges, dams, radio towers, oil refineries, and cultural landmarks.* By definition, increased target value carries with it the possibility of increased political effect.

Along with the recognition that such targets contain greater political value comes the additional recognition that the political value of offbattlefield targets can be either positively or negatively charged. For example, while the political effect of striking an enemy's ministry of defence might be positive (from our perspective), the political effect of striking an enemy school or place of worship would be just the opposite. In either case, offbattlefield targets generally contain more political value (visàvis the achievement of wartime objectives) than they do military value.

There may be military targets outside the limits of the battlefield that, if struck, have a potentially similar effect on the outcome of the battle (an air defence sector operations center situated in an underground bunker miles from the battlefield would be one example). But, in general, targets outside the immediate area of the battlefield are of less military value, unless they directly contribute to the ongoing conduct of the battle. Of course, that is not to say that targets outside the immediate area of the battlefield do not potentially contain military value, but whatever military value they contain is outweighed—in most cases—by their potential political value.

The second reason the destruction of offbattlefield targets contains a potentially greater political (rather than military) effect stems from the increased likelihood that a target will have dual uses for both civilian and military needs. Examples of dualuse targets include a power plant, telephone exchange, or railway station. While the destruction of such targets might affect the enemy military's ability to fight, their destruction also affects the enemy's civil population. Whether or not such an effect is considered acceptable, or even desirable, depends on the situation. The potential dual use of offbattlefield targets increases the inherent political sensitivity attendant to their destruction.

The third and perhaps most important reason offbattlefield targets receive such a high degree of political oversight involves the increased probability of civilians in and around target areas as we progress further from the lateral limits of the traditional battlefield. This consideration remains, of course, a function of both culture and situation. While political and military leaders of the United States agonized over the prospect of shooting into crowds of civilians in Somalia in 1993, they showed less concern for greater numbers of civilians killed in the firebombing of Dresden during World War II. Generally, the greater the stakes involved in war, the less effect civilian casualties (or collateral damage) will have on the subsequent criteria for determining how, when, and what measure of force will be applied. Conversely, when the stakes involved in war are less compelling, the aims are more circumspect, and when the degree of oversight and transparency available to independent news media is more pervasive, then the degree to which civilian casualties undermine the achievement of war aims will be significant.

When these three factors occur in combination—hightarget value, dual civil and military use of the target, and the potential for high numbers of civilian casualties—the resulting convergence of political concerns may preclude the application of destructive force against the target in all but the most extreme cases. A fully operating nuclear power plant would be a good example of such a target.

Although the political value of a target may exceed its military value, this does not mean its destruction necessarily contributes any more or less to the achievement of the overall aims of war, since war is a political act conducted with military means. Instead, military planners assume that destroying such targets will have a more pronounced effect on the political end of the spectrum of war aims than it will on the military end of the spectrum. In either case, if the political and military goals appropriately complement one another, the effects should not contravene the overall aims of war. The problem is that political effects are subjective and more difficult to predict than military effects. Hence, there is an inevitable increase in the stake the politician bears in the process when the destructive effects of aerial warfare are applied beyond the lateral limits of the traditional battlefield.

FUTURE OF AEROSPACE POWER

Let me start by being the devil's advocate and making two points to this audience. One: that this seminar is about "Aerospace Power" and not "Air Force Power". The army and the navy, therefore too, have a stake in it, even though it may be a relatively small one.

History has repeatedly confirmed that air power is decisive in conflict, and there can be little doubt that "aerospace power" will certainly dominate the battlefield. However, by itself, airpower has not been able to prevail in any conflict. Look at WW II, Vietnam, Gulf Wars I and II, Afghanistan and lately in Lebanon. A major limitation of air power is that it is inherently transient; you can operate "through" the medium of air but not "from" it. Therefore, in a conflict, you cannot do without what the army calls "boots on the ground" and the navy refers to as "forward presence". We all, therefore, need to move together participatively or jointly.

While the Arab-Israeli wars and the conflicts on our own subcontinent contributed a great deal to the repository of air warfare knowledge and experience, it is the deployments of air power in the Balkans and the Persian Gulf that opened a radically new chapter in air power.

We cannot look at the world through monochromatic lenses, because each nation and each region is faced by its own set of challenges. And just as there is no single panacea for all problems, we need to define a future for aerospace power that is relevant to our conditions and environment.

Aircraft were used in offence for the very first time in 1911, when the Italians bombed the Turks in Tripoli from the air. And WW I was only three weeks old when the first aerial combat took place over France.

This war was to be the first and last major conflict of the 20th century in which infantry made horrendous sacrifices for gaining or losing a few yards of territory; the total casualties of this war, to machine gun fire, poison gas and barbed wire, exceeding those in all previous conflicts put together. Although extensively deployed, aircraft played a generally defensive and not very crucial role in the outcome of war, perhaps due to lack of doctrine and experience.

All too often in history, the conclusion of each conflict has served as a prelude to the next one, and so it was with WW I. The script of WW II was said to have been written in June 1919, in the peace Treaty of Versailles, and the inter-war years were spent by strategists working out ways to fight future wars with minimum casualties. And of course, air power offered the greatest promise in this area.

Few events in the history of air power, which can be termed as defining moments because of the momentous impact they had on the course of aerial warfare; World War I and its aftermath are:-

- The merger of the RFC and RNAS in 1918 produced the world's first force, independent of army or navy command for the conduct of air operations; the RAF.
- Naval air power became an established reality, with the first aircraft carrier being completed in 1918, thus giving impetus to a new branch of air warfare with profound implications in the years to come.
- Air power captured the imagination of military theorists like Guilio Douhet, Billy Mitchell and Hugh Trenchard, who staunchly advocated strategic bombing of the enemy heartland to shatter his morale, cripple his war fighting ability: and thus obtain early victory, with the least casualties.

Asymmetric wars involving terrorism, low intensity conflict, and insurrections are going to be far more frequent than conventional wars between nation states. A major challenge for air forces will, therefore, be to adapt some of the advanced capabilities at their disposal to sub-conventional applications

Between the Great wars there were many wars. The French, Italians and the British experimented with air power to put down insurrections in their colonies. Interestingly, as far back as 1922, the RAF was practicing a concept called "air control" in Iraq to avoid committing ground troops against the local tribes. The Spanish Civil War and the Sino-Japanese wars were the proving grounds for new flying machines as well as new aerial tactics.

All this was a useful prelude to WW II. Three different events during World War II which were to have far reaching implications with regard to employment of air power are:-

- The first one, which heralded the opening campaign of WW II, was the German concept of Blitzkrieg or lightning war. Fast moving armoured columns on the ground, supported by furious air assault by the Luftwaffe resulted in the swift conquest of half of Europe in a few months, and set the bar for future army-air cooperation.
- The second was the commencement of a new phase in 1940, of strategic bombing in the hope of breaking the enemy's will to fight and bringing the war to an early conclusion. While the bomber offensive certainly caused immense damage to life and property, and also to German morale, whether its impact was enough to shorten the war remains a hotly debated issue.
- The third was the two atomic bomb detonations over Hiroshima and Nagasaki in August 1945. Both bombs were delivered by a single B-29, and their destructive power was enough to result in instant capitulation by the Japanese. This heralded a terrifying new capability of air power, and ensured a place for the manned bomber in the armoury of nuclear powers for many decades to come.

The Vietnam War constituted a watershed for deployment of air power in the 20th century and beyond. It saw a decade and a half of slowly escalating conflict, in which huge air assets were committed and the US lost over 8500 aircraft and helicopters. Smart weapons were tried out for the first time, and tactics evolved for jet fighters, bombers and attack helicopters, which were to transform air warfare.

The defining moments that have been highlighted were significant in that they contained seminal lessons, both positive and negative, and were instrumental in the formulation of air power doctrines and strategies, and in shaping its future. Most of these lessons were learnt and internalised by practitioners of air power, but humans are imperfect; and there are probably still many mistakes, which get repeated, and many lessons that are re-learnt again and again. The army and the navy presume that air power is just an extension of their artillery, and the air force, should therefore be the handmaiden of land and maritime forces.

The Kosovo operations and the recent Israeli campaign against the Hezbollah in Lebanon, with the subsequent resignation of the Chief of Defence Staff Lt Gen Dan Halutz would possibly throw up their own lessons.

Closer home, the growth of our own air force has remained intimately linked with India's evolution as a nation state, and her slow but steady graduation from somewhat utopian ideologies in the early years after independence, to the harsh world of realpolitik today.

8

Information Technology and War

TECHNOLOGICAL EVOLUTION

New weapons development can dramatically alter the face of war. In prehistoric times, fighting occurred by usage of clubs and spears, as early as 35,000 BC. Arrows, maces, and slings were developed around 12,000 BC. Chariots, pulled by animals like the onager, ox, donkey, and later the horse, originated around 2,000 BC. The chariot was an effective weapon for speed; while one man controlled the maneuvering of the chariot, a second bowman could shoot arrows at enemy soldiers. These became crucial to the maintenance of several governments, including the New Egyptian Kingdom and the Shang dynasty.

Some of the military unit types and technologies which were developed in the ancient world are:

- Slinger
- Hoplite
- Auxiliaries
- Infantry
- Crossbowmen
- Chariots
- Cavalry.

For settled agrarian civilizations, the infantry would become the core of military action. The infantry started as opposing armed groups of soldiers underneath commanders. The Greeks used rigid, heavily-armed phalanxes, but the Romans used mobile legions that were easily maneuverable.

Cavalry would become an important tool. In the Sicilian Expedition, led by Athens in an attempt to subdue Syracuse, the well-trained Syracusan cavalry became crucial to the success of the Syracusans. Macedonian Alexander the Great effectively deployed his cavalry forces to secure victories. In later battles, like the Battle of Cannae of the Second Punic War, the importance of the cavalry would be repeated. Hannibal was able to surround the Romans on three sides and encircled them by sending the cavalry to the rear of the army. There were also horse archers, who had the ability to shoot on horseback- the Mongols were especially fearsome with this tactic. In the Middle Ages, armored cataphracts continued to fight on horseback. Even in the First World War, cavalry was still considered important; the British mobilized 165,000 horses, the Austrians 600,000, the Germans 715,000, and the Russians more than a million.

The early Indo-Iranians developed the use of chariots in warfare. The scythed chariot was later invented in India and soon adopted by the Persian Empire.

War elephants were often deployed for fighting in ancient warfare. They were first used in India and later adopted by both the Persians and Alexander the Great against one another. War elephants were also used in the Battle of the Hydaspes River, and by Hannibal in the Second Punic War against the Romans.(The effectiveness of war elephants in a battle is a matter of debate)

There were also organizational changes, made possible by better training and intercommunication. Combined arms was the concept of using infantry, cavalry, and artillery in a coordinated way. The Romans, Swiss, and others made advances with this, which arguably led to them being unbeatable for centuries.

Naval warfare was often crucial to military success. Early navies used sailing ships without cannons; often the goal was to ram the enemy ships and cause them to sink. There was human oar power, often using slaves, built up to ramming speed. Galleys were used in the 3rd millennium BC by the Cretans. The Greeks later advanced these ships.

In 1210 BC, the first recorded naval battle was fought between Suppiluliuma II, king of the Hittites, and Cyprus, which was defeated. In the Persian Wars, the navy became of increasing importance. Triremes were involved in more complicated sea-land operations. Themistocles helped to build up a stronger Greek navy, composed of 310 ships, and defeated the Persians at the Battle of Salamis, ending the Persian invasion of Greece. In the First Punic War, the war between Carthage and Rome started with an advantage to Carthage because of their naval experience. A Roman fleet was built in 261 BC, with the addition of the corvus that allowed Roman soldiers onboard the ships to board the enemy ships. The bridge would prove effective at the Battle of Mylae, resulting in a Roman victory. The Vikings, in the 8th century AD, invented a ship propelled by oars with a dragon decorating the prow, hence called the Drakkar. The 12th century CE Song Dynasty invented ships with watertight bulk head compartments while the 2nd century BCE Han Dynasty invented rudders and sculled oars for their warships.

Fortifications are important in warfare. Early hill-forts were used to protect inhabitants in the Iron Age. They were primitive forts surrounded by ditches filled with water. Forts were then built out of mud bricks, stones, wood, and other available materials. Romans used rectangular fortresses built out of wood and stone. As long as there have been fortifications, there have been contraptions to break in, dating back to the times of Romans and earlier. Siege warfare is often necessary to capture forts.

Some of the military unit types and technologies which were used in the medieval period are:

- Artillery
- Cataphract
- Condottieri
- Fyrd
- Janissary
- Knight (see also: Chivalry)

- Crossbow
- Pikeman
- Samurai
- Sipahi.

Bows and arrows were often used by combatants. Egyptians shot arrows from chariots effectively. The crossbow was developed around 500 BC in China, and was used a lot in the Middle Ages. The English/Welsh longbow from the 12th century also became important in the Middle Ages. It helped to give the English a large early advantage in the Hundred Years' War, even though the English were eventually defeated. It dominated battlefields for over a century.

In the 10th century, the invention of gunpowder led to many new weapons that were improved over time. Blackpowder was used in China since the 4th century, but it was not used as a weapon until the 11th century. Until the mid-15th century, guns were held in one hand, while the explosive charge was ignited by the other hand.

Then came the matchlock, which was used widely until around the 1720s. Leonardo da Vinci made drawings of the wheel lock which made its own sparks. Eventually, the matchlock was replaced by the flintlock. Cannons were first used in Europe in the early 14th century, and played a vital role in the Hundred Years' War. The first cannons were simply welded metal bars in the form of a cylinder, and the first cannonballs were made of stone. By 1346, at the battle of Crécy, the cannon had been used; at the Battle of Agincourt they would be used again.

At the beginning of the 16th century, the first European fire ships were used. Ships were filled with flammable materials, set on fire, and sent to enemy lines. This tactic was successfully used by Francis Drake to scatter the Spanish Armada at the Battle of Gravelines, and would later be used by the Chinese, Russians, Greeks, and several other countries in naval battles. Naval mines were invented in the 17th century, though they were not used in great numbers until the American Civil War. They were used heavily in the First World War and Second World War.

The first model of submarine was invented in 1624 by Cornelius Drebbel, which could go to depth of 15 feet (5 m). However, the first war submarine as we presently think of it was constructed in 1885 by Isaac Peral.

The Turtle was developed by David Bushnell during the American Revolution. Robert Fulton then improved the submarine design by creating the Nautilus (submarine).

The Howitzer, a type of field artillery, was developed in 17th century to fire high trajectory explosive shells at targets that could not be reached by flat trajectory projectiles.

Bayonets also became of wide usage to infantry soldiers. Bayonet is named after Bayonne, France where it was first manufactured in the 16th century. It is used often in infantry charges to fight in hand-to-hand combat. General Jean Martinet introduced the bayonet to the French army. They were used a lot in the American Civil War, and continued to be used in modern wars like the Invasion of Iraq.

Balloons were first used in warfare at the end of the 18th century. It was first introduced in Paris of 1783; the first balloon traveled over 5 miles (8 km). Previously military scouts could only see from high points on the ground, or from the mast of a ship. Now they could be high in the sky, signalling to troops on the ground. This made it much more difficult for troop movements to go unobserved.

At the end of the 18th century, iron-cased rockets were successfully used militarily in India against the British by Tipu Sultan of the Kingdom of Mysore during the Anglo-Mysore Wars. Rockets were generally inaccurate at that time, though William Hale, in 1844, was able to develop a better rocket. The new rocket no longer needed the rocket stick, and had a higher accuracy.

In the 1860s there were a series of advancements in rifles. The first repeating rifle was designed in 1860 by a company bought out by Winchester, which made new and improved versions. Springfield rifles arrived in the mid-19th century also. Machine guns arrived in the middle of the 19th century. Automatic rifles and light machine guns first arrived at the beginning of the 20th century.

Also in the 1860s came the first boats that would later be known as torpedo boats. These were first used in the American Civil War, but generally were not successful. Several Confederates used spar torpedoes, which were bombs on long poles designed to attach to boats. In the later part of the 19th century, the self-propelled torpedo was developed.

At the start of the World Wars, various nations had developed weapons that were a surprise to their adversaries, leading to a need to learn from this, and alter how to combat them. Flame throwers were first used in the first world war. The French were the first to introduce the armored car in 1902. Then in 1918, the British produced the first armored troop carrier. Many early tanks were proof of concept but impractical until further development. In World War I, the British and French held a crucial advantage due to their superiority in tanks; the Germans had only a few dozen A_7V tanks, as well as 170 captured tanks. The British and French both had over several hundred each. The French tanks included the 13 ton Schnedier-Creusot, with a 75 mm gun, and the British had the Mark IV and Mark V tanks.

On December 17, 1903, the Wright Brothers performed the first controlled, powered, heavier-than-air flight; it went 39 meters (120 ft). In 1907, the first helicopter flew, but it wasn't practical for usage. Aviation became important in World War I, in which several aces gained fame. In 1911 an aircraft took off from a warship for the first time. It was a cruiser. Take-offs were soon perfected, but deck landings on a cruiser were another matter. This led to the development of an aircraft carrier with a decent unobstructed flight deck.

Chemical warfare exploded into the public consciousness in World War I but may have been used in earlier wars without as much human attention. The Germans used gas-filled shells at the Battle of Bolimov on January 3, 1915. These were not lethal, however. In April 1915, the Germans developed a chlorine gas that was highly lethal, and used it to great effect at Second Battle of Ypres.

World War II gave rise to even more technology. The worth of the aircraft carrier was proved in the battles between the United States and Japan like the Battle of Midway. Radar was independently invented by the Allies and Axis powers. It used radio waves to detect nearby objects. Molotov cocktails were invented by the Finns in 1939, during the Winter War. The atomic bomb was developed by the Manhattan Project and launched at Hiroshima and Nagasaki in 1945, ultimately ending World War II.

During the Cold War, even though fighting did not actually occur, the superpowers- the United States and Russia- engaged in a race to develop and increase the level of technology available for military purposes. In the space race, both nations attempted to launch human beings into space to the moon. Other technological advances centered around intelligence (like the spy satellite) and missiles (ballistic missiles, cruise missiles). Nuclear submarine, invented in 1955. This meant submarines no longer had to surface as often, and could run more quietly. They evolved into becoming underwater missile platforms. Cruise missiles were invented in Nazi Germany during World War II in the form of the V-1.

MEASURING TECHNOLOGICAL PROGRESS

Many sociologists and anthropologists have created social theories dealing with social and cultural evolution. Some, like Lewis H. Morgan, Leslie White, and Gerhard Lenski, declare technological progress to be the primary factor driving the development of human civilization. Morgan's concept of three major stages of social evolution (savagery, barbarism, and civilization) can be divided by technological milestones, like fire, the bow, and pottery in the savage era, domestication of animals, agriculture, and metalworking in the barbarian era and the alphabet and writing in the civilization era.

Instead of specific inventions, White decided that the measure by which to judge the evolution of culture was energy. For White "the primary function of culture" is to "harness and control energy." White differentiates between five stages of human development: In the first, people use energy of their own muscles. In the second, they use energy of domesticated animals. In the third, they use the energy of plants (agricultural revolution). In the fourth, they learn to use the energy of natural resources: coal, oil, gas. In the fifth, they harness nuclear energy. White introduced a formula P=E*T, where E is a measure of energy consumed, and T is the measure of efficiency of technical factors utilizing the energy. In his own words, "culture evolves as the amount of energy harnessed per capita per year is increased, or as the efficiency of the instrumental means of putting the energy to work is increased". Russian astronomer, Nikolai Kardashev, extrapolated his theory creating the Kardashev scale, which categorizes the energy use of advanced civilizations.

Lenski takes a more modern approach and focuses on information. The more information and knowledge (especially allowing the shaping of natural environment) a given society has, the more advanced it is. He identifies four stages of human development, based on advances in the history of communication. In the first stage, information is passed by genes. In the second, when humans gain sentience, they can learn and pass information through by experience.

In the third, the humans start using signs and develop logic. In the fourth, they can create symbols, develop language and writing. Advancements in the technology of communication translates into advancements in the economic system and political system, distribution of wealth, social inequality and other spheres of social life. He also differentiates societies based on their level of technology, communication and economy: (1) hunters and gatherers, (2) simple agricultural, (3) advanced agricultural, (4) industrial (5) special (like fishing societies).

Finally, from the late 1970s sociologists and anthropologists like Alvin Toffler (author of Future Shock), Daniel Bell and John Naisbitt have approached the theories of post-industrial societies, arguing that the current era of industrial society is coming to an end, and services and information are becoming more important than industry and goods. Some of the more extreme visions of the post-industrial society, especially in fiction, are strikingly similar to the visions of near and post-Singularity societies.

BY PERIOD AND GEOGRAPHY

Early Technology

Agriculture preceded writing in the history of technology.

- Olduvai stone technology (Olduwan) 2.5 million years ago (scrapers; to butcher dead animals)
- Acheulean stone technology 1.6 million years ago (hand axe)
- Fire used since the Paleolithic, possibly by Homo erectus as early as 1.5 Million years ago
- Clothing possibly 100,000 years ago.
- Stone tools, used by Homo floresiensis, possibly 100,000 years ago.
- Ceramics ca. 25,000 BC
- Domestication of Animals, ca. 15,000 BC
- Bow, sling ca. 9th millennium BC
- Microliths ca. 9th millennium BC
- Copper ca. 8000 BC
- Agriculture and Plough ca. 8000 BC
- Wheel ca. 4000 BC
- Gnomon ca. 4000 BC
- Writing systems ca. 3500 BC
- Bronze ca. 3300 BC
- Salt
- Chariot ca. 2000 BC
- Iron ca. 1500 BC
- Sundial ca. 800 BC
- Glass ca. 500 BC
- Catapult ca. 400 BC
- Horseshoe ca. 300 BC
- Stirrup first few centuries AD

Stone Age

During the Stone Age, all humans had a lifestyle which involved limited use of tools and few, if any, permanent settlements. The first major technologies, then, were tied to survival, hunting, and food preparation in this environment. Fire, stone tools and weapons, and clothing were technological developments of major importance during this period. Stone Age cultures developed music, and engaged in organized warfare. A subset of Stone Age people developed ocean-worthy outrigger ship technology, leading to an eastward migration across the Malay archipelago, across the Indian ocean to Madagascar and also across the Pacific Ocean, which required knowledge of the ocean currents, weather patterns, sailing, celestial navigation, and star maps. The early Stone Age is described as Epipaleolithic or Mesolithic. The former is generally used to describe the early Stone Age in areas with limited glacial impact.

The later Stone Age, during which the rudiments of agricultural technology were developed, is called the Neolithic period. During this period, polished stone tools were made from a variety of hard rocks such as flint, jade, jadeite and greenstone, largely by working exposures as quarries, but later the valuable rocks were pursued by tunnelling underground, the first steps in mining technology. The polished axes were used for forest clearance and the establishment of crop farming, and were so effective as to remain in use when bronze and iron appeared.

Although Paleolithic cultures left no written records, the shift from nomadic life to settlement and agriculture can be inferred from a range of archaeological evidence. Such evidence includes ancient tools, cave paintings, and other prehistoric art, such as the Venus of Willendorf. Human remains also provide direct evidence, both through the examination of bones, and the study of mummies. Though concrete evidence is limited, scientists and historians have been able to form significant inferences about the lifestyle and culture of various prehistoric peoples, and the role technology played in their lives.

Copper and Bronze Age

The Stone Age developed into the Bronze Age after the Neolithic Revolution. The Neolithic Revolution involved radical changes in agricultural technology which included development of agriculture, animal domestication, and the adoption of permanent settlements. These combined factors made possible the development of metal smelting, with copper and later bronze, an alloy of tin and copper, being the materials of choice, although polished stone tools continued to be used for a considerable time owing to their abundance compared with the less common metals (especially tin).

This technological trend apparently began in the Fertile Crescent, and spread outward over time. It should be noted that these developments were not, and still are not, universal. The Three-age system does not accurately describe the technology history of groups outside of Eurasia, and does not apply at all in the case of some isolated populations, such as the Spinifex People, the Sentinelese, and various Amazonian tribes, which still make use of Stone Age technology, and have not developed agricultural or metal technology.

Iron Age

The Iron Age involved the adoption of iron smelting technology. It generally replaced bronze, and made it possible to produce tools which were stronger and cheaper to make than bronze equivalents. In many Eurasian cultures, the Iron Age was the last major step before the development of written language, though again this was not universally the case.

It was not possible to mass manufacture steel because high furnace temperatures were needed, but steel could be produced by forging bloomery iron to reduce the carbon content in a controllable way. Iron ores were much more widespread than either copper or tin. In Europe, large hill forts were built either as a refuge in time of war, or sometimes as permanent settlements. In some cases, existing forts from the Bronze Age were expanded and enlarged. The pace of land clearance using the more effective iron axes increased, providing more farmland to support the growing population.

By 1000 BC - 500 BC, the Germanic tribes had a Bronze Age civilization, while the Celts were in the Iron Age by the time of the Hallstatt culture. Their cultures collided with the military and agricultural practices of the Romans, leading those Europeans who were conquered to adopt Roman technological advances.

Ancient Civilizations

It was the growth of the ancient civilizations which produced the greatest advances in technology and engineering, advances which stimulated other societies to adopt new ways of living and governance.

The Egyptians invented and used many simple machines, such as the ramp to aid construction processes. The Indus Valley Civilization, situated in a resource-rich area, is notable for its early application of city planning and sanitation technologies. Ancient India was also at the forefront of seafaring technology - a panel found at Mohenjodaro, depicts a sailing craft. Indian construction and architecture, called 'Vaastu Shastra', suggests a thorough understanding of materials engineering, hydrology, and sanitation.

The Chinese made many first-known discoveries and developments. Major technological contributions from China include early seismological detectors, matches, paper, sliding calipers, the double-action piston pump, cast iron, the iron plough, the multi-tube seed drill, the wheelbarrow, the suspension bridge, the parachute, natural gas as fuel, the magnetic compass, the raised-relief map, the propeller, the crossbow, the South Pointing Chariot, and gun powder.

Greek and Hellenistic engineers invented many technologies and improved upon pre-existing technologies, particularly during the Hellenistic period. The Romans developed an intensive and sophisticated agriculture, expanded upon existing iron working technology, created laws providing for individual ownership, advanced stone masonry technology, advanced road-building (exceeded only in the 19th century), military engineering, civil engineering, spinning and weaving and several different machines like the Gallic reaper that helped to increase productivity in many sectors of the Roman economy.

Roman engineers were the first to build monumental arches, amphitheatres, aqueducts, public baths, true arch bridges, harbours, reservoirs and dams, vaults and domes on a very large scale across their Empire. Notable Roman inventions include the book (Codex), glass blowing and concrete. Because Rome was located on a volcanic peninsula, with sand which contained suitable crystalline grains, the concrete which the Romans formulated was especially durable. Some of their buildings have lasted 2000 years, to the present day.

The engineering skills of the Inca and the Mayans were great, even by today's standards. An example is the use of pieces weighing in upwards of one ton in their stonework placed together so that not even a blade can fit in-between the cracks. The villages used irrigation canals and drainage systems, making agriculture very efficient. While some claim that the Incas were the first inventors of hydroponics, their agricultural technology was still soil based, if advanced. Though the Maya civilization had no metallurgy or wheel technology, they developed complex writing and astrological systems, and created sculptural works in stone and flint. Like the Inca, the Maya also had command of fairly advanced agricultural and construction technology. Throughout this time period much of this construction, was made only by women, as men of the Maya civilization believed that females were responsible for the creation of new things. The main contribution of the Aztec rule was a system of communications between the conquered cities. In Mesoamerica, without draft animals for transport (nor, as a result, wheeled vehicles), the roads were designed for travel on foot, just like the Inca and Mayan civilizations.

MEDIEVAL AND MODERN TECHNOLOGIES

Medieval Europe

European technology in the Middle Ages may be best described as a symbiosis of *traditio et innovatio*. While medieval technology has been long depicted as a step backwards in the evolution of Western technology, sometimes willfully so by modern authors intent on denouncing the church as antagonistic to scientific progress, a generation of medievalists around the American historian of science Lynn White stressed from the 1940s onwards the innovative character of many medieval techniques. Genuine medieval contributions include for example mechanical clocks, spectacles and vertical windmills. Medieval ingenuity was also displayed in the invention of seemingly inconspicuous items like the watermark or the functional button. In navigation, the foundation to the subsequent age of exploration was laid by the introduction of pintle-and-gudgeon rudders, lateen sails, the dry compass the horseshoe and the astrolab.

Significant advances were also made in military technology with the development of plate armour, steel crossbows, counterweight trebuchets and cannon. Perhaps best known are the Middle Ages for their architectural heritage: While the invention of the rib vault and pointed arch gave rise to the high rising Gothic style, the ubiquitous medieval fortifications gave the era the almost proverbial title of the 'age of castles'.

Muslim Agricultural Revolution

From the 8th century, the medieval Islamic world witnessed a fundamental transformation in agriculture known as the "Muslim Agricultural Revolution", "Arab Agricultural Revolution", or "Green Revolution". Due to the global economy established by Muslim traders across the Old World during the "Afro-Asiatic age of discovery" or "Pax Islamica", this enabled the diffusion of many crops, plants and farming techniques between different parts of the Islamic world, as well as the adaptation of crops, plants and techniques from beyond the Islamic world, distributed throughout Islamic lands which normally would not be able to grow these crops. Some have referred to the diffusion of numerous crops during this period as the "Globalisation of Crops", which, along with an increased mechanization of agriculture, led to major changes in economy, population distribution, vegetation cover, agricultural production and income, population levels, urban growth, the distribution of the labour force, linked industries, cooking and diet, clothing, and numerous other aspects of life in the Islamic world.

Muslim engineers in the Islamic world were responsible for numerous innovative industrial uses of hydropower, the early industrial uses of tidal power, wind power, and petroleum, and large factory complexes (*tiraz* in Arabic). The industrial uses of watermills were in widespread use since the 8th century. A variety of industrial mills were developed in the Islamic world, including fulling mills, gristmills, hullers, paper mills, sawmills, shipmills, stamp mills, steel mills, sugar mills, tide mills, and windmills. By the 11th century, every province throughout the Islamic world had these industrial mills in operation, from al-Andalus and North Africa to the Middle East and Central Asia. Muslim engineers also developed crankshafts and water turbines.

A significant number of inventions were produced by Muslim scientists and engineers during this time, including inventors such as Abbas Ibn Firnas, Taqi al-Din, and especially al-Jazari, who is considered the "father of robotics" and "father of modern day engineering". Some of the developments from the Islamic Golden Age include the camera obscura, coffee, hang glider, hard soap, shampoo, nitric acid, alembic, valve, reciprocating, combination lock, quilting, pointed arch, surgical catgut, windmill, inoculation, fountain pen, cryptanalysis, frequency analysis, quartz glass, Persian carpet, modern cheque, celestial globe, explosive rockets and incendiary devices.

Renaissance

The era is marked by such profound technical advancements like the printing press, linear perspectivity, patent law, double shell domes or Bastion fortresses. Note books of the Renaissance artist-engineers such as Taccola and Leonardo da Vinci give a deep insight into the mechanical technology then known and applied. Architects and engineers were inspired by the structures of Ancient Rome, and men like Brunelleschi created the large dome of Florence Cathedral as a result. He was awarded one of the first patents ever issued in order to protect an ingenious crane he designed to raise the large masonry stones to the top of the structure. Military technology developed rapidly with the widespread use of the cross-bow and ever more powerful artillery, as the city-states of Italy were usually in conflict with one another. Powerful families like the Medici were strong patrons of the arts and sciences.

Age of Exploration

The sailing ship (Nau or Carrack) enabled the Age of Exploration with the European colonization of the Americas, epitomized by Francis Bacon's *The New Atlantis*. Pioneers like Vasco de Gama, Cabral, Magellan and Christopher Columbus explored the world in search of new trade routes for their goods and contacts with Africa, India and China which shortened the journey compared with traditional routes overland. They also re-discovered the Americas while doing so. They produced new maps and charts which enabled following mariners to explore further with greater confidence. Navigation was generally difficult however owing to the problem of longitude and the absence of accurate chronometers. European powers rediscovered the idea of the Civil code, lost since the time of the Ancient Greeks.

TECHNOLOGY SHAPES WARFARE

Technology shapes *warfare,* not war. War is timeless and universal. It has afflicted virtually every state known to human history. Warfare is the conduct of war. It is the clash of arms or the maneuver of armed forces in the field. It entails what military professionals call operations, whether or not the opposing forces actually unleash their organized violence on one another. War is a condition in which a state might find itself; warfare is a physical activity conducted by armed forces in the context of war. Of course, many kinds of group violence, from gang fights to terrorism, might display some or all of the characteristics of warfare without rising to this definition of war, but more often than not these violent conflicts use instruments of war. To understand the technology of warfare is to understand the technology of most public violence.

Wording is also important in articulating exactly what impact technology has on warfare. A number of verbs suggest themselves. Technology defines, governs, or circumscribes warfare. It sets the stage for warfare. It is the instrumentality of warfare.

The most important verb describing the impact of technology on warfare is that it *changes* warfare. Technology has been the primary source of military innovation throughout history. It drives changes in warfare more than any other factor. Consider a simple thought experiment. Sun Tzu and Alexander the Great are brought back to life and assigned to lead coalition forces in Afghanistan in 2008. These near contemporaries from the fourth century BCE would understand almost everything they would need to know.

Alexander actually fought in Afghanistan, and Sun Tzu (if such a person really existed) fought in comparably mountainous terrain in China. Both were masters of strategy and tactics. What came to be called the "principles of war" are simply the tacit knowledge that all successful commanders throughout history have carried around in their bank of experience: an understanding of intelligence, surprise, maneuver, command and control, concentration of force, unity of command, terrain, etc. Even Clausewitz's seminal contributions to military art and science—chance, violence, the "fog of war," and "friction"—were concepts that Alexander and Sun Tzu knew by different names.

The only modern tool of command they would not know and could not readily assimilate would be the technology of war. Airplanes, missiles, tanks, drones, satellites, computers, GPS, and all the remaining panoply of the modern high-tech battlefield would be incomprehensible to them. A sergeant from their operations staff could exploit these resources more fully and effectively than either of our great captains. Sun Tzu and Alexander would be incompetent on the modern battlefield.

The point is even more obvious in humankind's other two fields of battle—the sea and the air—to say nothing of space, perhaps the battlefield of the future. Naval warfare does not occur without ships, which, through most of human history, were the most complex of human technological artifacts. Of course the same is true of planes for air warfare, missiles for strategic warfare, and spacecraft for star wars. In each case, the vehicle defines the warfare. Horatio Nelson, perhaps the greatest naval commander of all time, would have been powerless to understand the strategy and tactics of World War II's air warfare in the Pacific or submarine warfare in the Atlantic. The cat-and-mouse contest of Soviet and American attack submarines in the Cold War would have been even more incomprehensible to him. He might have gone back in time and intuited the essence of galley warfare, but he could not command in the age of steam, let alone the nuclear age, without a solid grounding in modern science and technology.

The more modern, or postmodern, the warfare becomes, the more the generalization holds true. Technology defines warfare.

Air warfare was not even possible before the twentieth century, save for the vulnerable and inefficient reconnaissance balloons that were pioneered in Europe and America in the nineteenth century.

In the twenty-first century, air warfare ranges from strategic bombing to close air support of ground troops to dog fights for air superiority to pilotless drones that carry the eyes and ears, and sometimes the ordnance, of operators hundreds, even thousands, of miles away.

The U.S. boasts a missile defense installation that can stop the unstoppable, an intercontinental ballistic missile. Space-faring nations flirt with anti-satellite weapons launched from earth and even the prospect of space-based weapons to fight one another and threaten the earth below. Air warfare differs from naval warfare, not because the strategy and tactics of conflict in those realms differs, but because planes differ from ships. And, of course, both differ from tanks and rockets and satellites. Each technology shapes, defines, circumscribes, and governs a new kind of warfare.

Nor is it just the evolution of weaponry that changes warfare. It is the distribution of the weaponry. Throughout history, states have usually fought one another in weapons symmetry. In the first Gulf War, for example, Saddam Hussein attempted to defeat a conventional, industrialized, mechanized American army with a conventional, industrialized, mechanized Iraqi army. The quality and quantity of the American technology prevailed.

In the second Gulf War, however, the insurgents resorted to asymmetrical warfare, fighting the high-tech American arsenal with low-tech instruments of assassination, sabotage, and terror. Only when the United States adjusted its technology to meet the new threat did the enemy tactics lose their edge. Of course training, morale, numbers, will, and politics also contributed to the outcome in Iraq, but the nature of the technology set the stage for the struggle.

Technology Does Not Determine Warfare

However much technology may *change* warfare, it never *determines* warfare—neither how it will be conducted nor how it will turn out. Technology presides in warfare, but it does not rule. The whole notion of "technological determinism" is a red herring. Humans can always resist the historical forces surrounding them. To believe in determinism is to believe in inevitability. This begs the question, "Why"?

What historical force or law pushes events to some inescapable outcome? In hindsight, events may appear predetermined or inevitable, but nothing in human activity can be predicted with certainty. Think about the instances in history when technology appeared to determine the nature and even the result of warfare. Chariots were perhaps the most dominant instrument of warfare before nuclear weapons. Indeed, historian William H. McNeill has called them the superweapon of their day.

When they appeared in the Levant in the eighteenth century BCE, they swept all before them. From Egypt to Mesopotamia, states either adopted chariots or ceased to compete in interstate war. The chariot craze bred an international chariot aristocracy, the Maryannu, who sold their services to the highest bidder. States built up enormous chariots corps with attendant supply and maintenance trains, culminating in the battle of Kadesh in 1275 BCE, when the contending Egyptian and Hittite forces committed an estimated 5,000 chariots to a cataclysmic but ultimately indecisive day of battle.

Western warfare through most of the second millennium BCE was chariot warfare. The chariot defined, drove, governed, circumscribed ground warfare. And then it was gone. Within a century after the Armageddon at Kadesh, the chariot disappeared as the dominant technology of Levantine warfare. Just as there is no sure evidence of where the chariot came from and why it ruled, so is its fall from dominance a mystery.

Robert Drews notes that it lost power in "The Catastrophe," the wave of wars, raids, and forced migrations that swept the eastern Mediterranean around 1200 BCE. William McNeill believes that the introduction of iron weapons at just this time gave infantry new power to stand up to chariots. Another possible explanation is state bankruptcy brought on by the arms race in chariots and the horses to pull them. Still another is a change in infantry tactics, perhaps coupled with McNeill's iron weapons. In any case, the apparent determinism of the chariot evaporated.

Countless other examples through history of seemingly irresistible weapons leading to inevitable triumph have similarly risen and fallen in their turn, from gunpowder through the "*Dreadnought* revolution" and strategic bombing to the recent enthusiasm for the "revolution in military affairs," a technological superiority that was to have given the U.S. unassailable military prowess.

The Open Door

A better conceptual model for the technology of war is "the open door." This metaphor was introduced by medieval historian Lynn White, Jr., in his classic study *Medieval Technology and Social Change* (Oxford, 1962). Seeking to demonstrate that medieval society spawned its share of technological innovation, White presented a series of interrelated case studies. One revisited and refined the discredited claim by Heinrich Brunner that the appearance of the heavily armed and armored mounted knight on the battlefields of eighth-century Europe had bred feudalism.

Brunner had imagined that Charles Martel first conceived the scheme of a feudal array and the social, political, and economic system to sustain it at or immediately following the battle of Poitiers in 732, when his posse of mounted warriors drove off Muslim raiders spilling into southern France from the Iberian Peninsula. But White showed that Martel had begun confiscating church property for distribution to a new class of mounted warriors before the battle of Poitiers.

What, then, asked White, might have inspired Martel, if not his victory over the lightly armed and armored Muslim mounted warriors? White's answer was the stirrup, an Asian innovation just making its first appearance in Europe about the time of Poitiers. White imagined that this technology allowed the heavily armed and armored mounted knight to lean into his lance and overwhelm mounted and unmounted warriors alike with irresistible force.

White's argument was widely and roundly attacked, especially by Marxist historians. Most of his critics accused him of technological determinism, of arguing that the stirrup produced feudalism.

But White had gone out of his way to avoid any such claim. He called the stirrup a "catalyst." It did not create feudalism out of whole cloth. Rather, when it was added to the complex soup of medieval society, feudalism precipitated out.

Other societies with different ingredients and different chemistries would produce different residues. Technology does not determine outcomes, said White, it opens doors. People must decide if they want to pass through. The availability of the stirrup in Europe did not mean that Martel would adopt it to make the heavily armed and armored mounted knight the mainstay of an emergent military system. The "open door" is a powerful conceptual tool for thinking about all technology, especially military technology. It adds what most accounts of technological innovation lack: human agency. Humans must decide if they are going to, or can, take up a given military innovation.

And they must adapt it to their circumstances. Technology is a possibility, not an imperative. The varieties of technology—think, for example, of the different models of automobiles in the world—testify to the countless contexts in which people will apply the same fundamental innovation with differing results. In the years between the world wars, for example, the U.S. and Britain, geographically isolated from continental Europe, developed strategic bombers with which to project their military power, while the major continental powers concentrated on fighter aircraft to contend with each other for air superiority over the battlefields in their back yards.

What White did *not* discern was that human agency intervenes not once, but twice, at the moment of innovation. When discovering who chooses to walk through a door opened by technological innovation, it is equally important to understand who opened it for them.

People invent and innovate. People open the door. Often there is a relationship between those who open the door and those who pass through it. In modern military experience we often think of that relationship as the military-industrial complex. This byproduct of the Cold War reminds us that the door can be swinging, even revolving.

People who are anxious to pass through may hire agents to open the door for them. Likewise, those who figure out how to open doors may entice others to pass through. None of this makes the technology itself deterministic, but it can make the social system attending the door self-replicating and self-sustaining.

In time, the participants may pass into realms that they would not otherwise have chosen to enter and that do not serve their interests. The reasons for their decisions, even the bad ones, however, lie not in the technology but in the personal, political, economic—in sum, contextual—forces already at work. The catalyst precipitates the consequences dictated by the ingredients and the chemistry. This raises my fourth point.

9

Electronic and Information Warfare

SIGNALS INTELLIGENCE TECHNIQUES IN ELECTRONIC AND INFORMATION WARFARE

Before communications can be attacked, the enemy's network must be mapped. The most expensive and critical task in signals intelligence is identifying and extracting the interesting material from the cacophony of radio signals and the huge mass of traffic on systems such as the telephone network and the Internet. The technologies in use are extensive and largely classified, but some aspects are public.

In the case of radio signals, communications intelligence agencies use receiving equipment, that can recognize a huge variety of signal types, to maintain extensive databases of signals — which stations or services use which frequencies.

In many cases, it is possible to identify individual equipment by signal analysis. The components can include any unintentional frequency modulation, the shape of the transmitter turn-on transient, the precise center frequency and the final-stage amplifier harmonics.

This *RF fingerprinting*, or RFID, technology was declassified in the mid-1990s for use in identifying cloned cellular telephones, where its makers claim a 95% success rate. It is the direct descendant of the World War 2 technique of recognizing a wireless operator by his *fist* — the way he used Morse Code.

Radio Direction Finding (RDF) is also critical. In the old days, this involved triangulating the signal of interest using directional antennas at two monitoring stations. So spies might have several minutes to send a message home before having to move. Modern monitoring stations use *time difference of arrival* (TDOA) to locate a suspect signal rapidly, accurately and automatically by comparing the phase of the signals received at two sites; anything more than a second or so of transmission can be a giveaway.

Traffic analysis — looking at the number of messages by source and destination — can also give very valuable information, not just about imminent attacks (which were signalled in World War 1 by a greatly increased volume of radio messages) but also about unit movements and other more routine mat- ters. However, traffic analysis really comes into its own when sifting through traffic on public networks, where its importance (both for national intelligence and police purposes) is difficult to overstate. Until a few years ago, traffic analysis was the domain of intelligence agencies — when NSA men referred to themselves as 'hunter-gatherers', traffic analysis was much of the 'hunting'. In the last few years, however, traffic analysis has come out of the shadows and become a major subject of study.

One of the basic techniques is the *snowball search*. If you suspect Alice of espionage (or drug dealing, or whatever), you note everyone she calls, and everyone who calls her. This gives you a list of dozens of suspects. You eliminate the likes of banks and doctors, who receive calls from too many people to analyze (your *whitelist*), and repeat the procedure on each remaining number. Having done this procedure recursively several times, you have a mass of thousands of contacts — they accumulate like a snowball rolling downhill. You now sift the snowball you've collected — for example, for people already on one of your blacklists, and for telephone numbers that appear more than once. So if Bob, Camilla and Donald are Alice's contacts, with Bob and Camilla in contact with Eve and Donald and Eve in touch with Farquhar, then all of these people may be considered suspects. You now draw a *friendship tree* which gives a first approximation to Alice's network, and refine it by collating it with other intelligence sources. *Covert community detection* has become a very hot topic since 9/11, and researchers have tried all sorts of hierarchical clustering and graph partitioning methods to the problem. As of 2007, the leading algorithm is by Mark Newman ; it uses spectral methods to partition a network into its natural communities so as to maximise modularity.

But even given good mathematical tools for analysing abstract networks, reality is messier. People can have several numbers, and people share numbers.

When conspirators take active countermeasures, it gets harder still; Bob might get a call from Alice at his work number and then call Eve from a phone box. (If you're running a terrorist cell, your signals officer should get a job at a dentist's or a doctor's or some other place that's likely to be whitelisted.) Also, you will need some means of correlating telephone numbers to people. Even if you have access to the phone company's database of unlisted numbers, prepaid mobile phones can be a serious headache, as can cloned phones and hacked PBXs. Tying IP addresses to people is even harder; ISPs don't always keep the Radius logs for long. I'll discuss all these issues in more detail in later chapters; for now, I'll just remark that anonymous communications aren't new. There have been letter boxes and public phone booths for generations. But they are not a universal answer for the crook as the discipline needed to use anonymous communications properly is beyond most criminals. It's reported, for example, that the 9/11 mastermind Khalid Sheikh Mohammed was caught after he used in his mobile phone in Pakistan a prepaid SIM card that had been bought in Switzerland in the same batch as a SIM that had been used in another Al-Qaida operation.

Signals collection is not restricted to getting phone companies to give access to the content of phone calls and the itemised billing records. It also involves a wide range of specialized facilities ranging from expensive fixed installations that copy international satellite links, down to temporary tactical arrange- ments. A book by Nicky Hagar describes the main fixed collection network operated by the USA, Canada, the UK, Australia and New Zealand. Known as *Echelon,* this consists of a number of fixed collection stations that monitor international phone, fax and data traffic with computers called *dic- tionaries* which search passing traffic for interesting phone numbers, network addresses and machine-readable content; this is driven by search strings entered by intelligence analysts. One can think of this as a kind of Google for the world's phone system (though given the data volumes nowadays, content generally has to be selected in real time; not even the NSA can afford to store all the data on the Internet and the phone networks).

This fixed network is supplemented by tactical collection facilities as needed; Hagar describes, for example, the dispatch of Australian and New Zealand navy frigates to monitor domestic communications in Fiji during military coups in the 1980s. Koch and Sperber discuss U.S. and German installations in Germany in Fulghum describes airborne signals collection in ; satellites are also used to collect signals, and there are covert collection facilities too that are not known to the host country.

But despite all this huge capital investment, the most difficult and expensive part of the whole operation is traffic selection rather than collection . Thus, contrary to one's initial expectations, cryptography can make communications more vulnerable rather than less (if used incompetently, as it usually is). If you just encipher all the traffic you consider to be important, you have thereby marked it for collection by the enemy. And if your cryptosecurity were perfect, you've just helped the enemy map your network, which means he can collect all the unencrypted traffic that you share with third parties.

Now if everyone encrypted all their traffic, then hiding traffic could be much easier (hence the push by signals intelligence agencies to prevent the widespread use of cryptography, even if it's freely available to individuals). This brings us to the topic of attacks.

ATTACKS ON COMMUNICATIONS

Once you have mapped the enemy network, you may wish to attack it. People often talk in terms of 'codebreaking' but this is a gross oversimplification.

First, although some systems have been broken by pure cryptanalysis, this is fairly rare. Most production attacks have involved theft of key material, as when the State Department code book was stolen during World War 2 by the valet of the American ambassador to Rome, or errors in the manufacture and distribution of key material, as in the 'Venona' attacks on Soviet diplomatic traffic . Even where attacks based on cryptanalysis have been possible, they have often been made much easier by operational errors, an example being the attacks on the German Enigma traffic during World War 2 . The pattern continues to this day. The history of Soviet intelligence during the Cold War reveals that the USA's technological advantage was largely nullified by Soviet skills in 'using Humint in Sigint support' — which largely consisted of recruiting traitors who sold key material, such as the Walker family .

Second, access to content is often not the desired result. In tactical situations, the goal is often to detect and destroy nodes, or to jam the traffic. Jamming can involve not just noise insertion but active deception. In World War 2, the Allies used German speakers as bogus controllers to send German nightfighters confusing instructions, and there was a battle of wits as authentication tech- niques were invented and defeated. More recently, as I noted in the chapter on biometrics, the U.S. Air Force has deployed more sophisticated systems based on voice morphing. I mentioned in an earlier chapter the tension between intelligence and operational units: the former want to listen to the other side's traffic, and the latter to deny them its use . Compromises between these goals can be hard to find. It's not enough to jam the traffic you can't read as that tells the enemy what you can read!

Matters can be simplified if the opponent uses cryptography — especially if they're competent and you can't read their encrypted traffic. This removes the ops/intel tension, and you switch to RDF or the destruction of protected links as appropriate. This can involve the hard-kill approach of digging up cables or bombing telephone exchanges (both of which the Allies did during the Gulf War), the soft-kill approach of jamming, or whatever combination of the two is economic. Jamming is useful where a link is to be disrupted for a short period, but is often expensive; not only does it tie up facilities, but the jammer itself becomes a target. Cases where it is more effective than physical attack include satellite links, where the uplink can often be jammed using a tight beam from a hidden location using only a modest amount of power.

The increasing use of civilian infrastructure, and in particular the Internet, raises the question of whether systematic denial-of-service attacks might be used to jam traffic. (There were anecdotes during the Bosnian war of Serbian information warfare cells attempting to DDoS NATO web sites.) This threat is still considered real enough that many Western countries have separate intranets for government and military use.

Protection Techniques

As should be clear from the above, communications security techniques involve not just protecting the authenticity and confidentiality of the con- tent — which can be achieved in a relatively straightforward way by encryp- tion and authentication protocols — but also preventing traffic analysis, direction finding, jamming and physical destruction. Encryption can stretch to the first of these if applied at the link layer, so that all links appear to have a constant-rate pseudorandom bitstream on them at all times, regardless of whether there is any message traffic. But link layer encryption alone is not always enough, as enemy capture of a single node might put the whole network at risk.

Encryption alone cannot protect against RDF, jamming, and the destruction of links or nodes. For this, different technologies are needed. The obvious solutions are:

- redundant dedicated lines or optical fibers;
- highly directional transmission links, such as optical links using infrared lasers or microwave links using highly directional antennas and ex- tremely high frequencies;
- *low-probability-of-intercept* (LPI), *low-probability-of-position-fix* (LPPF) and anti-jam radio techniques.

The first two of these options are fairly straightforward to understand, and where they are feasible they are usually the best. Cabled networks are very hard to destroy completely, unless the enemy knows where the cables are and has physical access to cut them. Even with massive artillery bombardment, the telephone network in Stalingrad remained in use (by both sides) all through the siege.

The third option is a substantial subject in itself, which I will now describe (albeit only briefly).

A number of LPI/LPPF/antijam techniques go under the generic name of *spread spectrum* communications. They include *frequency hoppers, direct sequence spread spectrum* (DSSS) and *burst transmission*. From beginnings around World War 2, spread spectrum has spawned a substantial industry and the technology (especially DSSS) has been applied to numerous other problems, ranging from high resolution ranging (in the GPS system) through copyright marks in digital images (which I'll discuss later). I'll look at each of these three approaches in turn.

Frequency Hopping

Frequency hoppers are the simplest spread spectrum systems to understand and to implement. They do exactly as their name suggests — they hop rapidly from one frequency to another, with the sequence of frequencies deter- mined by a pseudorandom sequence known to the authorized principals.

They were invented, famously, over dinner in 1940 by actress Hedy Lamarr and screenwriter George Antheil, who devised the technique as a means of controlling torpedos without the enemy detecting them or jamming their transmissions . A frequency hopping radar was independently developed at about the same time by the Germans.

Hoppers are resistant to jamming by an opponent who doesn't know the hop sequence. If the hopping is slow and a nearby opponent has capable equipment, then an option might be *follower jamming* — observing the signal and following it around the band, typically jamming each successive frequency with a single tone. However if the hopping is fast enough, or propagation delays are exces- sive, the opponent may have to jam much of the band, which requires much more power. The ratio of the input signal's bandwidth to that of the transmitted signal is called the *process gain* of the system; thus a 100 bit/sec signal spread over 10MHz has a process gain of 107 /102 = 105 = 50dB. The *jamming margin,* which is defined as the maximum tolerable ratio of jamming power to signal power, is essentially the process gain modulo implementation and other losses (strictly speaking, process gain divided by the minimum bit energy-to- noise density ratio). The optimal jamming strategy, for an opponent who can't predict or effectively follow the hop sequence, is *partial band jamming* — to jam enough of the band to introduce an unacceptable error rate in the signal.

Frequency hopping is used in some civilian applications, such as Bluetooth, where it gives a decent level of interference robustness at low cost. On the military side of things, although hoppers can give a large jamming margin, they give little protection against direction finding. A signal analysis receiver that sweeps across the frequency band of interest will usually intercept them (and depending on the relevant bandwidths, sweep rate and dwell time, it might intercept a hopping signal several times).

Since frequency hoppers are simple to implement and give a useful level of jam-resistance, they are often used in combat networks, such as man pack radios, with hop rates of 50 – 500 per second. To disrupt these communications, the enemy will need a fast or powerful jammer, which is inconvenient for the battlefield. Fast hoppers (defined in theory as having hop rates exceed- ing the bit rate; in practice, with hop rates of 10,000 per second or more) can pass the limit of even large jammers. Hoppers are less 'LPI' than the techniques I'll describe next, as an opponent with a sweep receiver can detect the presence of a signal; and slow hoppers have some vulnerability to eavesdropping and direction finding, as an opponent with suitable wideband receiving equipment can often follow the signal.

DSSS

In direct sequence spread spectrum, we multiply the information-bearing sequence by a much higher rate pseudorandom sequence, usually generated by some kind of stream cipher. This spreads the spectrum by increasing the bandwidth.

The technique was first described by a Swiss engineer, Gustav Guanella, in a 1938 patent application , and developed extensively in the USA in the 1950s. Its first deployment in anger was in Berlin in 1959.

Like hopping, DSSS can give substantial jamming margin (the two systems have the same theoretical performance). But it can also make the signal significantly harder to intercept. The trick is to arrange things so that at the intercept location, the signal strength is so low that it is lost in the noise floor unless the opponent knows the spreading sequence with which to recover it. Of course, it's harder to do both at the same time, since an antijam signal should be high power and an LPI/LPPF signal low power; the usual tactic is to work in LPI mode until detected by the enemy (for example, when coming within radar range) and then boost transmitter power into antijam mode.

CHINESE CONCEPTS AND CAPABILITIES OF INFORMATION WARFARE

The People's Liberation Army (PLA) has been sensitive to continuous changes in geo-political and geo-strategic contexts, as well as the changing nature of warfare. It has fashioned its responses by evolving appropriate military doctrines and strategies to meet future threats and challenges. Thus, China's military doctrine has over the years undergone a transition from people's war to 'people's war under modern conditions' and thereafter from 'limited local war' to 'limited war under high tech conditions'.

The concept of limited war under high tech conditions was formulated as a response to 'Operation Desert Storm' and the lessons learnt from it, especially in the areas of information technologies and knowledge-based warfare. China's November 2004 White Paper on National Defence outlines the acceleration of a Revolution in Military Affairs (RMA) with Chinese characteristics by building an 'informationalised' force. 'Limited war under high tech conditions', which remained in force for over 10 years, has now been replaced by 'local war under informationalised conditions'' after studying the lessons of the Second Gulf War, 'Operation Enduring Freedom' in Afghanistan and 'Operation Allied Force' in Kosovo. The White Paper mentions the main objective of PLA as:

"The PLA, aiming at building an informationalised force and winning an information war, deepens its reforms, dedicates itself to innovation, improves its quality and actively pushes forward the RMA with Chinese characteristics with informationalisation at its core."

Though the term 'informationalisation' has not been clearly defined, what can be inferred is that it covers a wide ambit and includes intelligencebased weaponry besides all elements of command, control, computer, communications, intelligence, surveillance and reconnaissance (C4ISR) and traditional components of information warfare. While informationalisation is only a sub-set of the RMA, with Chinese characteristics, information warfare is a sub-set of informationalisation. But at the national and strategic levels, it transcends the military aspects and becomes an important tool for shaping perceptions and belief systems of adversaries and competitors on a higher plane. The 2004 White Paper, among other things, makes certain observations and places emphasis and focus on:

Means of information operations and automated command systems, information measures, sound organisational structures and advance weaponry and equipment, which possesses an integrated and complete array of information support and operational means. Promotion of informationalisation of missiles and equipment, and improvements in communications and reconnaissance capabilities, especially of the. Second Artillery Force.

A series of projects on military information systems have been completed and information technology elements have been incorporated into battle systems and development support to military information structure has been guaranteed.

Development of new military and operational theories and increased emphasis on training for information warfare.

Integration of military and civil resources for efficient information mobilisation mechanisms for exploiting synergies.

Importance of Information Warfare

Given the above context, one can get an insight into evolution of Chinese theories and concepts on Information Warfare (IW). As with all its military theories and strategic perspectives, Chinese traditional wisdom and strategic thought is applied to all new concepts and precepts originating from the US, Russia or elsewhere. The first wave of Chinese writings on IW appeared in the mid-1990s following the success of US information technologies in the first Gulf War of 1991. Though this war was a defining event for all militaries of the world, its impact on the PLA was greater because of the aspirations of the Chinese political and military leadership towards acquiring comprehensive national strength. The PLA was first off the block in developing theories of IW and adapting Western concepts to suit local conditions. A PLA General, writing on challenges and importance of IW, observed:

In near future, Information warfare will control the form and future of war. We recognise this developmental trend of information warfare and see it as a driving force in China's military and combat readiness. This trend will be highly critical to achieve victory in future wars.

The General further emphasised that China must use a practical combination of IW and Maoist and Marxist military thought to guide IW issues under military construction. The military must study ways of using inferior equipment to achieve victory over the enemy's superior equipment. He advocated study on how to conduct 'People's war in IW domain'. The underlying theme of Chinese concepts on IW has been emphasis on devising ways and means to attack an enemy's weaknesses and vulnerabilities, and on exploiting own strengths. The other fundamental assumption is that superior tactics can compensate for inferior technology.

PEOPLE'S WARFARE IN INFORMATION WARFARE CONTEXT

According to some Chinese military analysts, because of the increasing relevance of information technology (IT) to people's lives, individuals who take part in IW are not all soldiers and that anybody who understands computers may become a fighter. IW is inexpensive as the targeted party can be delivered a paralysing blow through the net and it may be difficult for the latter to discern where the attack originated.

Large amount of useless information can be created to block or stop the functioning of an adversary's information system. Thus, a People's War in context of IW can be carried out by hundreds of millions of people, using open-type modern information systems. Even political mobilisation for war can be achieved via the internet, by sending patriotic e-mail messages and by setting up databases for education.

This finds further support from another Chinese author, who observes that "even as ... government mobilised troops, the numbers and roles of traditional warriors will be sharply less than those of technical experts...since thousand of personal computers can be linked up to perform a common operation, to perform many tasks in in place of a large-scale military computer, an IW victory will very likely be determined by which country can mobilise the most computer experts and part-time fans... That will be a real People's War."

Preparing for people's war is a recurring theme in Chinese writing, as IW will be carried out by the PLA and society as a whole. This concept has found practical expression in turning some of the 1.5 million reserve forces into mini-IW regiments. The People's Armed Forces Department (PAFD) has reportedly organised militia/ reserve IW regiments at district levels in many provinces. For instance, in Echeng district of Hubei province, the PAFD has a network warfare battalion as well as electronic warfare, intelligence and psychological warfare battalions, and also a training base for IW activities. The PAFD has also carried out 'Informaticised People's Warfare Network Simulation Exercise'. A version of this concept was also put into practice following the bombing of the Chinese embassy in Belgrade on May 8, 1999, during 'Operation Allied Force'. The Chinese hacked a number of US political, military and diplomatic web sites, and also carried out a network battle by mobilising thousands of net users for sending emails and viruses. This caused servers to crash, paralysing a large number of web sites.

Cyber Warfare

Concerns about China's net force were heightened after the aforementioned attacks on US computer systems and after the Chinese militia carried out IW exercises, which included India, the US, Taiwan and Japan as target countries. The aim of such training was to disrupt critical infrastructure like banking, power supply and telecommunication networks in the target country as part of China's strategy of asymmetric approach to warfare. In the cyber domain, the Chinese have adopted three methods for targetting such networks; the first is the use of e-mails for planting viruses; then phishing and lastly, the introduction of 'intelligent trojans' and 'vacuum trojans'. Diverse routes of planting trojans and viruses have been used to attack critical PCs, which in turn send out files or cause Chinese Concepts and Capabilities of Information Warfare 785 malfunction. Hackers' tools are becoming more robotic and simple; for instance, a vacuum trojan will extract information from a pen drive automatically when connected to a USB port. It is also believed that the next step could be planting the targeted sites with the more difficult to detect fake data or partially fake data.

In Nanjing, the PLA has developed more than 250 trojans and similar tools. Here, it needs to be remembered that foreign companies like Network Solutions, were made to hand over 300 computer viruses by the Ministry of Public Security's lab in an effort to speed up the certification of antivirus products . Further, the Chinese Academy of Sciences, which provides suggestions about national information security policy and law, has established the State Lab for Information Security. The lab has 'National Attack Project' as one of its research programmes. Also, select professionals have been inducted into militia organisations to boost combat capabilities in future wars. Thus, China has been paying much attention to offensive strategies in cyberspace even as it concentrates on defensive IW.

DEFINITION AND GOALS OF INFORMATION WARFARE

The Chinese understanding of IW, which was initially based on western concepts, has increasingly moved towards evolving its own orientation. Chinese experts believe that IW's essence is the sum of information capabilities capable of breaking the will to resist by attacking an enemy's cognitive understanding and convictions, forcing it to give up all resistance and terminate the war. The goal is to "force enemy to regard their goal as our goal, to force the opponent to give up the will to resist and end confrontation and stop fight by attacking enemy's perceptions and belief via information energy." Xie Guang, the then Vice Minister of Science and Technology and Industry for National Defence, defined IW in December 1999 thus: "IW in military sense means overall use of various types (of) information technologies, equipment and systems, particularly his command systems, to shake determination of enemy's policy makers and at the same time, the use of all the means possible to ensure that that one's own systems are not damaged or disturbed." This definition apparently includes the aspects of IW's goals at the larger national level. A further elaboration was done by two senior PLA colonels, who described IW as consisting of five major elements and two general areas. The five elements are:

- Substantive destruction, the use of hard weapons to destroy enemy headquarters, command posts, and command and control (C2) information centres
- Electronic warfare, the use of electronic means of jamming or the use of anti-radiation [electromagnetic] weapons to attack enemy information and intelligence collection systems such as communications and radar
- Military deception, the use of operations such as tactical feints [simulated attacks] to shield or deceive enemy intelligence collection systems
- Operational secrecy, the use of all means to maintain secrecy and keep the enemy from collecting intelligence on our operations.
- Psychological warfare, the use of TV, radio, and leaflets to undermine the enemy's military morale.

The two general areas are information protection (defence) and information attack (offence). Information defence means preventing the destruction of one's own information systems, ensuring that these systems can perform their normal functions. In future wars, key information and information systems will become "combat priorities", the key targets of enemy attack. It also includes many other manifestations of IW like computer virus warfare, precision warfare and stealth warfare, all dependent in some manner on information and software programmes.

Information Operations

Information Operations (IO) are specific operations and are considered to be at the core of IW, in the same manner as IW is considered to be at the core of informationalisation. In fact, IO is a manifestation of IW on the battlefield. It can be both of the defensive and offensive types, and can be conducted at the strategic, operational, campaign and tactical levels at times of peace, wars and crises. Principles of IO have been defined by Chinese military authors to include centralised command, decentralised control (multi-level power delegation), multi-dimension inspection and testing, timely decision-making and integration of military and civil actions with focus on key links. Major General Dai Qingmin, Director of PLA's General Staff responsible for IW and IO (and also ex-Commander of PLA's IW Centre in Wuhan) observes that integrated and joint information operations give more scope and purpose to people's war. (In fact, jointness and integration is a major theme of the 2004 White Paper). He defines IO as a series of operations with an informationalised environment as the basic battlefield condition, with military information and information systems as the direct operational targets and electronic warfare (EW) and computer networks as the principal form. He has outlined various IO strategies because, as mentioned earlier, according to the traditional Chinese approach strategies can compensate for inferior equipment and technologies and, in the case of IO, it may also compensate for gaps in information or poor information about the enemy.10 Some of the IO strategies are:

- Jamming or sabotaging an enemy's information or information system.
- Sabotaging an enemy's overall information operational structure.

- Weakening an enemy's information fighting capacity.
- Dispersing enemy forces, arms and fires while concentrating own forces, arms and fire.
- Confusing or diverting an enemy and creating an excellent combat opportunity for on self.
- Diverting an enemy's reconnaissance attempt and making sufficient preparations for it.
- Giving the enemy a false impression and launching surprise information attack on him at the same time.
- Blinding or deafening an enemy with false impressions.
- Confusing an enemy or disrupting his thinking.
- Making an enemy believe that what is true is false and what is false is true.
- Causing an enemy to make a wrong judgement or take wrong action.

In the IW exercises conducted by PAFD, 10 methods of IO were practised and these can be viewed as tactics in the electronic battlefield. These are:

- Planting information mines
- Conducting information reconnaissance
- Changing network data
- Releasing information bombs
- Dumping information garbage
- Disseminating propaganda
- Applying information deception
- Releasing clone information
- Organising information defence
- Establishing network spy stations

Computer Network Operations

In Chinese writings on Information Warfare, networking has also been the focus of discussions. The recent emphasis on jointness and integration apply equally to integrating various military networks. A critique by Timothy Thomas notes that the Chinese feel it necessary to prepare for a "network people's war". Computer network warfare has been included by Dai Qing as one of the six forms of IW (i.e. operational security, military deception, psychological warfare, electronic warfare, computer network warfare and physical destruction). Though there is no evidence of a formal Chinese doctrine, Chinese theorists have coined the term "Integrated Network Electronic Warfare" (INEW) and this has also been referred to by Timothy Thomas as a half cousin, given its similarities and points of divergences to the US approach.

INEW has been described as a series of combat operations that integrate electronic warfare and computer network warfare measures to disrupt the normal operation of an enemy's battlefield systems while protecting one's own with the objective of attaining information superiority. The essence of computer network warfare (CNW) is "to disrupt layers in which information is processed, by seizing and maintaining control of network space". EW is targeted at networked information systems and informationalised weapon systems in order to increase combat effectiveness. According to Dai, INEW is necessary for system to system confrontation on the informationalised battlefield, as systems are centres of gravity. Any disruption in system will lead to a disconnect between the people and weapons. Thus, INEW lays stress on coordinating and integrating all aspects of C4ISR and weapon platforms and weapon systems to produce the desired effects at the target end. The effectiveness of weapon platforms and network systems is directly proportional to its levels of integration. As in other spheres, integration produces a combat capability greater than the sum of its parts and, this is true for information operations as well.

China's computer network operations (CNO) comprise network attacks, defence, and exploitation. According to the Pentagon's Annual Report for 2005 to the Congress on China's military power, the PLA views CNO as critical to seize the initiative and "electromagnetic dominance" early in a conflict, and as a force multiplier. This concept outlines the integrated use of electronic warfare, CNO and limited physical strikes against key C4ISR nodes to disrupt an enemy's battlefield network information systems. It is believed that the PLA has established information warfare units to develop viruses to attack enemy computer systems and networks, and tactics to protect friendly computer systems and networks. The PLA has increased the role of CNO in its military exercises. Although initial training efforts focused on increasing the PLA's proficiency in defensive measures, recent exercises have incorporated offensive operations, primarily as first strikes against enemy networks.

The main area of weakness that the Chinese espy, especially with regard to US forces, is the deployment phase. US forces are largely dependent upon computer and communication systems, both military and nonmilitary, and the particularly weak links in the logistics network systems make them susceptible to computer network attacks. Logistics network systems may be relatively easy to penetrate compared to other C4 systems though it will be more useful to penetrate command and information links. However, the priority of Chinese CNW seems to be to prevent the force from deploying at the first place and thereafter breaking the linkages between decision-makers and weapon platforms. This approach rhymes with the oft-stated Chinese strategy of attacking weaknesses and avoiding strengths of the enemy. As observed by James Mulvenon, Chinese strategists theorise that:

- Computer network attack is the most effective means for a weak adversary to fight a strong one.
- It can be used as a means to deter the enemy.

It has longer range than the conventional power projection assets, as long distance surveillance and precise powerful and long distance attacks are available to the military.

PSYCHOLOGICAL OPERATIONS AND INFORMATION WARFARE

Another important component of information Warfare with Chinese characteristics is psychological warfare. Chinese doctrine has traditionally focused more attention on the psychological dimensions of IW, including deception, though of late they have also been paying equal, if not more, attention to the technological dimensions.15 The target in psychological operations is always the people and decision-makers, so that their will and perceptions are attacked to alter their beliefs, goals and behaviour. This is aimed at both military and civil components of an adversary's populace. Psychological operations comprise of manipulation of media to support military efforts and include conventional methods of propaganda like distribution of leaflets, radio and TV broadcasts, and other means of communication. Like most of the components of IW, psychological operations are a continuum of actions in peacetime, crisis time and war time.

In August 2005, the PLA conducted a joint exercise, involving not only all its services but also troops from Russia. The exercise involved distribution of leaflets over the opponent, electronic warfare to confuse incoming missiles and adoption of electronic counter measures.

These exercises involved the use of live missiles and ammunition, and showcased precision warfare capabilities as well as the latest military equipment.16 These exercises could also be said to have had a psychological dimension for deterring Taiwan or those aiding it in its political objectives. Here, it can be argued that the Chinese appear to have taken a leaf out of the US forces' tom-tomming of the awesome power of their arsenal and military capabilities before the start of 'Operation Iraqi Freedom', which had the effect of lowering the morale of the Iraqi military. The US forces also air dropped over 31 million leaflets for propaganda purposes besides physically attacking Iraqi forces' command and control networks based on fibre optic lines and radio and computer servers.

US forces had been issued cyber-guidance as early as February 2003 for operations in Iraq. The PLA has thus been quick to absorb lessons on IW from 'Operation Iraqi Freedom'.

The Chinese also observed the power of media when CNN's broadcast of a US soldier's body being dragged through the streets of Mogadishu transformed perceptions of victory into defeat. Authors of the Chinese book titled Unrestricted Warfare reflected on the incident thus: Did CNN's broadcast of an exposed corpse of a US soldier in the streets of Mogadishu shake the determination of the Americans to act as the world's policeman, thereby altering the world's strategic situation? And should an assessment of wartime actions look at the means or the results?

PLA's IW/EW Capabilities

The 2004 White Paper shows that the Chinese military has understood that there is a large and expanding technology gap between it and modern militaries, especially that of the US. China's leaders, including President Hu Jintao, have ordered the PLA to pursue "leap ahead" technologies and "informationalised" capabilities to increase weapons' mobility, firepower and precision. This perspective applies to IW also.

The Central Military Commission's (CMC) Third or Technical Department of General Service Headquarters is responsible for strategic SIGINT and has established a number of monitoring stations to intercept signals from countries like India, Taiwan, Japan, South Korea and others. The PRC also established a Fourth Armed Forces Department in 1990 to look after offensive and defensive IW activities. It has also built "an information warfare simulation centre" for training its corps of network warriors. The centre uses high technology simulation skills and equipment to simulate information warfare and its environment. The Fourth Department has special detachments and units that manage and direct SIGINT and EW operations for the PLA at all levels and includes operations of the Air Force and the Navy.

The PRC has completed one million km of fibre optics line and communication infrastructure called "Eight Horizontal Grids and Eight Vertical Grids" supported by satellite, ground mobile receiving stations and ground to air data links.19 With technologies obtained from Western countries and by exploiting its booming commercial IT and telecommunications sector, it has improved the quality of its military programmes. The PLA has acquired and deployed a wide variety of air, sea and land-based intelligence, surveillance and reconnaissance (ISR) systems to enhance its ability to detect monitor and target military activities in Asia and West Pacific Ocean. Some of the latest programmes include electro-optics, synthetic aperture radar, over the horizon radars, and surveillance systems that can detect stealth aircraft.

EW is a key element in the PLA's 'Three Attacks and Three Defences' strategy (attack stealth aircraft, cruise missiles and helicopters; defend against precision strikes, electronic warfare, and enemy reconnaissance) to meet the requirements of 'local war under high tech conditions' which has now progressed to 'local war under informationalised conditions'. Both military and civil sectors are actively exploring IW concepts which could lead to developing a corps of network warriors to defend China's telecommunication, command and information networks while uncovering vulnerabilities of adversaries' networks.

At the national level, China has a C3I system based on fibre optic cables, satellite communications, micro-wave links, tropo-scatter communications and automated command and control systems. The PLA has both secured and non-secured telecommunications and has an army wide data communication network and integrated field operations communication system. Its WAN is capable of supporting peacetime operations within Chinese borders and limited pre-planned operations along China's periphery but is inadequate for large-scale joint operations.

The Chinese Army has a family of battlefield ELINT systems like DZ 9002 that detect, intercept, analyse and record an adversary's signal emissions. DZ 9001 has been developed both for defensive and offensive electronic counter measures (ECM). DZ 9300 is a man-packed radar reconnaissance system meant for special operations forces and rapid reaction forces. A bodyguard laser countermeasures system has also been developed to counter precision-guided munitions guided by laser emissions.21 There are also a variety of jamming systems with the ground forces.

The PLA Air Force is developing capabilities in airborne warning and control systems (AWACS), airborne early warning, and ECM aircraft and UAVs. Shaanxi Y-8 has been designed for special EW, ELINT and ECM missions. This aircraft was first observed in operation in the summer of 2004 and it is believed that some of its equipment may be from the US Navy's EP-3 ELINT aircraft that made an emergency landing in Hainan in April 2001. Another version of the Y-8 aircraft is 'Balance Beam' airborne early warning aircraft meant for tactical ISR, EW and ELINT missions. It made its maiden flight in 2001 and its finalised version Y-8 F600 flew in January 2005. The PLA Air Force is planning for 4-6 AWACS and has about 20 other dedicated ELINT aircraft like HD-5, TU-154M and HZ-6. HD-5, an older version, is being replaced by HZ-6 which has improved capabilities. UAV's configured for ELINT and EW missions are also in use. In July 2002, the PLA inducted the Israeli anti-radar hunter killer HARPY UAV.

The Chinese Navy also has over a dozen ships and several trawlers for various electronic warfare missions. Four Yuan Wang and Shiyan class ships monitor space events and are capable of collecting and monitoring missile and satellite telemetry data and communications. Chinese industry has developed three types of systems, based on Soviet-era systems, which have been further upgraded and modernised.

Space is another area where the Chinese have been making rapid advances, especially in the field of ISR and anti-satellite technologies. China considers space as a 'commanding height' and it plans to control space and win the information war after having built up an informationalised PLA. In 2003, the PLA had six dual-use dedicated satellites for military purposes. In 2004, China placed 10 satellites into orbit and has a similar schedule through 2006. It hopes to have more than 100 satellites in orbit by 2010, and launch an additional 100 satellites by 2020. In the next decade, Beijing will most likely field radar, ocean surveillance, and improved filmbased photo-reconnaissance satellites. China will eventually deploy advanced imagery, reconnaissance, and Earth resource systems with military applications. China's ZY-2 payloads have digital imagery reconnaissance capabilities and have worldwide coverage. Beijing also tested new film-based imagery satellites and small digital imagery satellites in 2003 and 2004. It is also developing its own GPS navigation system based on the Beidou series of navigational satellites. The PLA possesses anti-GPS jammers obtained from Russia, which however may not be very effective against the NAVSAT satellite system of the US.

China is also developing electronic intelligence (ELINT) and signals intelligence (SIGINT) reconnaissance satellites. These digital data systems will be able to transmit directly to ground sites, and China may be developing a system of data relay satellites to support global coverage. Furthermore, Beijing has acquired mobile data reception equipment that can support more rapid data transmission to deployed military forces and units. China is developing micro satellites for remote sensing as well as for putting into place networks of electro-optical and radar satellites. In April 2004, Beijing launched a micro satellite with a probable imagery mission. China is also conducting research to develop ground-based laser ASAT Weapons. All these capabilities will contribute to China's prowess in the field of information warfare.

Implications for India

Attaining information superiority has become one of the most important objectives to be achieved in the era of knowledge age warfare. The concept of information superiority is somewhat analogous to similar concepts of air, sea or space superiority. This is because proper use of information is as lethal as other kinds of power. Further, the concept of information superiority leads us to attainment of decision superiority. Information operations are increasingly being considered as important as sea, land and air operations. Information operations can vary from physical destruction to psychological operations to computer network defence. Wellconducted joint information operations with new RMA technologies, improved organisations and doctrine will greatly contribute to a successful and decisive outcome.

It is in this context that a Defence Information Warfare Agency (DIWA) under the Integrated Defence Staff Headquarters has been formed to coordinate efforts of the three services and certain other agencies to handle all aspects of information warfare.25 The Indian concepts of IW are generally based on Western concepts and according to the 2004 Army Doctrine, IW encompasses the elements of command and control warfare, intelligencebased warfare, electronic warfare, cyber warfare, psychological warfare and network centric warfare, military deception and secrecy as well as media support. Though the three Services have different set ups for IW activity, DIWA is the nodal and apex policy-making body to formulate joint and integrated responses to IW challenges. Therefore, an IW doctrine needs to be formulated, which it is believed, is under the process of being evolved by DIWA. However, it is at operational levels that weaknesses in our IW efforts exist.

There is a need for joint linkages and joint planning to synchronise our response to all elements of information warfare.

SURVEILLANCE AND TARGET ACQUISITION

Although some sensor systems use passive direction finding, the main methods used to detect hostile targets and guide weapons to them are sonar, radar and infrared. The first of these to be developed was sonar, which was invented and deployed in World War 1 (under the name of 'Asdic') . Except in submarine warfare, the key sensor is radar. Although radar was invented in 1904 as a maritime anti-collision device, its serious development only occurred in the 1930s and it was used by all major participants in World War 2 . The electronic attack and protection techniques developed for it tend to be better developed than, and often go over to, systems using other sensors. In the context of radar, 'electronic attack' usually means jamming (though in theory it also includes stealth technology), and 'electronic protection' refers to the techniques used to preserve at least some radar capability.

Types of Radar

A wide range of systems is in use, including search radars, fire-control radars, terrain-following radars, counter-bombardment radars and weather radars. They have a wide variety of signal characteristics. For example, radars with a low RF and a low *pulse repetition frequency* (PRF) are better for search while high frequency, high PRF devices are better for tracking. A good textbook on the technology is by Schleher.

Simple radar designs for search applications may have a rotating antenna that emits a sequence of pulses and detects echos. This was an easy way to implement radar in the days before digital electronics; the sweep in the display tube could be mechanically rotated in synch with the antenna. Fire control radars often used *conical scan*: the beam would be tracked in a circle around the target's position, and the amplitude of the returns could drive positioning servos (and weapon controls) directly. Now the beams are often generated electronically using multiple antenna elements, but tracking loops remain central. Many radars have a *range gate,* circuitry which focuses on targets within a certain range of distances from the antenna; if the radar had to track all objects between (say) zero and 100 miles, then its pulse repetition frequency would be limited by the time it takes radio waves to travel 200 miles. This would have consequences for angular resolution and tracking performance generally.

Doppler radar measures the velocity of the target by the change in frequency in the return signal. It is very important in distinguishing moving targets from *clutter*, the returns reflected from the ground. Doppler radars may have *velocity gates* that restrict attention to targets whose radial speed with respect to the antenna is within certain limits.

Jamming Techniques

Electronic attack techniques can be passive or active. The earliest countermeasure to be widely used was *chaff* — thin strips of conducting foil that are cut to a half the wavelength of the target signal and then dispersed to provide a false return. Toward the end of World War 2, allied aircraft were dropping 2000 tons of chaff a day to degrade German air defenses. Chaff can be dropped directly by the aircraft attempting to penetrate the defenses (which isn't ideal as they will then be at the apex of an elongated signal), or by support aircraft, or fired forward into a suitable pattern using rockets or shells. The main counter-countermeasure against chaff is the use of Doppler radars; as the chaff is very light it comes to rest almost at once and can be distinguished fairly easily from moving targets.

Other decoy techniques include small decoys with active repeaters that retransmit radar signals and larger decoys that simply reflect them; sometimes one vehicle (such as a helicopter) acts as a decoy for another more valuable one (such as an aircraft carrier). These principles are quite general. Weapons that home in on their targets using RDF are decoyed by special drones that emit seduction RF signals, while infrared guided missiles are diverted using flares.

The passive countermeasure in which the most money has been invested is *stealth* — reducing the *radar cross-section* (RCS) of a vehicle so that it can be detected only at very much shorter range. This means, for example, that the enemy has to place his air defense radars closer together, so he has to buy a lot more of them. Stealth includes a wide range of techniques and a proper discussion is well beyond the scope of this book. Some people think of it as 'extremely expensive black paint' but there's more to it than that; as an aircraft's RCS is typically a function of its aspect, it may have a fly-by-wire system that continually exhibits an aspect with a low RCS to identified hostile emitters.

Active countermeasures are much more diverse. Early jammers simply generated a lot of noise in the range of frequencies used by the target radar; this technique is known as *noise jamming* or *barrage jamming*. Some systems used systematic frequency patterns, such as pulse jammers, or swept jammers that traversed the frequency range of interest (also known as *squidging oscillators*). But such a signal is fairly easy to block — one trick is to use a *guard band* receiver, a receiver on a frequency adjacent to the one in use, and to blank the signal when this receiver shows a jamming signal. It should also be noted that jamming isn't restricted to one side; as well as being used by the radar's opponent, the radar itself can also send suitable spurious signals from an auxiliary antenna to mask the real signal or simply overload the defenses.

At the other end of the scale lie hard-kill techniques such as *anti-radiation missiles* (ARMs), often fired by support aircraft, which home in on the sources of hostile signals. Defenses against such weapons include the use of decoy transmitters, and blinking transmitters on and off.

In the middle lies a large toolkit of *deception jamming* techniques. Most jammers used for self-protection are deception jammers of one kind or another; barrage and ARM techniques tend to be more suited to use by support vehicles.

The usual goal with a self-protection jammer is to deny range and bearing information to attackers. The basic trick is *inverse gain jamming* or *inverse gain amplitude modulation*. This is based on the observation that the directionality of the attacker's antenna is usually not perfect; as well as the main beam it has *sidelobes* through which energy is also transmitted and received, albeit much less efficiently. The sidelobe response can be mapped by observing the transmitted signal, and a jamming signal can be generated so that the net emission is the inverse of the antenna's directional response. The effect, as far as the attacker's radar is concerned, is that the signal seems to come from everywhere; instead of a 'blip' on the radar screen you see a circle centered on your own antenna. Inverse gain jamming is very effective against the older conical-scan fire-control systems.

More generally, the technique is to retransmit the radar signal with a systematic change in delay and/or frequency. This can be non-coherent, in which case the jammer's called a *transponder*, or coherent — that is, with the right waveform — when it's a *repeater*. (It is now common to store received waveforms in *digital radio frequency memory* (DRFM) and manipulate them using signal processing chips.)

An elementary countermeasure is *burn-through*. By lowering the pulse repetition frequency, the dwell time is increased and so the return signal is stronger — at the cost of less precision. A more sophisticated countermeasure is *range gate pull-off* (RGPO). Here, the jammer transmits a number of fake pulses that are stronger than the real ones, thus capturing the receiver, and then moving them out of phase so that the target is no longer in the receiver's range gate. Similarly, with Doppler radars the basic trick is *velocity gate pull-off* (VGPO). With older radars, successful RGPO would cause the radar to break lock and the target to disappear from the screen. Modern radars can reacquire lock very quickly, and so RGPO must either be performed repeatedly or combined with another technique — commonly, with inverse gain jamming to break angle tracking at the same time.

An elementary counter-countermeasure is to jitter the pulse repetition frequency. Each outgoing pulse is either delayed or not depending on a *lag sequence* generated by a stream cipher or random number generator. This means that the jammer cannot anticipate when the next pulse will arrive and has to follow it. Such *follower jamming* can only make false targets that appear to be further away. So the counter-counter-countermeasure, or (counter)3 - measure, is for the radar to have a *leading edge tracker*, which responds only to the first return pulse; and the (counter)4 -measures can include jamming at such a high power that the receiver's automatic gain control circuit is captured. An alternative is *cover jamming* in which the jamming pulse is long enough to cover the maximum jitter period.

The next twist of the screw may involve tactics. Chaff is often used to force a radar into Doppler mode, which makes PRF jitter difficult (as continuous wave- forms are better than pulsed for Doppler), while leading edge trackers may be combined with frequency agility and smart signal processing. For example, true target returns fluctuate, and have realistic accelerations, while simple transponders and repeaters give out a more or less steady signal. Of course, it's always possible for designers to be too clever; the Mig-29 could decelerate more rapidly in level flight by a rapid pull-up than some radar designers had anticipated, so pilots could use this manoeuvre to break radar lock. And now of course, CPUs are powerful enough to manufacture realistic false returns.

10

Defensive Information Warfare

The revolution in military affairs has elevated the role of information in military operations to center stage. Information is now a primary instrument in national power. In response to the challenges posed by the increasing power of information and information systems, Information Warfare is emerging as a major new area of conflict. The first official directive on information warfare is Department of Defense Directive TS3600. "Information Warfare," 21 December 1992. This document provided a definition, but Information Warfare stakeholders are still hotly debating its meaning and scope. One working definition provided by the Office of the Assistant Secretary of Defense (C3I) is "actions taken to achieve information superiority by affecting adversary information, information-based processes, information systems and computer-based networks while defending oneís own information, information-based processes, information systems and computer-based networks.." Dr. Frederick Cohen, SAIC, provided another more general, and perhaps more powerful, definition of information warfare. Beginning with dictionary definitions of information and warfare he defines Information Warfare as ìthe role of symbolic representations in conflict between opposing forces.

The purpose of this chapter is to frame defensive information warfare in terms of protecting data quality. It will be shown that information warriors are handicapped by the imprecision of current terminology to specify expected and desired defensive states and that data quality concepts can provide for more precise attack assessment and security targeting. An information warrior system architecture for providing this capability is described.

OPERATIONAL NEED

One warfare goal is to decrease the enemy's ability to wage war. Successfully bombing a runway will immediately reduce the enemyís short term ability to get planes in the sky. Bombing the water supply to a base will not affect its immediate capabilities, but is likely to reduce the staying power of its forces. If such attacks cannot be prevented by defensive measures, they must be quickly detected, and recovery measures initiated as quickly as possible.

The defense of information systems requires similar measures, but providing them is often much more complex. Information systems tend to have more layers of abstraction and more interdependencies between nodes. Some attacks are easily detected and their implications readily understood. However, many types of attacks are very difficult to detect until the consequences are noted from effects that have rippled through the information network to another component or location. Even when an attack is detected, it is often difficult to track it to its source. Additionally, it can be very difficult to understand all the implications of such an attack.

Just as bombing attacks on physical assets have an impact and blast zone, information attacks can also be thought of as having an initial information impact and corresponding secondary information effects. A method is needed for rapidly assessing the implications of an information attack. In this paper we discuss a framework and system for automatically performing this analysis.

Background

The National Institute of Standards and Technology (NIST) and the Organization for Economic Co-operation and Development (OECD), among others, provides assistance in securing computer-based resources. A NIST handbook and OECD guidelines provide a broad overview of computer security and the selection of appropriate security controls. Common threats include: errors and omissions, fraud and theft, employee sabotage, loss of physical and infrastructure support, malicious hackers, industrial espionage, malicious code, and foreign government espionage. This paper deals with the impact of those threats that alter data and thus data quality attributes.

One set of technical tools are those that can identify system vulnerabilities. Many are available on the internet. One highly publicized tool is SATAN, Security Administrator Tool for Analyzing Networks.

Another set of tools tests for intrusions and misuse. (Misuse refers to actions by people who have access to a system for specific tasks, but are performing functions or accessing data which exceed their authority.) Currently most intrusions and misuse are identified by smart security administrators who use audit data to identify anomalies in system and user behavior patterns. Tools are available to assist in analyzing the audit data by incorporating security rules and checking for violations and by checking for changes in behavioral trends. An example of one commercial tool to assist in these analyses is Computer Misuse Detection System (CMDS) by SAIC. Such tools identify the specific behavior, e.g. requesting root access, but do not attempt to predict the consequences of a successful break-in.

In practice, most of these tools and techniques are useful for supporting off-line risk analysis, designing security systems and procedures, and identifying computer misuse. However, none attempts to address the effects of information attacks on information quality and the potential for widely distributed consequences.

Defensive information warfare, framed as data quality states and changes to data quality clarify security attributes that currently are ignored or ambiguous. Typically security guidance specifies that the goal of information protection is to maintain availability, integrity, and confidentiality.

- Availability, meaning accessible for use, is also an important data quality attribute. The attack on availability is denial of services. Even short eclipse of service can reduce the effectiveness of communications, weapon systems, and command and control.

- ntegrity is a security term for an information system that has not been tampered with, i.e. corrupted. Corruption causes information systems to make decisions they were not originally designed to make. Current automated information systems have little or no integrity protection and thus are susceptible to viruses, Trojan horses, errors etc. To say a system is corrupted leads to the next, more interesting question: What is the alteration?-- Is the data accuracy reduced? Is the data precision reduced? Is the data timeliness reduced? These are data qualities of interest to information warfare.
- Confidentiality is ability to make information available only to those expressly given access and out of sight of all others. Leakage, unfortunately, is a common phenomena. Confidentiality is the inverse of availability. Confidentiality reducing availability of our information to our enemies. The data quality attribute of availability will capture the meaning of leakage or confidentiality.

Organization of Paper

To explain the unique contribution of data quality concepts, a Scud missile attack during Desert Storm is used as the military operational context. Key Scud missile-related events are presented in the Scenario section of this paper. Then data quality concepts are defined, their relationships specified and propagation rules developed. An architecture is then described for a system to support the information warrior in analyzing information attacks in terms of changes in data quality attributes. A summary of the contribution of a data quality framework applied to defensive information warfare concludes the paper.

Scenario

Desert Storm often proved that the image becomes the reality. The war on CNN was televised in real-time. Thus the narrow focus and random selection of the unfiltered, real-time images distorted the true scope and nature of events. What was really known about the enemyís relative strengths and weaknesses was often erroneously-shaped by television.

A murderous dictator of a fifth-rate country is put on the same plane as the democratically elected President of the most powerful nation on Earth. The perception of invincibility was so strong however, that many well-informed Americans really believed that the ìelite republican guardsî would make the US forces ìswim in a river of bloodî in the ìMother of All Battles.

Saddam Hussein attacked our sense of vulnerability by using it to send a message of terror to the Israeli people via Scud missile attacks and threats of gas warfare to the US press. On day two of the war, as Israel came under Scud attack, CNN went live to its Jerusalem Bureau showing the bedlam of newsmen who believed they were being gassed, trying to don gas masks, earpieces and microphones simultaneously, while the camera bucked and panned wildly. They were completely wrong about the gas attack, but the perception scared the watching public.

Israeli officials responded to the Scud attacks with threats of military retaliation. Pressure from the Israeli government and from graphic imagery of Scud missiles hurtling toward Israeli population centers can be viewed as information attacks on the US. The US government controls this information attack with information controls. One shaping event was of a Scud being intercepted by Patriots over Israel at night. More important militarily was the shelling of Khafji, but reality was skewed because there was more action, drama and suspense in the Scud tape.

First attempts at countering Scuds were to try to knock them out of the air with a Patriot missile after Iraq fired them. The Patriot missile guidance radar increased the availability of launched missile data. Then direct linkage of the radar to the missiles increased the timeliness with which the data reached the missile guidance. And a local radar aboard the Patriot missile increased the precision of target location data.

Attempts were also made to visually find and destroy Scud launchers on the ground. Saddam decreased the availability of Scud visual location data by hiding his missiles and moving them only at night. He would move them frequently to decrease the timeliness of Scud location data to the US forces. The US response was to use F-16ís equipped with radar and infrared sensors provided availability of radar and infrared imagery of the missiles even in the dark. Saddam decreased the accuracy of this data by deploying a host of decoys with similar radar and IR signatures.

Scud ìeyes and earsî were attacked by eliminating scud radar, relays and telecommunication links. Scud ìbrainsî were attacked when the US used Saddamís centralized command and control against him by cutting communication links between himself and his troops, leaving the Scud operators to plan alone.

Concepts

To fight a war of information, it is useful to conceptualize the assets being protected are data units and their associated data qualities.

Vulnerabilities

Vulnerabilities are specific events which can potentially result in a change in the quality of a unit of data. A system may be vulnerable to events initiated by attackers, accidents, improper use by legitimate users, system failures, etc. As will be shown later, a particular vulnerability can imply other vulnerabilities. In the Desert Storm example cited above, the US was vulnerable to Saddamís propaganda because he had unfiltered access to US news cameras which could rapidly spread his messages and to US reporters who had much to gain by presenting sensational footage of the war.

Vulnerability Propagation

Vulnerabilities which are known to apply to particular data units can automatically be deduced to apply to other units - depending on their interrelations. For example:

- If a data unit is vulnerable to availability increase to the enemy, then each unit of which it is an copy is also vulnerable.
- If a data unit is vulnerable to availability increase to the enemy, then each unit which is a copy of it is also vulnerable.

- If the credibility of a data unit is increased, then each data unit which it is an aggregation of may also be vulnerable.
- If a data unit is vulnerable to a decrease in timeliness, then every unit which is a future function of it is also vulnerable.
- f a data unit is vulnerable to a decrease in accuracy, then each data unit which is a future function of it is also vulnerable.

EXPOSURE PROPAGATION

In the example, both Saddam and the US exploited the existing vulnerabilities and the vulnerabilities which followed from the relations of the data units to one another. The resulting exposures worked first in favor of Saddam by increasing the availability and credibility of his message, then in favor of the US by decreasing the credibility of Saddam's message.

Some characteristic exposure propagation are listed below:

- An exposure occurs if there is an attack on a vulnerability, but no control.
- An exposure can cause further attacks.
- An exposure can degrade the effectiveness of a control.
- An exposure can cause further vulnerabilities.

Perhaps the most basic of these is that an exposure occurs given an attack on a vulnerability with no control. For our system this allows successful attacks to be distinguished from unsuccessful attempts. Also of interest, an exposure can cause further attacks. Consider, for example the increased availability to the enemy of a page of data when he exploits the vulnerability of data left in the trash by conducting a "dumpster diving" attack. This "attack" on the page of data is also an attack on all the units of data on the page of which it is an aggregation.

The basic premise of considering each of the propagation rules is that together they can flesh out the implications of attacks on a given information flow. It is important to note that different data qualities propagate differently through a data flow. Each must be considered separately.

System Architecture

The system is structured as shown in Figure 4. The processing center of the system is an inference engine with complementary fact and rule bases.

The fact base stores information about system hardware, software and data interdependencies as well as vulnerabilities of these assets. At run time, the fact base can receive updates to the basic structure of the system as well as updates concerning newly discovered or published vulnerabilities (as are typically published by CERT). These updates can be entered manually by users observing the situation, or automatically from system interrogators such as COPS or SATAN. Furthermore, knowledge concerning observed or detected attacks to the system infrastructure can also be entered as facts.

The rule base stores knowledge concerning the propagation of effects of changes in system structure, vulnerabilities, attacks or exposures throughout the rest of the system. A basic structure of the rule base as it affects the facts is shown in Figure 5. The fact types are shown with curved edges and the rule types are shown as rectangles. For example, at the center of the diagram is a type of "exposure" rule.

The diagram shows that an exposure results when an attack occurs on a vulnerability without a control. Under such conditions, an exposure rule actually generates a new exposure fact. The diagram also shows a rule "vulnerability" with a two way arrow to a class of fact vulnerabilities. This is to say that there are "vulnerability rules" that generate vulnerability facts. These rules are, in turn, dependent on vulnerability facts. For example, consider that a given frequency and modulation scheme are known to be vulnerable to jamming. There is a vulnerability rule which says that if a physical communication method can be jammed, then the message units which traverses the medium can be jammed. Consider further that a given message unit contains sub-units - as a file folder that contains many files. In this case, if a message folder is jammed, then all the data units which it contains are jammed. These examples demonstrate rules which can propagate the existence of a given vulnerability to others.

Given the rules and facts the inference engine deduces the logical conclusions and implications of new vulnerabilities, attacks and exposures. These implications are communicated to the user via the user interface, and potentially to automated attack response systems. Users can also enter hypothetical situations - a "what if" capability - and check to see what the ultimate effects might be.

NATIONAL SECURITY AND DEFENSIVE INFORMATION WARFARE

In 1990, President Bush issued National Security Directive 42, portions of which were declassified on April 1, 1992. This directive recognized the vulnerability to national telecommunications and information processing systems. The directive calls them "highly susceptible to interception, unauthorized access, and related forms of technical exploitation as well as other dimensions of the foreign intelligence threat." The directive also notes that "the technology to exploit these electronic systems is widespread and is used extensively by foreign nations and can be employed, as well, by terrorists groups and criminal elements." On June 5, 1996 the U.S. Senate Government Affairs Committee Permanent Committee on Investigations released the Minority Staff Report, Security in Cyberspace, that called for swift attention to the defense of our National Information Infrastructure (NII). On June 25, 1996, former Director of Central Intelligence (DCI) John Deutch testified before this committee warning that the country will face some "very large and uncomfortable" incidents at the hands of foreign computer terrorists. Deutch testified that these information attacks could not only "disrupt our daily lives, but also seriously jeopardize our national or economic security." Deutch also noted that "virtually any 'bad actor' can acquire the hardware and software needed to attack some of our critical information-based infrastructures."

The government has clearly recognized the national security threat involved with information warfare and the NII. Articles and papers abound laced with the fear of a "digital Pearl Harbor," a phrase coined by Winn Schwartau in his 1991 testimony before Congress. But, what has been proposed to protect us against a digital Pearl Harbor and what has the government done in attempting to accomplish this task? And, perhaps most importantly what remains to be done?

The Day After in Cyberspace, RAND Corporation

RAND Corporation calls for cooperation between the U.S. government and the computer industry to develop security standards that would make networked civilian computers more secure. They also call for the creation of a national clearinghouse, similar to the Center for Disease Control (CDC), that would collect and assess information on disparate cyberspace security incidents. RAND would like to see an institution created for the testing and evaluation of security provisions of infrastructure software and systems. Finally, they call for a study of the ability to sterilize data passing through the NII, in such a manner that the NSA could assist in the monitoring and tracking of perpetrators without collecting intelligence on U.S. citizens.

Security in Cyberspace, Senate Permanent Subcommittee on Investigation

This Senate report calls for the creation of a national policy that clarifies the roles and missions of agencies concerned with the NII. The report also claims that robust encryption must become part of the NII security process, thus the debate concerning cryptography must be addressed and settled. The report also calls for the creation of a National Information Infrastructure Threat Center with representatives from law enforcement, the intelligence community, the defense community, and a liaison from the private sector. This center would also serve as a clearinghouse for intrusion reports. According to the subcommittee, the DCI should complete an NII threat estimate, with an unclassified version to be disseminated among private industry. Finally the government should create an agency to perform regular vulnerability assessments of the NII.

Martin Libicki, Information Warfare Expert (Author of What is Information Warfare? Currently at the National Defense University) Libicki wants the government to determine how vulnerable the NII actually is. He wants the funding of research and development on enhanced security practices and their timely dissemination. He believes the U.S. government should work toward an international consensus on what constitute bad behavior on the part of a state and what appropriate reprisals might be. He stresses that the government should not waste much more effort on traditional intelligence for information warfare. It takes very little to be a hacker, mostly intelligence and motive, two things that are not visible. A skilled hacker can use a home computer system to infiltrate many systems.

Government Action

In 1990, President Bush issued National Security Directive 42, recognizing the vulnerabilities of telecommunications and information processing systems. In 1993, President Clinton issued Executive Order #12864. This established the Information Infrastructure Task Force (IITF), the body was to address "national security, emergency preparedness, system security, and network protection implications" concerning the NII among other things. In 1995, a secret report was drafted by the Security Policy Board, an interagency body established by President Clinton with former DCI John Deutch as its chairman. The report concluded that at least 30 countries are actively working on information warfare programs. In 1996, the NSA formed the Information Warfare Technology Center with a charter to serve domestic and military security. President Clinton also issued Executive Order #13010 which established a commission to conduct a risk assessment of and recommend ways to mitigate unacceptable risks to eight critical infrastructure elements. While the Commission conducts its study, the FBI will manage an interagency task force to coordinate, as needed, existing Federal agency responsibilities to respond to an incident involving the infrastructure elements. Congress passed the National Information Infrastructure Protection Act of 1996 which revises Federal criminal code provisions regarding fraud and related activity in connection with computers.

The federal government has responded well to this Post-Cold War era national security threat, including the IC (namely, the CIA who assisted in collecting intelligence that documented 30 foreign information warfare programs and the NSA who is operating the new Information Warfare Technology Center). But there are still serious improvements that can and must be made in order to keep this Post-Cold War threat at bay.

Recommendations and Discussion

Due to our nation's dependence on the NII and it's demonstrated vulnerability, we must implement a five part strategy, in addition to what's already been done, to prepare properly for an information warfare attack.

Make Private Sector Adequately Responsible. The private sector must bear the majority of the burden for its own protection. Remember, information warfare is the application of a destructive force on a large scale against the nation's critical infrastructures. The private sector must protect itself against targeted hacker attacks. Consider it in this manner. If a family left its doors and windows open and found all of their valuables stolen, they would not contact the DoD. They would start locking their doors and windows. However, if the country was invaded and the invading forces looted their home, they would be justified in contacting the DoD. The same applies for networked computers. The private sector cannot leave their systems vulnerable to targeted crime and expect the DoD to protect them. The private sector needs to begin locking their windows and doors. However, in the information and economic age knowledge is precious. Economic espionage, theft of information, etc. can pose serious economic security risks for the nation. This provides proper incentive for the government to assist the private sector in protecting themselves. Therefore, I recommend that the National Institute of Standards and Technology (NIST) set security standards (or objectives) for the private sector to follow. NIST's primary mission is to promote U.S. economic growth by working with industry to develop and apply technology, measurements, and standards. Its location in the commerce department will remove a stigma from the standards that would exist if they were handed down from the DoD. The NSA and DISA should lend NIST any guidance or assistance it may need. Both organizations have extensive experience in computer and network security. Furthermore, NIST and NSA have worked together in the past, working to develop the Clipper Chip. There should be no need for additional funding or manpower for this addition to the mission of NIST. They boast 3,300 scientists, engineers, technicians, and support personnel, plus an additional 1,250 visiting researchers each year. With the wealth of knowledge that the NSA and DISA should be able to provide from the work they are already tasked to do, NIST should assume this responsibility fairly smoothly.

Resist IW funding becoming the next Manhattan Project. Adequate, but not excessive, resources should be devoted to the collection of intelligence on possible foreign information warfare threats. Despite abundant literature referring to a digital Pearl Harbor, information warfare, though a legitimate national security concern, is not threatening to destroy us all and no Manhattan Project size effort is required to provide adequate defense. The RAND Corporation did recently publish "The Day After in Cyberspace" report, exploring current U.S. ability to respond to an information warfare attack. RAND used the same "Day After" methodology to develop policy in the event of a full scale nuclear holocaust. Martin Libicki at the National Defense University, however, sees information warfare attacks more as a national nuisance and inconvenience, rather than the next paramount national security threat. Libicki says that paranoia about the threat of an information warfare attack is unwarranted. He does not, however, dismiss completely the threat of a Digital Pearl Harbor. But he notes that in RAND's "Day After in Cyberspace" over twenty incidents befall the United Stated and their allied information infrastructures, many that stretch the limits of plausibility.

Resolve the Encryption Debate. Encryption provides a reasonably reliable method of protection for the private sector to use for their own computer networks and systems, which they certainly have a vested interest and responsibility to do. However, robust encryption may remove from the government its long held ability to tap into communication channels of criminals. Therefore, a joint and powerful commission, with representatives from law enforcement, industry, and the scientific community, as well as ranking members of Congress who carry political weight, should review the current policy on encryption and the political impasse that surrounds it. This commission's focus should be on ironing out the politics of the matter and producing a viable solution that can be passed into law immediately.

Provide alternative for Government Communication. The most dangerous and frightening aspect of our vulnerabilities is the way that it could affect our military. The military's dependence on the NII has reached a critical dependence with now over 95% of the military's communications traveling through the NII. During the Persian Gulf War, for example, commercial communication satellites carried 24% of Central Command's long-haul communications. Logistics planning for Operation Desert Shield made extensive use of the Saudi and international civil telephone networks. In the event of an information warfare attack the military's ability to communicate and thus, mobilize efficiently would be jeopardized. Adversaries may be able to appreciably undermine U.S. military power by attacking the information systems upon which it depends for deployment and sustenance. A well executed information warfare strike might very well be the leveling force for a less equipped army. Or it might lower the national defenses and allow for the occurrence of another physical Pearl Harbor. If the military is going to maintain such a heavy dependence on the NII, then it must develop a secure, emergency form of communication. If not, then the military must decrease its dependence on the NII and develop a more extensive Defense Information Infrastructure (DII) that will remain functional in the event of an information warfare attack.

Declassify the NII Threat Assessment. The NII threat assessment required of the DCI by the Intelligence Authorization Act for Fiscal Year 1997 should be prepared in a declassified format to be released to the public. As the public assumes the responsibility of protecting itself, it must know the scope of its vulnerabilities. This declassification can be done in accordance with Director of Central Intelligence Directive (DCID) 1/7, which encourages producing reports in an easy to declassify format.

Continue Coordination. Continued close coordination, namely Dual Use Technology, between DoD, especially the NSA, and industry can only benefit both parties and ensure the maximum possible security.

11

Information Warfare: Combating the Threat in the 21st Century

INFORMATION – THE NEW BATTLESPACE WEAPON

Many theorists believe we are in the midst of an information age. Although the weapons of warfare have changed, the ultimate objective remains the same: conquering one's adversary. The information age has created new targets of opportunity thus changing the way in which war in the 21st century will be fought.

For example, what happens when the new battlespace frontier becomes the mind of the individual commander and the information he uses to make critical decisions? George Gilder, author of *The Quantum Revolution in Economics and Technology*, said "the most valuable capital is now the capital of human mind and spirit." Dr George J. Stein, director of International Security Studies at Air War College, Maxwell Air Force Base, Alabama, said "The target of Information Warfare...is the human mind, especially those minds that make key decisions of war or peace."

When we think of the mind, thoughts of Plato and Aristotle surface to the forefront.

The mind and its mental processes have fascinated philosophers throughout the ages. Random House defines the mind as "the agency or part in a human or other conscious being that reasons, understands, wills, perceives..." Man is distinguished from the rest of nature by his highly developed capacity for thought. His ability to rationalize and process information received are characteristics of a sound mind. The "information" becomes the centerpiece of this transaction. However, when the information becomes damaged, corrupted or unreliable, it threatens his ability to make sound and accurate decisions. IW, thus with its focus on destroying information becomes a legitimate and perhaps preferred tactic for use by potential adversaries.

British armor theorist, J.F.C. Fuller, author of the famous tank Plan 1919 recognized the benefits of attacking the brain within an organization. He believed that attacking the brains of an organization and severing it from the remainder of its organization would produce enough chaos to create what he called "strategic paralysis." Although he referred to the brain as the headquarters' unit, it is easy to understand how disrupting the information flow can paralyze a warfighting force.

Although there is much evidence to suggest that the information age has changed warfare, in his book, *What is Information Warfare,* Martin Libicki describes the difficulty involved in determining the nature of IW.

In the fall of 1994, I was privileged to observe an Information Warfare game sponsored by the Office of the Secretary of Defense. Red, a middle- income nation with a sophisticated electronics industry, had developed an elaborate five-year plan that culminated in an attack on a neighboring country. Blue, the United States, was the neighbor's ally and got wind of Red's plan. The two sides began an extended period of preparation during which each conducted peacetime information warfare and contemplated wartime information warfare. Players on each side retreated to game rooms to decide on moves.

Upon returning from the game rooms, each side presented its strategy. Two troubling tendencies emerged: First, because of the difficulty each side had in determining how the other's information system was wired, for most of the operations proposed (for example) no one could prove which actions might or might not be successful, or even what "success" in this context meant. Second, conflict was the sound of two hands clapping, but not clapping on each other.

Blue saw information warfare as legions of hackers searching out the vulnerabilities of Red's computer systems, which might be exploited by hordes of viruses, worms, logic bombs, or Trojan horses. Red saw information warfare as psychological manipulation through media. Such were the visions in place even before wartime variations on information warfare came into the discussion. Battle was never joined, even by accident. This game illustrated a fundamental difficulty in coming to terms with information warfare, deciding on its nature.

Although the nature of IW may be in question, "History tells us that with each phase of new technology comes a new type of crime." The advances made in technology over the past decade have enabled our military to literally revolutionize the battlefield. The Army's *Force XXI*, the Navy's *Forward...From the Sea,* and the Air Force's *Global Engagement: A Vision for the 21st Century Air Force* represents the Service's architectures for implementing this new technology. However, as these architectures are implemented over the next several years, our growing dependency on this technology will create open-doors for potential attacks by hostile adversaries.

Let's look at an example of a hypothetical IW situation. Suppose a terrorist organization wanted to influence the will of the American populace regarding a specific situation. A possible course of action would be to infiltrate the computer systems of the Cable News Network (CNN), and begin sending something as simple as subliminal messages through the network. This scenario may appear improbable; however a few years ago, subliminal practices were carried out in the music industry. Several news broadcasts reported customers complaining of hidden messages being discovered in cassette recordings. For irrational actors such as terrorist organizations, nothing is beyond their scope of reason.

INSIDER THREATS: HOMEGROWN TERRORISM IN THE 21ST CENTURY

Homegrown terrorism is a major national security threat to the United States in the 21st century because of the combination of violent extremist ideology—especially violent Islamist extremism and its suicidal terrorism—with the Internet accelerating an individual's radicalization and with the proliferation of technology enabling an individual to cause mass casualties or widespread disruption. In other words, the scope of the insider threat to the United States in the 21st century is virtually unprecedented. An individual within the United States, segregated within his or her own Internet community of sympathizers, can potentially radicalize to violent extremism and then utilize modern technology to kill millions of people or hobble critical infrastructure. This insider threat requires a greater emphasis on preventing potentially catastrophic attacks before they occur.

The attacks of September 11, 2001, heightened America's consciousness to the threat posed by violent Islamist extremism. "Violent Islamist extremism" refers to the ideology advocating creation of a global state that would impose the most radical version of Islamic law and the use of violence against non-Muslim military personnel and civilians and even against Muslim opponents of this ideology.

To recruit adherents, violent Islamist extremism utilizes a narrative that the West, led by the United States, is at war with Islam. The process by which individuals adopt violent Islamist extremism is commonly called radicalization.

Violent Islamist extremists demonstrated on 9/11 and in subsequent plots that they seek to kill large numbers of U.S. civilians domestically, and al Qaeda leadership has sanctioned the use and pursued the development of weapons of mass destruction. Moreover, the 9/11 attacks showed violent Islamist extremists' willingness to commit suicide while attacking, thus making them difficult to deter. These characteristics make violent Islamist extremism the most dangerous terrorist threat to the United States. Indeed, the Obama Administration has identified this threat, which it calls "violent extremism and terrorism inspired by al Qa'ida and its affiliates and adherents," as the "preeminent" violent extremist threat to the United States.

The 9/11 hijackers came from outside the United States to attack. During the initial years after 9/11, the U.S. government assumed that the United States' experience as a melting pot of immigrants pursuing the American dream was a bulwark against U.S. citizens—native and immigrant—radicalizing to violent Islamist extremism. This assumption seemed generally correct because there were only 21 cases of homegrown violent Islamist extremism—that is, terrorist attacks or plots by U.S. citizens, permanent residents, or visitors radicalized largely within the United States—from 9/11 until April of 2009.5

But since May of 2009, there have been 32 cases of homegrown violent Islamist extremism. Two of these post–2009 cases have resulted in deaths on U.S. soil. On June 1, 2009, Carlos Bledsoe killed one service member and wounded a second at a military recruiting station in Little Rock, Arkansas. And on November 5, 2009, 12 service members and one Department of Defense civilian were killed and 32 wounded at Fort Hood, Texas. Army-trained psychologist Major Nidal Hasan, who reportedly had radicalized to violent Islamist extremism during his military medical training, is being court-martialed for the attack. Other notable plots have included a 2008 plot led by Najibullah Zazi to attack the New York City subway system and the attempt on May 1, 2010, by Faisal Shahzad to detonate a car bomb in Manhattan's Times Square. The vast majority of these cases have not involved plans for suicide, but Zazi and his fellow plotters did plan their attack as a suicide mission, and several Americans who joined the al-Shabaab terrorist group in Somalia reportedly became suicide attackers there.

These cases of homegrown violent Islamist extremism represent a tiny percentage of the estimated six million Muslim-Americans. Moreover, as Presidents George W. Bush and Barack Obama have stressed since 9/11, the United States is not at war with Islam but rather with adherents to an ideology that perverts it. However, this upward trend in cases is worrisome, particularly when combined with the role of the Internet and the proliferation of destructive and disruptive technology.

The Internet has facilitated radicalization to violent Islamist extremism and resulting terrorist activity. To be sure, the Internet has provided billions of people with access to information, and social media has played a critical role in democratic revolutions across the world. However, the Internet has also enabled radicalization, with violent Islamist extremists becoming adept at using the Internet to spread their propaganda. Violent Islamist extremists originally used password-protected forums, but they are now present on mainstream sites such as YouTube. The Internet enables individuals who are vulnerable to radicalization to find violent Islamist extremist material easily and to self-segregate and interact only with individuals who share that ideology—and in the privacy of their own homes.

Homegrown violent Islamist extremist plots to date have not involved weapons of mass destruction but rather conventional explosives and firearms. Of course, firearms can cause significant casualties, such as the terrorist attack that killed 168 people in Mumbai, India, in November of 2008. But the proliferation of mass destructive and disruptive technology enables even a single individual to wreak havoc domestically. For example, a single terrorist with microbiologicaltraining and access to a laboratory with dangerous pathogens—or equipment enabling the synthesis of a new pathogen—could release a pathogen that could kill millions. In addition, an individual with cyber skills could cause extensive damage to infrastructure and even loss of life through a cyber attack, such as by interfering with supervisory control and data acquisition systems that control the underpinnings of modern society, such as electrical power transmission, communications, and airports. An individual could also gain access to radiological material—such as held by hospitals for medical purposes—and create a "dirty bomb" that renders several city blocks or larger areas uninhabitable and sow panic. The vector of technological development thus continually increases the power of an individual to cause mass destruction and disruption.

The result of the combination of violent extremism, especially violent Islamist extremism, the role of the Internet, and the proliferation of destructive technology is that the government must increasingly emphasize prevention of homegrown terrorism. This task is complicated by the fact that, although an overall four-stage model of radicalization to violent Islamist extremism does exist, individuals who have radicalized have not necessarily followed the model's sequence of stages, and an analysis of homegrown terrorism cases does not reveal a profile to predict who will radicalize except that homegrown terrorists are predominantly male and approximately two-thirds are under 30 years old.

Immediately after the 9/11 attacks, Federal Bureau of Investigation (FBI) Director Robert Mueller declared that the FBI, which had previously focused on investigating terrorism after its occurrence, now had the top priority of preventing terrorist attacks. To do so, the FBI needed to reorient itself from prosecutions after an attack to an intelligence-driven effort to detect and dismantle terrorist threats prior to an attack. For example, Director Mueller charged each of the 56 FBI field offices with "domain awareness," defined as "a 360- degree understanding of all national security and criminal threats in any given city or community. It is the aggregation of intelligence, to include what we already know and what we need to know, and the development of collection plans to find the best means to answer the unknowns. With this knowledge, we can identify emerging threats, allocate resources effectively, and identify new opportunities for intelligence collection and criminal prosecution." Director Mueller also declared that every counterterrorism lead would be pursued.

However, prior to the 9/11 attacks, the FBI was not authorized to conduct investigative activity without sufficient factual predication that a crime was being or had been committed. For the FBI to become "intelligence-driven," it had to develop a protocol for collecting intelligence information, that is, information concerning potential threats even if there was no factual predication of criminal activity. Without such a protocol, the FBI would have limited ability to track down counterterrorism leads that lacked predication of criminal activity or to gather information to be able to analyse the nature and trend of violent extremist threats above and beyond the FBI's ongoing criminal cases.

Accordingly, in 2008, Attorney General Michael Mukasey authorized and Director Mueller instituted a new FBI operational protocol permitting "assessments" when there is "no particular factual predication" that a crime has been committed and instead based on an "authorized purpose" such as "to detect, obtain information about, or prevent or protect against federal crimes or threats to the national security or to collect foreign intelligence."

According to the protocol: Limited investigative tools are permitted, including reviewing publicly available information and conducting physical surveillance not otherwise requiring a warrant, as opposed to intrusive tools such as wiretaps, which require a warrant.

Assessments are prohibited "based solely on the exercise of First Amendment protected activities or on the race, ethnicity, national origin or religion of the subject."

FBI agents must use the "least intrusive" investigative mechanisms possible. As stated in Attorney General Mukasey's authorization to the FBI, "For example, assessment activities may involve proactively surfing the Internet to find publicly accessible websites and services through which recruitment by terrorist organizations and promotion of terrorist crimes is openly taking place." The use of assessments does raise the risk of abuse, such as that the FBI's guidelines for use of assessments will be ignored in practice and that the assessments will be conducted based solely on First Amendment activity or that racial and ethnic profiling will be done. However, three counterbalancing forces provide the necessary checks:

First, FBI and other law enforcement personnel need adequate training concerning the nature of violent extremism and in particular violent Islamist extremism and how it differs from the peaceful practice of Islam. Training has often focused on behavioral indicators of radicalization—such as whether an individual is isolating himself or herself from friends and family—and not the ideology of violent Islamist extremism. As the Senate investigation of the Fort Hood attack found, "Understanding the ideology of violent Islamist extremism would assist agents in determining, in conjunction with an individual's conduct, what degree of risk an individual might present and whether to pursue further inquiry." In addition, state and local law enforcement are the first lines of defense against terrorism because of their knowledge of and constant contact with local communities, and anecdotal evidence raises concerns about the quality of training that they receive. Such training by outside experts has reportedly included that "Islam is a highly violent religion" and that if an individual has "different spellings of a name . . . that's probably cause to take them in." Preventing terrorism from violent Islamist extremism requires accurate training so that law enforcement agents can focus their efforts on extremists and not on Americans practicing Islam.

Second, oversight of law enforcement intelligence activities is essential. The FBI is overseen by the Department of Justice, especially the Department of Justice Inspector General, and by various congressional committees. The Department of Justice Inspector General has issued a variety of reports including a report on FBI agents cheating on tests concerning the new FBI investigative authorities discussed above, FBI investigations of domestic advocacy groups (which did not find systemic abuses), and errors and management failures in the use of FBI authorities to request information from communications providers. Congress exercises oversight via hearings, requests for briefings, appropriation of the FBI's funding, and launching special investigations. The criticality of preventing homegrown terrorism, combined with the new authorities granted to the FBI, require that oversight of the FBI be rigorous and sustained.

And third, the FBI's attempts to prevent terrorist activity by utilizing its authorities must take place alongside vigorous U.S. government outreach to local communities and in particular Muslim-American communities. This outreach is designed to build relationships with local communities, provide them with information that they need to develop communal efforts to prevent and respond to radicalization in their midst, and elicit concerns about particular government actions or policies, including the FBI's conduct of assessments. This outreach is conducted by a range of agencies, including the Department of Homeland Security's Civil Rights and Civil Liberties office and the FBI. The Obama Administration released an overall framework in August of 201130 and an implementation plan in December of 2011 that listed tasks along with leading and supporting government agencies. The challenge now is to ensure that this plan is implemented aggressively and with clear leadership and commensurate resources, thus providing the greatest chance of preventing terrorism especially motivated by violent Islamist extremism.

THE MEASURE OF A SUPERPOWER: A TWO MAJOR REGIONAL CONTINGENCY MILITARY FOR THE 21ST CENTURY

How much military force does a global superpower require? Answering this question has challenged U.S. leaders and defense planners for more than 20 years. With the collapse of the Soviet Union and the end of the Cold War, the United States found itself the world's sole superpower, but one without a significant adversary against which to measure the adequacy of its military capabilities. In the immediate aftermath of the first Gulf War, U.S. leaders decided to use the requirement to conduct two major regional conventional contingencies (MRCs) at the same time as the basis for sizing the U.S. military. Every subsequent review of U.S. defense policy and programs has reaffirmed the two-war standard. In fact, every Administration for the past two decades found that a force sized to fight two wars was essential for meeting the ongoing demands for forward presence, crisis response, regional deterrence, humanitarian assistance, building partnership capacity, homeland defense, and support to civil authorities.

Based on some 20 years of analyses and studies as well as the experiences of Desert Storm, Operation Iraqi Freedom, and Operation Enduring Freedom, a two-MRC force should generally consist of 10 Active and eight Reserve Component Army divisions, two to three Marine Expeditionary Forces, 11 aircraft carriers, 120 large surface naval combatants, 38 large amphibious warfare ships, 200 strategic bombers, 20 tactical fighter wings, 400–500 tankers, and 250 airlifters. Such a force would need support from a wide range of enabling capabilities, such as special operations forces; intelligence, surveillance, and reconnaissance systems; cyber defenses; air and missile defenses; and space systems.

Today's military is too small to meet the two-MRC test credibly. Moreover, the qualitative advantage that the U.S. military has long enjoyed is eroding as advanced military capabilities proliferate around the world. The capabilities of U.S. forces are also deteriorating as platforms and systems age and as critical modernization programs are delayed or even cancelled.

Building a two-MRC force for the 21st century means increasing the size of the U.S. military, modernizing existing platforms and systems, and investing in advanced air, sea, and land capabilities. This will require resources above the levels proposed by the Obama Administration. Over the next decade, building a reasonable two-MRC force for the 21st century will cost roughly $70 billion more per year than the projected cost of the current defense program, which averages approximately $550 billion per year.

What It Takes to Be a Military Superpower

Since the end of the Cold War, the United States has measured the fundamental adequacy of its force posture in terms of the ability of U.S. forces, without national mobilization, to defeat two nation-state adversaries in geographically separate theaters nearly simultaneously. From the time it was first articulated in 1991, the two-theater-war standard has undergone repeated reviews and revisions. The fundamental reason that the two-theater-war standard still survives is because no credible alternative has ever been proposed. Senior decision makers across five Administrations, Republican and Democrat, have been unable to avoid the reality that, in a world of continuing globalization and growing political and military uncertainty, the U.S. needs a military that is large enough and has a sufficient range of capabilities to cover multiple major military contingencies in overlapping time frames. Such a military would not only fit the character of the post–Cold War threat environment, but also serve a critical deterrence function in an era in which the scale of potential conventional conflicts was seen as decreasing and the ability to resort to nuclear weapons had become less plausible. The 1997 Quadrennial Defense Review (QDR) provided one of the best formulations of the rationale for the two-theater-war standard:

As a global power with worldwide interests, it is imperative that the United States now and for the foreseeable future be able to deter and defeat large-scale, cross-border aggression in two distant theaters in overlapping time frames, preferably in concert with regional allies. Maintaining this core capability is central to credibly deterring opportunism—that is, to avoiding a situation in which an aggressor in one region might be tempted to take advantage when U.S. forces are heavily committed elsewhere—and to ensuring that the United States has sufficient military capabilities to deter or defeat aggression by an adversary that is larger, or under circumstances that are more difficult, than expected. This is particularly important in a highly dynamic and uncertain security environment. We can never know with certainty when or where the next major theater war will occur, who our next adversary will be, how an enemy will fight, who will join us in a coalition, or precisely what demands will be placed on U.S. forces. Indeed, history has repeatedly shown that we are often unable to predict such matters. A force sized and equipped for deterring and defeating aggression in more than one theater ensures the United States will maintain the flexibility to cope with the unpredictable and unexpected. Such a capability is the sine qua non of a superpower and is essential to the credibility of our overall national security strategy. It also supports our continued engagement in shaping the international environment to reduce the chances that such threats will develop in the first place.

If the United States were to forego its ability to defeat aggression in more than one theater at a time, our standing as a global power, as the security partner of choice, and as the leader of the international community would be called into question. Indeed, some allies would undoubtedly read a one-war capability as a signal that the United States, if heavily engaged elsewhere, would no longer be able to help defend their interests. Such a capability could also inhibit the United States from responding to a crisis promptly enough, or even at all, for fear of committing the bulk of our forces and making ourselves vulnerable in other regions. This fact is also unlikely to escape the attention of potential adversaries. A one-theater war capacity would risk undermining both deterrence and the credibility of U.S. security commitments in key regions of the world. This, in turn, could cause allies and friends to adopt more divergent defense policies and postures, thereby weakening the web of alliances and coalitions on which we rely to protect our interests abroad.

Some 15 years later, the 2012 new strategic guidance for the Department of Defense acknowledged the same basic reality: As a nation with important interests in multiple regions, our forces must be capable of deterring and defeating aggression by an opportunistic adversary in one region even when our forces are committed to a large-scale operation elsewhere.... Even when U.S. forces are committed to a large-scale operation in one region, they will be capable of denying the objectives of—or imposing unacceptable costs on—an opportunistic aggressor in a second region.

Every Administration has put its own spin on the two-war standard, sometimes repeatedly. The initial formulation was based on the concern that the United States might need to deal with aggression at the same time in both Southwest and Northeast Asia. Over time, the requirement evolved from maintaining the capability to defeat two conventionally armed aggressors to a more complex formulation in which the U.S. military was asked to be able to conduct a single campaign against a conventional adversary while waging a long-duration counterinsurgency and stability campaign or protecting the homeland against attack and providing support to civil authorities.

This evolution culminated in the 2010 Quadrennial Defense Review, which explicitly attempted to move away from the two-theater-war standard. However, it failed to provide a clear alternative metric for determining the size and shape of U.S. forces. Rather, the 2010 QDR proposed to determine force sizing and composition by using the requirements of a diverse and complex set of scenarios, including long-duration stability operations and the defense of the homeland on par with a major regional conflict (MRC). The Obama Administration clearly acknowledged the inadequacy of this approach in its 2012 new strategic guidance, which returned to the two-theater-war construct, although U.S. operations in the second conflict would be limited to countering an aggressor's objectives or inflicting unacceptable damage. In his announcement of the new defense strategy in January 2012,

Secretary of Defense Leon Panetta clearly articulated the need to maintain capabilities to deal with two major regional conflicts at one time:

> Our strategy review concluded that the United States must have the capability to fight several conflicts at the same time. We are not confronting, obviously, the threats of the past; we are confronting the threats of the 21st century. And that demands greater flexibility to shift and deploy forces to be able to fight and defeat any enemy anywhere. How we defeat the enemy may very well vary across conflicts. But make no mistake, we will have the capability to confront and defeat more than one adversary at a time.

Secretary Panetta even more explicitly advocated the two-conflict standard in his speech to the 2012 Munich Security Conference in front of America's major allies:

> We will ensure that we can quickly confront and defeat aggression from any adversary, any time, any place. It is essential that we have the capability to deal with more than one adversary at a time, and we believe we have shaped a force that will give us that capability.

Experience also suggests the need for the U.S. military to be prepared to conduct two major long-term operations at a time. Three times since the end of the Cold War, the United States has found itself involved in major theater conflicts. For Desert Shield/ Desert Storm in 1990–1991, the U.S. deployed nearly a million soldiers (73 percent were U.S. personnel) from 34 countries. The United States conducted decisive theater operations in Afghanistan (Operation Enduring Freedom or OEF) in 2001 and in Iraq (Operation Iraqi Freedom or OIF) in 2003, overthrowing the regimes in both countries. These two operations morphed into long-term counterinsurgency campaigns involving at their zeniths around 150,000 U.S. troops each as well as significant contingents from allied and partner nations.

An essential premise of U.S. national security since the end of the Cold War has been this nation's role as the guarantor of global security. The Clinton Administration sought to take advantage of the opportunities provided by the demise of the

Soviet Union to define a new approach to U.S. security policy—one based on the opportunities created by the end of the East-West divide to expand the community of democratic states and improve global engagement on a host of issues. U.S. military preeminence was essential to this new strategy and the U.S. role in the world:

First and foremost, we must exercise global leadership. We are not the world's policeman, but as the world's premier economic and military power, and with the strength of our democratic values, the U.S. is indispensable to the forging of stable political relations and open trade.

Almost two decades later, as it sought to articulate its vision for U.S. defense and foreign policies, the Obama Administration had to acknowledge the close intertwining of U.S. military power and peace in the world:

Our country possesses the attributes that have supported our leadership for decades—sturdy alliances, an unmatched military, the world's largest economy, a strong and evolving democracy, and a dynamic citizenry. Going forward, there should be no doubt: the United States of America will continue to underwrite global security—through our commitments to allies, partners, and institutions; our focus on defeating al-Qaeda and its affiliates in Afghanistan, Pakistan, and around the globe; and our determination to deter aggression and prevent the proliferation of the world's most dangerous weapons.

The two-MRC standard also provided a useful hedge against both the near-term danger of a resurgent Russia and the longer-term rise of a true peer competitor, either a single "superstate" or a confederation of adversaries. With respect to the latter, discussions in the early 1990s when the standard was first proposed did not foresee such a situation for at least 20 years. Conceptually, a force structure designed to conduct two relatively large and intense theater campaigns could serve as a counterweight to a hostile, militarizing Russia and simultaneously as the base for an expanded military capability to deter a peer adversary.

The two-MRC standard was never considered a perfect guide to force sizing and modernization. In the absence of a clear and driving threat, such as that provided by the Soviet Union, its role was as a placeholder, allowing defense planners and budgeters to define a useful and affordable military capability that could respond to the range of known demands and unknown future contingencies.

In truth, there have always been some doubts about the ability of the post–Cold War U.S. military to conduct two MRCs precisely at the same time and in the absence of national mobilization. The temporal relationship between the two conflicts was recognized as a problem. Overlapping conflicts placed particular stress on so-called high-demand/low-density systems, the critical enablers that were central to the ability of U.S. forces to gather intelligence, deploy forces, and conduct high-intensity precision operations. In addition, there was continuing uncertainty about the capacity and willingness of regional allies to support U.S. operations. Turkey's refusal to allow U.S. forces to use it as a staging base for a northern offensive against Iraq confirmed the validity of this concern.

Of far greater concern has been the gap between the appetite of successive post–Cold War Administrations for military forces and their willingness to invest the resources necessary to support the required force structure. Over the past 20 years, the size of the U.S. military has declined by 50 percent while its activity level has increased fourfold, excluding recent conflicts in Iraq and Afghanistan. Even as successive force structure and strategy reviews have reconfirmed the centrality of the two-MRC construct to America's global leadership, defense budgets have been cut; modernization programs have been reduced, delayed, or even canceled; and maintenance and upgrades of older equipment have been deferred. This process led two senior defense experts to conclude about the ritualized process of the Quadrennial Defense Review:

> There is an air of unreality about the whole process, particularly because the last three administrations systematically underfunded America's armed forces while increasing their deployments and missions abroad. As a result, the military is too small and is forced to use equipment that is too old. Consistent with ongoing obligations in Iraq and Afghanistan, the military cannot fight one regional contingency like Desert Storm, much less two.

Nevertheless, the two constants in U.S. national security policy for the past two decades have been, first, the centrality of U.S. military preeminence to this nation's position of global leadership and its goal of a stable international environment and, second, the value of the two-MRC force-sizing construct as both a symbol of that preeminence and a measure of overall adequacy of the force to perform the range of its missions.

Nothing in the evolving global security environment suggests that the U.S. military will be unshackled from the basic requirement to deter if possible, but fight and win if necessary, two geographically separated major theater conflicts in overlapping time frames. Rather the opposite appears to be the case. Core U.S. national security interests and objectives have changed very little since the end of the Cold War and the formulation of the two-theater-war sizing construct. These interests include protecting the U.S. homeland and U.S. citizens everywhere, partnering with allies and friends to provide regional security, ensuring access to areas of vital national interest, securing the global commons, and countering efforts by aggressive powers to dominate important regions of the world.

At the same time, challenges to these interests and threats to U.S. forces abroad and U.S. allies are increasing, not declining. The canonical Southwest and Northeast Asia scenarios remain. Iran is pursuing a hegemonic strategy in the Persian Gulf, supporting terrorist organizations and rogue regimes and continuing a sustained military buildup. North Korea shows no signs of easing its hard-line stance or curtailing its efforts to acquire long-range ballistic missiles and a stockpile of nuclear weapons. Over the past two decades, Pyongyang has engaged in a series of provocative military actions that caused the deaths of South Korean military personnel and civilians. In addition, other parts of the Greater Middle East from Libya and Egypt to Syria and even Pakistan are experiencing political instability, social upheavals, and increased conflict.

The possibility of major theater conflicts in other parts of the world can no longer be ignored. Russia's new national security strategy identifies the North Atlantic Treaty Organization (NATO) as that country's principal security challenge. Moscow maintains a military presence in a number of former Soviet republics and fought a short, inconclusive conflict with Georgia in 2008. Russia's defense minister recently warned that his country might respond to the deployment of theater missile defenses in Europe with a preemptive strike on those sites. China continues to expand and improve its military forces deployed opposite Taiwan. In addition, that country and its southern neighbours have sparred over territorial rights in the South China Sea.

Looking ahead, if the U.S. will be required to conduct a theater campaign along the lines of Desert Storm, OIF, or OEF, it will likely do so under more challenging circumstances than envisioned when the standard was first articulated. Potential adversaries have studied the strategies, tactics, and technologies that the United States employed to win decisively in prior theater conflicts. These countries are participating in the global proliferation of advanced conventional weapons. A number of these regional actors are investing heavily in anti-access/area denial (A2/AD) capabilities primarily to counter the ability of the United States and its allies to project power into regions of interest using their traditional advantages in air and naval power to achieve decisive military outcomes as they did in earlier major theater conflicts.

A number of prospective regional adversaries also are investing in a range of unconventional capabilities and operational methods to counter or circumvent traditional U.S. advantages in conventional military forces. Some of these countries have extensive programs to develop, stockpile, and deploy weapons of mass destruction (WMDs). A number of prospective adversaries also have developed extensive ties with non-state actors and terrorist groups seeking to develop what some analysts have termed a "hybrid threat," such as the military relationship between Iran and Hezbollah.

Even as prospective theater adversaries build up their military capabilities and acquire more advanced weapons and systems, the ability of regional allies to contribute to their own defense and the security of their regions is changing. Some U.S. allies are reducing their defense budgets and cutting their military capabilities.

Budgetary pressures in Europe have forced a number of NATO allies to reduce the size of their armed forces and scale back modernization programs. However, many U.S. allies in the Middle East and East Asia are expanding and modernizing their force structures.

Future major theater conflicts will likely be more challenging than those of the past several decades, and they may not be limited to foreign theaters. A theater conflict could easily involve actions against the U.S. homeland or overseas bases outside the primary region of hostilities. Such attacks on the homeland could either be preemptive à la Pearl Harbor, intended to undermine a U.S. response, or in retaliation for U.S. actions against a theater adversary. Possible homeland events could range from terrorism and acts of sabotage to cyber attacks to the use of a WMD.

Not all of the trends are negative. Since the inception of the two-MRC standard, the United States has invested in a range of platforms, systems, and capabilities that have significantly enhanced its ability to conduct large-scale joint and combined operations. In this regard, the contrast between Desert Storm in 1991—the first MRC in Southwest Asia—and Operation Iraqi Freedom in 2003 is telling. The 1991 coalition to liberate Kuwait deployed nearly 1 million combatants, more than half of them U.S. personnel. In 2003, the march to Baghdad employed only 248,000 U.S. personnel along with some 50,000 allied soldiers, primarily from Great Britain.

Improvements in military equipment significantly affected the conduct of the two MRCs. In 1991 only 7.5 percent of the air-delivered ordnance was precision-guided, but the proportion had increased to nearly 65 percent in 2003. Over this period similar radical changes occurred in unmanned aerial systems, real-time strategic and tactical communications, stealth aircraft, and theater missile defenses.

Today, the two-MRC standard, the sine qua non of superpower status and possibly the most critical measure of a viable U.S. national security strategy, is at risk. The new defense strategy attempts to have it both ways. It professes to adhere to the two-major-theater-war standard while proposing for the second contingency something a great deal less. In the 1990s, this lesser standard was tried and found wanting. Given the number, variety, and war-waging potential of current and emerging threats to U.S. national security, maintaining a U.S. force structure sized against any standard less than fighting and winning two nearly simultaneous major theater conflicts invites the very instability that U.S. defense strategy is intended to deter. For the foreseeable future even more than in the recent past, the U.S. military's ability to meet a two-MRC standard will be the measure of this nation's status as a superpower and a primary engine driving its role as a global leader.

This paper defines the essential quantitative and qualitative characteristics of a U.S. force structure required to meet the two-MRC standard for the near term and midterm. Section II examines the evolving character of the two-MRC standard in the post–Cold War era with a particular focus on future theater conflicts and criteria for sufficiency. Section III examines the evolving military threat to regional security and U.S. vital interests and its effect on the two-MRC standard. Section IV defines a 21st-century standard for a two-MRC force structure. Section V develops a top-level assessment of the costs associated with sculpting the planned force structure to meet the two-MRC test. Finally, Section VI recommends the steps that the Administration should take to address the shortfalls of the current U.S. force structure, one based on the new defense strategy, so as to enable that force to meet the goal of fighting and winning two nearly simultaneous MRCs.

The Evolving Character of the Two-MRC Standard, 1991–2012

The two-major-theater-war standard for sizing the U.S. military is hardly a new idea. It has its roots in the geopolitical situation that developed in the late 19th century. The United States had achieved the status of the world's leading industrial power, acquired a set of overseas territories as a consequence of the Spanish–American War, and finally settled the Western frontier, knitting together a transcontinental dominion from the Atlantic to the Pacific. In this context, the U.S. discovered that it had growing political, commercial, and security interests in geographically distinct regions. America's first tentative steps onto the world stage occurred during the first wave of globalization generated by rapid technological change, coupled with increased competition among the Great Powers to expand their investments in, influence over, and outright control of large parts of the world. The same conditions that called the United States out of its comfortable isolation also ended the sanctuary status the United States had enjoyed for the past century.

Alfred Thayer Mahan first articulated this new reality in his seminal work The Influence of Seapower on History. According to Mahan, the combination of expanded international commerce and the growing capability of the world's leading nations to project power globally required the United States to abandon its treasured notions of isolationism and the security afforded by two oceans. The United States needed to consider the possibility of involvement in conflicts in two widely separated regions of the globe as well as sorties by major adversaries against the East and West Coasts. The U.S. experience in the Spanish–American War, most notably the USS Oregon's circumnavigation of the globe and the acquisition of former Spanish colonies in the Caribbean and Western Pacific, appeared to confirm the correctness of the new doctrine. Mahan's thesis also resonated with the belief among political and military leaders in American exceptionalism and the requirement that the United States needed to prepare to address threats from both the Eastern and Western Hemispheres.

What were the implications of this new perspective on national security for the size and composition of the U.S. military? At the time, in the beginning of the 19th century, Mahan could argue that the United States required a Navy that could meet the greatest of any naval threat regardless of the direction from which it might come—the Pacific or the Atlantic. The construction of the Panama Canal reduced the risk of guessing wrong on which was the greatest threat by enabling the Navy to more easily "swing" ships to the other ocean as the magnitude of the threat changed. As a result, according to the prevailing military doctrine, the United States did not need a two-ocean Navy, although it had to focus on potential strategic threats from both the Atlantic and Pacific.

However, in the 1930s, with the rise of new regional powers such as Japan and the decline of the British Navy as a bulwark against threats to the United States, it became necessary for defense planners to consider the possibility of confronting threats in two theaters simultaneously. The result was the 1940 Vinson–Walsh Act, also known as the Two-Ocean Navy Act, which funded a 70 percent increase in the U.S. Navy, including construction of 18 aircraft carriers and construction or expansion of air and naval facilities across the Pacific. Proponents of the act argued that its fundamental purpose was to strengthen U.S. naval power to deter aggression by Japan and/or Germany.

World War II was a multi-adversary, multi-theater conflict and seemed to confirm Mahan's basic thesis. For many U.S. decision makers, this conflict also underscored the consequences of failing to acquire a military capable of meeting more than one adversary at a time. Notably, the Roosevelt Administration and the Joint Chiefs of Staff struggled to manage the flow of men and materials to both the European and Pacific Theaters. They made the strategic decision to give priority to winning the war in Europe, a choice ratified by the Allied powers.

Within a few years of defeating Germany and Japan, growing antagonism between the Western Allies and the Soviet Union and the ensuing Cold War resurrected the strategic requirement that U.S. forces be able to fight multiple, geographically dispersed, and possibly simultaneous conflicts. The early history of the Cold War—which involved a series of small wars beginning with the Korean conflict, insurgencies, and direct confrontations between the Soviet Union/Warsaw Pact and United States/NATO, such as over Berlin—underscored the centrality of a multi-conflict force-sizing standard. Even where Soviet forces were not present, there was growing concern that Moscow was directing the actions of revolutionary movements and fraternal communist regimes, such as the People's Republic of China and Cuba, to tie down U.S. forces and weaken the West's ability to confront Soviet aggression.

Throughout the Cold War, the United States struggled to define a relevant and affordable force-sizing standard. The fundamental strategic problem of the era was deterring central conflict between the two superpowers and their alliances, while still dealing with regional conflicts against Soviet forces or regional proxies. Faced with the growing Soviet strategic nuclear threat, U.S. defense planners abandoned reliance on nuclear weapons alone for deterrence and planned instead to counter, at least initially, conventional aggression at the regional level. Thus, under the Kennedy and Johnson Administrations, the United States formulated the two-and-a-half war sizing construct. One conflict would be in Europe, the decisive theater in the East–West standoff. A second would be in the Far East and could involve China or North Korea. The "half war" was a major counterinsurgency operation against a Soviet proxy. The U.S. deterrent strategy of graduated escalation relied on the ability to hold at bay, albeit temporarily, a Soviet attack on Europe or a proxy in the Far East, thereby creating intrawar firebreaks. Because it was never assumed that the United States and its allies could defeat a determined Soviet onslaught with conventional means alone, the force structure constructs deemed adequate to satisfy the requirements to fight in multiple theaters were lower than what a war-winning strategy would have necessitated.

Changes in the global threat environment allowed subsequent Administrations to make adjustments to the two-and-a-half-war standard. The Sino–Soviet split enabled the Nixon Administration to reduce the standard to the ability to fight one-and-a-half wars simultaneously. However, as the Soviet Union expanded its conventional military capabilities beginning in the 1970s, the Reagan Administration found it advisable to resurrect something akin to the old two-simultaneous-war standard. The Reagan Doctrine envisioned countering aggression by the Soviet Union or its proxies anywhere in the world. In addition, in the event of a conflict between the two superpowers in Europe or Asia, Reagan defense plans included options for expanding the scope of hostilities by escalating horizontally along the periphery of the Soviet Union.

Beginning in the late 1980s, U.S. defense planners began to rethink the character of a possible conflict with the Soviet Union, the central feature of U.S. force planning for more than four decades.

Monumental political changes in the Soviet Union and the Warsaw Pact and Moscow's withdrawal of military forces from Afghanistan caused the incoming Bush Administration to rethink the likelihood of a deliberate attack on Western Europe.

Political changes elsewhere in the world, including an improving relationship between the United States and China and the rise of political Islam, suggested that future threats to U.S. security lay elsewhere than a classic East–West confrontation. In addition, the Reagan-era defense buildup was clearly coming to an end, and significant reductions in defense spending were in the offing.

President George H. W. Bush framed the relationship between U.S. defense planning and future force structure and the strategic changes brought by the incipient Soviet reforms in advance of the collapse of the Communist Party of the Soviet Union and the fragmentation of the Soviet Union. Ironically, President Bush gave the speech on the same day that Saddam Hussein invaded Kuwait.

> Our task today is to shape our defense capabilities to these changing strategic circumstances. In a world less driven by an immediate threat to Europe and the danger of global war, in a world where the size of our forces will increasingly be shaped by the needs of regional contingencies and peacetime presence, we know that our forces can be smaller. Secretary Cheney and General Powell are hard at work determining the precise combination of forces that we need. But I can tell you now, we calculate that by 1995 our security needs can be met by an active force 25 percent smaller than today's. America's Armed Forces will be at their lowest level since the year 1950.

Bibliography

Ahuja, Vijay: *Network and Internet Security*. Academic Press, Inc.: Boston, 1996.

Allison, Graham: *Nuclear Terrorism: The Ultimate Preventable Catastrophe*, New York: Times Books, 2004.

Bellamy, C.: *Knights in White Armour: The New Art of War and Peace*, London, Random House, 1997.

Brooks, Constance : *Disaster Preparedness*, Washington, DC, Association for Research Libraries, 1993.

Carpenter, Stanley D. M., *Military Leadership in the British Civil Wars, 1642-1651: The Genius of This Age*, Routledge, 2005

Charlotte Waelde, *Law and the Internet: Regulating Cyberspace*. Hart Pub, 1997.

Crichton, Michael: *Electronic Life, How to Think About Computers*, New York, Alfred A. Knopf, 1983.

D'Aguilar, G.C., *Napoleon's Military Maxims*, free ebook, Napoleon's Military Maxims

David Post : *The Rise of Law in Cyberspace*, 48 Stan, L. Rev. 1367, 1996.

Duncan, Francis. *Rickover and the Nuclear Navy: The Discipline of Technology*. Annapolis: Naval Institute Press, 1990.

Eric Herring: *The Arms Dynamic in World Politics*, London: Lynne Rienner Publishers, 1998.

Friedman, G.: *The Future of War of Cyber Crimes*, N.Y., Random House, 1996.

Fuller, John F. C., *Foundations of the Science of War*. London, 1925.

Gerstell, Richard. *How to Survive an Atomic Bomb*. Washington, D.C.: Combat Forces Press, 1950.

Hasan-Askari Rizvi: *Nuclear Terrorism and South Asia*, Albuquerque, NM: Sandia National Laboratories, February 2003.

Herken, Gregg. *The Winning Weapon: The Atomic Bomb in the Cold War, 1945-1950*. Princeton: Princeton University Press, 1988.

Heuser, Beatrice, *The Evolution of Strategy: Thinking War from Antiquity to the Present,* Cambridge University Press, 2010.

Karanjit Siyan: *Internet Firewalls and Network Security.* New Riders Publishing: Indianapolis, 1996.

Kaufmann, Albert R. *Nuclear Reactor Fuel Elements: Metallurgy and Fabrication.* New York: Interscience Publishers, Inc., 1962.

Kurz, Raymond, *Internet and the Law: Legal Fundamentals for the Internet User.* Rockville, MD.: Government Institutes, 1996.

Lifton, Robert Jay and Mitchell, Greg. *Hiroshima in America: A Half Century of Denial.* New York: Avon Books, 1995.

Mary, W.: *Asian Power and Politics: the Cultural Dimensions of Authority,* Cambridge, Belknap Press, 1985.

Matloff, Maurice, *American Military History: 1775-1902,* Combined Books, 1996

McMahon, David: *Cyber Threat: Internet Security for Home and Business.* Warwick Publishing Inc.: Toronto, 2000.

Peter T.: *Manager's Guide to Internet Security.* CSI: San Francisco, 1994.

Posen, B.R.: *The Sources of Military Doctrine,* Ithaca, 1984, Cornell Univ. Press.

Robert L.: *Software Creativity,* Prentice Hall PTR, 1995.

Savkin, V. Y., *Basic Principles of Operational Art and Tactics,* Moscow, 1972.

Schroeer, Dietrich: *Science, Technology, and the Cyber Crimes,* Ontario: John Wiley & Sons, 1984.

Sherwin, Martin J. A World Destroyed: *The Atomic Bomb and the Grand Alliance.* New York: Vintage Books, 1977.

Spector, Leonard S., *Going Nuclear,* Cambridge, MA: Ballinger Publishing Company, 1987.

Sun-tzu, *The Art of War,* Oxford, 1963.

Tomes, Robert R., *US Defense Strategy from Vietnam to Operation Iraqi Freedom: Military Innovation and the New American Way of War, 1973–2003,* Routledge Press, 2007

Wilden, Anthony, *Man and Woman, War and Peace: The Strategist's Companion,* Routledge, 1987

William Aspray: *Computer, A History of the Information Machine,* New York, Basic Books, 1996.

Index

❑❑❑